TWO WINGS OF A NIGHTINGALE

Persian soul, Islamic heart

JILL WORRALL

EXISLE
PUBLISHING

For our mothers, Jocelyn and Sedighe,
who wave us goodbye and welcome us home.

First published 2011

Exisle Publishing Limited,
P.O. Box 60-490, Titirangi, Auckland 0642, New Zealand.
'Moonrising', Narone Creek Road, Wollombi, NSW 2325, Australia.
www.exislepublishing.com

National Library of New Zealand Cataloguing-in-Publication Data

Worrall, Jill.
Two wings of a nightingale : Persian soul, Islamic heart / Jill Worrall.
ISBN 978-1-921497-84-1
1. Worrall, Jill—Travel—Iran. 2. Mirkhalaf, Reza—Travel—Iran.
3. Iran—Social life and customs. 4. Iran—Description and travel. I. Title.
915.504—dc 22

10 9 8 7 6 5 4 3 2 1

Text and cover design by Christabella Designs
Map by Mark Roman
Printed in Singapore by KHL Printing Co Pte Ltd

This book uses paper sourced under ISO 14001 guidelines from well-managed forests
and other controlled sources.

CONTENTS

ACKNOWLEDGEMENTS

This book has consumed many hours of my life, so as always my heartfelt thanks to Derek, my husband, for his patience, unwavering support and encouragement and for reading, almost without complaint, the entire manuscript more than once.

Thank you also to Renée, my mentor and editor, and Carol and Elizabeth for finding all the missed commas (among other things) in the first draft.

How do I say thank you to everyone in Iran who, sometimes without knowing it, has played a part in making this book a reality? But thank you anyway.

To Reza's family – Sedighe, Mojik and Nasik and their extended family – you have accepted me as part of your family and that's a priceless gift.

Without Reza B our journey would have been impossible, and not nearly as much fun. Let's do it all again sometime, *inshallah*.

And finally, Reza, you are Iran for me. You have opened my eyes, ears, heart and soul to your country. Like Iran, you are in my heart forever.

GLOSSARY

arg citadel

azan call to prayer

badgir wind tower, a traditional ventilation system

bazaaris bazaar shopkeeper

begum honorific for women of high status

gaz Persian nougat usually containing pistachios

hijab head covering; modest Moslem dress style

hammam bathhouse, bathroom

Hosseini building used for ceremonies during *Moharram*

inshallah God willing

ivan vaulted space with walls on three sides and open on the
fourth side

madrasseh Moslem theological school

maidan open space

manteau long or short overcoat

mashallah God has willed it, used to show joy or praise or on
hearing good news

mihrab prayer niche in a mosque showing the direction of Mecca

Moharram Shia month of mourning commemorating the death
of Hossein

mohr small tablet used by Shia during prayers

muezzin person who calls worshippers to prayer

No Ruz Iranian New Year

qalyan waterpipe used for smoking

qanat underground water channel

sabzi germinated seeds associated with No Ruz

sob bekheihr good morning

takt throne

tarof an extreme form of politeness that involves repeatedly
refusing a gift, payment or hospitality

vozu washing ritual

zurkaneh house of strength

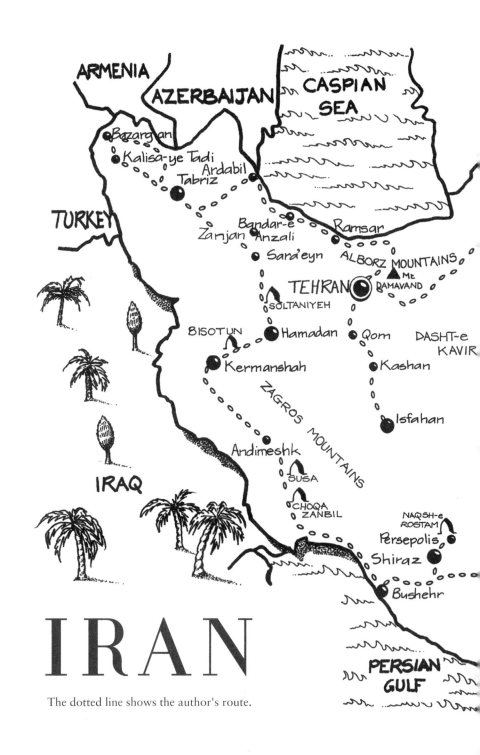

IRAN

The dotted line shows the author's route.

Key:

∧ – HISTORIC SITE

TURKMENISTAN

Sarakhs

Sabzevar

Neyshabur   Mashhad

Shahrood

Gonabad

AFGHANISTAN

Tabas

DASHT-e LUT

Yazd

Taft

Kerman

Mahan

Rayen

PAKISTAN

Life is not something to be left behind
by you or me on the edge of the habit's shelf.

Sohrab Sepehri

INTRODUCTION

Now that I have raised the glass of pure wine to my lips
The nightingale starts to sing!
Go to the librarian and ask for the book of this bird's songs,
And then go out into the desert.

Hafez, 14th century Persian poet

Iran is one of the largest countries in the world. Its geography is as varied as its history is long, making it a challenging place through which to journey. Mountain passes where the snow can lie for many months, bleak deserts that become all but incandescent in summer, and thousands of kilometres of borders shared with neighbours in turmoil mean travel can be arduous. Many millions of Iranians have not explored it fully, let alone the comparatively few visitors who come to visit its cultural and architectural highlights.

For centuries Iran was part of the ancient silk routes that linked the Far East and Europe. While camel caravans no longer plod their way across the vast expanses of the Iranian plateau, their memory lives on in the ruins of the unique caravanserais that provided shelter to these early entrepreneurs and their precious cargoes.

When my Iranian friend Reza Mirkhalaf and I decided to undertake a journey to view his homeland through Western and Iranian eyes we chose to follow, where possible, the footsteps of those early travellers. Our explorations took place at a time of high tension between Iran and the Western world as debate raged over Iran's nuclear ambitions, its perceived role in Iraq and in other Middle Eastern hot spots and against a backdrop of the West's deeply ingrained fear and misunderstanding of the people of this country.

Reza and I had met three years earlier, and over the course of working together as national guide and tour manager respectively for groups of overseas tourists, we'd become friends. The idea for the journey began in true Persian fashion over cups of tea and the gurgle of a *qalyan* (hubble-bubble or water pipe) while we unwound after a day introducing a tour party to the wonders of Isfahan. We were beside the 400-year-old Si-o-Se bridge. The tea is brewed in a cavernous kitchen under the bridge's arches, but most patrons of this famous teahouse choose to sit outside at ancient, wobbly metal tables set on the piers, where Reza and I were seated now. All day and late into the night waiters scurry across the precarious metal ramps that link the piers on which the teahouse sits, while the waters of the Zayandeh River surge through the narrow gaps just centimetres beneath. It must be one of the profession's most perilous postings.

While we awaited our tea by the bridge, our group was relaxing at the Abassi Hotel, one of Iran's finest, which had begun life in the 17th century as a caravanserai. Ruined or restored caravanserais are sprinkled right across Asia, but the word itself comes from two separate Persian words: 'caravan', meaning a company of travellers, and 'serai', a place. Perhaps the most tangible reminders of the silk routes (there was never one single route but a network of roads – arteries of commerce) that have intrigued travellers, including me, for centuries, the caravanserais were the silk route equivalents of the motor lodge; accommodation houses for the great caravans of camels that threaded their way from China west to Central Asia, India and the Middle East and were linked with important sea routes. In this way the silk routes were connected to southern Italy across the Mediterranean and were an important component of trade from the Persian Gulf ports.

At the Abassi where traders, travellers and merchants would once have slept in the arched rooms around a central courtyard, rested their camels, gossiped and intrigued as they plied the great silk routes of Asia more than 400 years ago, tourists now rest in five-star comfort. Conditions might be more luxurious now, but the hotel's romantic past lingers in the courtyard like woodsmoke from a camel herder's evening fire.

Meanwhile, down at the bridge the surroundings are just as atmospheric if a little more basic. Reza had just dipped a lump of sugar into his tea, then into his mouth before drawing deeply on the mouthpiece of the *qalyan*, which spluttered into life.

'Shah Abbas the Great, who made Isfahan Persia's capital in the seventeenth century, is supposed to have built nine hundred and ninety-nine caravanserais to help revive the importance of the silk routes through his empire,' said Reza, leaning back and passing me the *qalyan* mouthpiece. A beginner smoker then, I exhale at first, causing a minor eruption of water and smoke. Two men at a nearby table hear the spluttering, look at me and grin. I retreat inside my headscarf – sometimes *hijab* (meaning veil or cover and referring to the required modest dress for women in Iran where the body, from wrist to ankle, and hair have to be covered) has its advantages.

I loved the idea of such an impressive number of caravanserais. Apparently Shah Abbas thought that 999 sounded much grander than one thousand, hence his decree. Just the word caravanserai conjured up for me the sound of complaining camels, the smell of smoke from cooking fires, the glimpse of shadowy figures in dark archways, the glimmer of silk from a wrapped bundle. Caravanserais for me epitomised the romance of travel – and now I discovered Reza felt the same way.

'Few Iranians and even fewer foreigners have ever explored properly many of these remarkable buildings,' he added.

'Can you find them all over Iran?' I asked.

'Oh yes,' Reza said. 'From the Persian Gulf to the Caspian.'

'So it would be possible to explore a lot of Iran by following the ancient silk routes and visiting some of the nine hundred and ninety-nine along the way?'

'Quite possible,' was Reza's calm response as he puffed a small cloud of apple-flavoured smoke into the night air.

I thought back to my first visit to Iran that also marked the start of our friendship. Rather unconventionally I'd not arrived by air but by land across the border with Turkmenistan at Sarakhs in northeastern Iran, near Mashhad.

The terrain approaching the Iranian border from its northern neighbour is bleak and hard. A rubbly wasteland studded with struggling shrubs impaled with rubbish stretched into the heat haze on both sides of the road.

That morning I'd put on for the first time the floor-length black coat that I'd brought to make sure I passed muster at the Iranian border post. Covered from head to foot I had been quietly cooking and wishing that I'd waited until the border itself to don the garment. My driver's Soviet-era car did not run to air conditioning and even with the windows down the temperature was rising.

The Turkmen side of the border was something of an anticlimax. In fact, if I'd been on my own I'd probably have driven right past it. But my driver had been here before and so stopped the car beside a high wire fence into which was set a narrow gate. Leaning against the fence were two locals in faded T-shirts and jeans who half-heartedly asked me if I'd like to buy US dollars. When I declined they returned to puffing on their cigarettes and staring into the desert.

My escort pushed open the gate and dragged my bag though to the small square concrete-block building on the other side. Facing us was an open window behind which a Turkmen guard in a peaked cap was eating his lunch.

He didn't look up as I handed my passport and three slips of paper through the hatch. With a sigh he put down his hunk of bread and opened the passport. Only then did he glance at me. I didn't need any help in translating the look. 'The only tourist all day and she has to arrive at lunch-time.'

Turkmenistan, maybe because its tourist trade is so meagre, likes to make it as difficult as possible to get out of the country – once they get you in they are reluctant to let you leave. Obtaining an entry visa is time-consuming and expensive enough, but the

Turkmens save up the best of the bureaucratic mire for when you are trying to get out. When I arrived I was told that the three pieces of paper that had been tucked into my passport were absolutely crucial and must not be lost under any circumstances, otherwise I'd have trouble on departure. One of them had been printed on paper so thin it appeared in danger of disintegrating at any minute. As none of the documents contained any English translation I had no idea why they were so important, but I guarded them zealously. Now was their moment.

The border guard picked up all three slips and, without a glance at them, dropped them into a bin beside his desk. I decided to give him the benefit of the doubt – after all, what might have looked like a rubbish bin to me might have been some kind of sophisticated Turkmen filing cabinet. He then picked up his bread and my passport in one hand, and, holding the document open with the heel of one hand, thumped it with an exit visa (liberally sprinkling bread crumbs over the pages at the same time), thrust it through the open window and went back to his lunch.

'Is that it?' I said to the driver, rather aggrieved. Somehow, border crossings, especially into somewhere as exotic and supposedly dangerous as Iran, deserved more fanfare.

'Now we go to the customs building,' he said, pointing down the tarmac road to a slightly grander concrete-block edifice about a hundred metres away.

We trundled my bag down the slightly sticky tarmac and as we did so I realised that my Iranian coat was several centimetres too long. If I wasn't careful I'd be constantly tripping over the hem. I'd also not realised how incredibly hot black could be; under the coat sweat was trickling everywhere in a manner that hardly seemed fitting for entering an Islamic republic.

It was clearly a very slow day at the border as, on my arrival in the customs hall, all four occupants converged on me. We all helped put my bag up on a table. Among Turkmenistan's few claims to fame are its hand-knotted carpets and although buying and taking home new rugs is encouraged, removing antique ones is illegal. I'd been warned that it didn't matter what else I had in my bag; if I had an old carpet I could expect difficulties.

'Carpets?' one of the officials asked, hopefully.

I told him no. There ensued a brief discussion among them, but the four of them then decided that they should check my bag in case an illicit rug lurked within. I unlocked the bag and all of us peered in – even my escort and a truck driver who'd just strolled in. We all agreed there were no carpets hidden among my underwear, clothes and assorted headscarves. Everyone but me seemed rather disappointed. I guessed they'd been hoping to be entertained with some lively debate, multiple form-filling and maybe a confiscation.

'You can go to Iran now,' said the driver.

I headed back towards the door we had come through.

'No madam – Iran is that way,' he said, pointing to a door at the other end of the building.

He accompanied me through the doorway, and we contemplated the official border, a green smudge of trees that fringed the river several kilometres away.

'How do I get over there?' I asked. The driver said there was normally a bus for pedestrians parked around the side of the customs building and so we went to investigate.

We found a vehicle that certainly had wheels and a roof – but little else. The passenger door was tied up with wire, but that was entirely academic because there were no seats. There was also no sign of a driver.

The two of us contemplated the bus for a few minutes. The only sound came from the big rigs that were pulling up outside the customs house for clearance to cross the border.

'Maybe I can hitch a ride on a truck.'

I'd always wanted a ride in a long-haul truck and here were some beautiful chrome-encrusted monsters to choose from. My escort told me to wait with my bag while he went to find a driver who'd be willing to take me across the border. I'd spotted a particularly impressive red truck with a happy excess of gleaming metal and hoped it would be that one.

He was back in a few minutes to tell me he'd found a driver who'd pick me up soon. One by one the big rigs revved up and left, none of them coming near me. Finally, an elderly orange pick-up truck, brown smoke pouring from its exhaust, emerged from the belching throng of vehicles and pulled up in front of me.

The driver climbed down and heaved my bag onto the tray and motioned for me to climb up into the passenger seat. Another man was already sitting there.

'Who's he?' I asked the escort, thinking I should at least check out the identity of my travelling companion. 'Oh, he's just a local man who wants to travel with you across the border. He'll come back later. Your driver is Iranian, though.'

Short of walking through several kilometres of desert, then crossing a truck-laden one-lane bridge there was no option but to go with the men. I'd have to trust that the brevity of the journey and the volume of traffic would prevent any thought of robbery, and my sombre black garb and almost complete lack of any exposed flesh would be protection enough against any inflamed passions. I handed my daypack up to my fellow traveller, hitched up my coat and struggled up the ladder to the cab, almost strangling myself in the process with the long headscarf that I'd wrapped around my hair while waiting for the truck.

The driver got in and both men then engaged in a long debate punctuated with long stares at me. I asked my escort, who was still standing below, what was going on.

'They are saying that you do not need your headscarf until you reach the bridge – they will tell you when to put it on.'

I removed the scarf and we set off. When we reached the bridge a steady stream of trucks was heading in our direction from Iran and we had to wait for some time for them to cross. Up until this time my mind had been kept busy with the trivia of travel but now I started to become a little jittery. I'd brushed off all the jokes before I left about travelling to a country branded as part of the so-called Axis of Evil and told people, who were genuinely concerned about how a Western woman on her own would manage in a strict Islamic country, that the popular image of Iran in the West was nothing like the reality. Like a video on fast forward a stream of images was flicking through my brain – fanatical-looking demonstrators threatening death to America (the fact that I came from New Zealand might be a minor detail) and stony-faced women preaching the benefits of being swathed in black – along with sound bites about the nuclear weapons debate and possible military action against Iran. (After all, no world superpower considering a missile strike was going to take into account that I might be picking my away across a caravanserai ruin nearby.)

Then it was our turn on the bridge. We rumbled onto the wooden deck and the truck lurched towards the midway point. When we reached it both men suddenly turned to me and pointed to the headscarf. 'Yes!' they shouted, grinning.

My hair disappeared from view, and other than when I was in my hotel room at night, and during the occasional high wind or when I stood on a trailing scarf end, was never seen again during my stay in Iran.

When we reached the far bank, the driver pulled over at a small, grey concrete building, outside which was parked a black four-wheel-drive vehicle. I started to open the door but the driver, using the other half of his English vocabulary said 'No', and instead mimed that I should wind down the window. I obeyed and he then pointed at my passport. What did he want me to do – throw it out? But then I noticed, standing below me, was an Iranian immigration guard. I handed him my passport and immediately the driver put the truck into gear and began to drive away. 'No,' I said. 'Yes,' he replied. 'My passport!' I shrieked, but he shook his head and kept driving. I looked back out the window in time to see the border guard walking towards the four-wheel-drive vehicle and passing my passport in through the driver's window.

Great, I thought. I'm in a country almost everyone I know thinks I'm mad to visit and after less than five minutes my passport's been hijacked.

By now the driver was slowing down outside a sleek modern building, its smoky grey mirror-glass windows looking out blankly across an expanse of tarseal. This appeared to be the main Iranian immigration office. He signalled for me to get down.

'My bag?' I enquired.

'No,' he said.

'I need my bag,' I said, trying to sound masterful.

'No,' he repeated.

The other passenger leaned across me and opened my door.

I climbed down and resignedly watched the truck drive away, my bag bobbing gently on the tray.

Scarf, hem and heart trailing I went up the steps into the building. It was gleaming new, the floors shiny and pristine – but not a soul to be seen anywhere.

I looked in the doorways of several offices that led off the main hall, but they were all empty. I couldn't even hear any sign of life. I had no passport (and thus no visa), no bag and appeared to have been abandoned. The intrepid traveller was verging on tears. I stood in the middle of the hall, devoid of ideas, sticky with sweat and defeated.

There was a small cough behind me. I turned and a tall clean-shaven man with short, curling dark brown hair and an earnest expression leaned down to look under my headscarf which had slipped down low over my forehead. As upset as I was I couldn't help but notice his to-die-for eyelashes.

'Jill?' he said, 'I'm Reza, your guide. Welcome to Iran.'

'They've taken my passport and my bag's disappeared,' I blurted, immediately ashamed of sounding both pathetic and paranoid at the same time.

'Wait here just a moment, I'll be back.'

Reza disappeared through a doorway and once again I was marooned in silence. He came back a few minutes later.

'Here is your passport and your driver has just delivered your bag to the back door – he did not want you to have to carry it up the front steps. Let us do the formalities and then we will go to Mashhad. I think you will manage in that coat. I did not expect someone looking quite so, well, fundamental.'

As first impressions went I was doing badly. Weepy, suspicious, ungrateful and looking like a bedraggled black shuttlecock, I looked closely at Reza as we headed at a fast clip for the door and was not surprised to see him looking thoughtfully into the distance. He was probably trying to think of a prior engagement (not easy in such an isolated place) or whether he could claim to have mistaken me for another tourist.

Suddenly he stopped in his tracks.

'But, before we go much further, I think, maybe we will go and have some lunch?' Unbeknown to both of us at the time, he'd set a pattern for many of our future journeys – the principle that exploration and travel could only be improved by a succulent kebab, a good cup of tea, a puff or two on a *qalyan* and the occasional saffron ice cream.

Two Wings of a Nightingale is the story of our recent travels through a country with a Persian soul and an Islamic heart, a population with a public persona and a private life – a nightingale with two wings to keep it aloft and singing.

SAFFRON ICE CREAM
Mashhad

Those unable to grieve,
Or speak their love
Or to be grateful, those
Who can't remember God
As the source of everything,
Might be described as vacant wind,
Or a cold anvil, or a group
Of frightened old people
Say the Name. Moisten your tongue
With praise. And be the spring ground,
Waking. Let your mouth be given
Its gold-yellow stamen like the wild rose's.

Sanai, 12th century Persian poet

We are pilgrims. We are pilgrims in the holiest city in Iran and we're trying to finish our saffron-flavoured ice creams quickly so that we can enter the shrine complex.

Mashhad, in northeastern Iran, manages to combine spirituality with just a whiff of English seaside resort. Here it's possible not just to recharge yourself spiritually but you can also to replenish the household supplies of saffron, perfumes and prayer beads. In fact, you can shop until late and pray all night if you wish – Mashhad's shrine to Imam Reza is open 24 hours a day, every day.

Imam Reza (Ali ibn Musa al-Rida) was the eighth Shia imam. Iranian Shias believe there are 12 imams or leaders who are direct descendants of the Prophet Mohammad's cousin and brother-in-law Ali (who to Shias is the first imam). It is this core belief that separates them from the Sunni Moslems who dispute the right of Ali's descendants to be Islam's leaders. Instead, Sunnis believe that the Prophet's followers and friends were the rightful people to select his successor. To them Ali is simply the fourth Islamic caliph or ruler. Incidentally, the 12th imam is also known to Shias as the absent or hidden imam, who will appear again in the days of judgement and resurrection.

Imam Reza, a direct descendant of the Prophet Mohammad, was born in about AD 765 in Medina. A charismatic man, he became the eighth imam when he was 35. Shia Moslems believe he was poisoned by a rival spiritual leader, Caliph Ma'mun, in about AD 818. His burial site (known as Mashhad or place of martyrdom) quickly became a pilgrimage site and today it's the most important in Iran. He is the only one of the 12 imams to be buried in modern-day Iran. More than 14 million Shias from all over the world visit it every year. Along with the shrine itself, the vast precinct contains religious schools, mosques, libraries and museums.

Mashhad, with its pilgrims and glittering shrines, is not actually the start of my 8000-km journey around Iran following the routes plied by the caravans of old, but it represents the beginning of my love for Iran and my first steps on its soil. Its significance is intensified for me because it is also close to the place where I met Reza for the first time – a meeting that has led to a lasting and deep friendship.

When Reza brought me here that first time, I'd been in Iran less than 12 hours and was floundering in a sea of the unfamiliar. My memories of that visit include being refused entry to the shrine precinct by a wizened elderly lady on duty at the women's security gate.

'Moslem?' she enquired.

On my reply, she waved me imperiously out the way I'd come. I'd felt unaccountably inadequate and had to summon Reza back from the land of the believers to sort things out. Non-Moslems are allowed into the massive shrine precinct; it's the inside of the shrine itself that is forbidden to non-Moslems.

As we walk towards the shrine on this second visit, we reminisce about Reza's remonstration with the guards from the other side of the thick Persian carpet that hung down over the entrance to the women's checkpoint.

'The problem is,' says Reza, 'that people from all over Iran and of all ages and backgrounds volunteer to work at the shrine. They do it to show their love for Imam Reza but sometimes they do not know the proper regulations, although they can be very enthusiastic about the rules.'

We stop outside the ice-cream shop. Reza orders saffron-flavoured cones. Along with its spiritual importance to Shias, Mashhad is the centre of saffron production and many of the shops that line the main thoroughfares leading to the shrine are stocked with packets and jars of the dried squiggly anthers of the crocus flower. Taking saffron home to family and friends is a pilgrimage tradition.

Although it's after 10 pm the footpath is crammed with people. Tiny stores festooned with strings of prayer beads, blue evil-eye pendants and posters of Imam Ali and other religious heroes are doing a roaring trade. There are street vendors, too – we pass four young men, their arms encircled with a dozen watches, while nearby a man has attracted an attentive audience as he unwraps a roll of sparkling headscarves.

About a hundred metres in front of the shrine the road transforms into a roundabout. Traffic is careering around it – cars merging with the flow with just centimetres to spare while pedestrians dart through the chaos.

Reza prepares to launch us into the maelstrom of speeding metal.

'Just stay beside me and keep moving. I can't take your arm because it is not customary here,' he says, with a faint trace of irony.

Apparently, the authorities would rather I was flattened by a pilgrims' bus than risk any physical contact between unrelated men and women. We dodge between car bumpers, seemingly invisible to the vehicles' drivers. It's up to us to avoid them, not the other way round.

Close to the shrine two long pedestrian ramps lead to the main gates. The ramps are separated by a vehicle underpass that is choked with traffic travelling right under the holy site.

It's only at the top of the ramp that I remember I have not brought a chador with me. Without the all-encompassing piece of fabric I won't be going any further than the gate. I am wearing *hijab*, but my Iranian *manteau* (a mid thigh-length light coat) and headscarf are not sufficient here.

It would take us an hour to make the round trip to the pilgrims' hotel where we are staying. Reza stands, thoughtfully stroking his chin, then suddenly makes a run for the security booth at the top of the ramp.

Reza's style of running is one of his many endearing characteristics. It's the Irish dancing equivalent of running – while Reza's lower half runs, his upper body stays almost motionless. He glides to a stop outside the booth and begins a conversation with the guard. At one point, Reza turns around and points in my direction and they both contemplate the unsuitability of my attire.

The guard disappears from view but returns straight away with a cloth bundle that he hands to Reza.

'What a kind man, Reza says. 'He has lent this to you. Can you remember how to put it on?' he concludes, unfurling the sprigged blue cotton and almost completely circular chador.

Last time I was here we had to stop a woman passer-by to help me don the garment. Working out the intricacies of a chador is not something Iranian males get much practice in. But this time I'm determined not to have to ask for help.

I hold the chador out behind me and let it drop over my head, gather up a handful of fabric in my left hand and catch the edge on the right side with the same hand and grip it tight under my chin. This frees up my right hand for keeping the rest of the chador from gaping lower down. But of course now that both my hands are occupied, my shoulder bag promptly starts sliding down one arm.

Satisfied that I have the chador mostly under control, Reza checks for any sign of escaping hair. My hair is thick, blonde, unruly and unused to being tamed. It's always trying to make a break for it from the confines of my headscarf. So far it's behaving.

We head for the gates – Reza to the men's security check, I to the women's. I'm nervous; I don't want to be rejected again.

I haul back the thick carpet over the entrance and step in. This time it's a young woman in her early twenties sitting there behind a wooden table. I open my chador to uncover my bag and she leaps to her feet. I'm going to be evicted.

She walks around to my side of the table, reaches up with both hands and rearranges my chador. And smiles.

'Welcome,' she says.

She signals for me to go through. Halfway to the doorway her companion calls out to me. She's older, sterner, and I'm guessing she's not so sure about letting me in. But when I turn back to her she's gesticulating at my forehead, and signalling that I've covered up too much of my face.

Reza and I walk across the slippery smoothness of the first marble courtyard. Minarets and domes glitter under the spotlights and a loudspeaker broadcasts the voice of a mullah singing verses from the Koran. The Imam's shrine is surmounted by a golden dome and flanked by two golden minarets – stunning in daylight, breathtaking at night.

A man driving a floor-polishing machine is weaving his way around the groups of pilgrims heading in the same direction as us. Giggling teenage girls are struggling with their chadors – clearly they also are more used to wearing the *manteau*.

'They look more foreign than you do,' observes Reza. 'You are managing your chador just like my grandmother.'

I know he means it as a compliment, but I raise my eyebrows at him.

'But of course, I mean, when my grandmother was just 20,' he adds hurriedly.

We have reached another doorway where we take off our shoes. Reza hands them to a cloakroom attendant wearing gloves. There's a strong smell of hot feet in the air. Thick Persian carpets cover the floor of the prayer hall beyond the shoe station. People are sitting, praying here. The aroma of feet is replaced by the heady scent of rosewater. We sniff, trying to locate the source.

Reza points to a small machine about the size of a toaster sitting on a table in front of a mirrored pillar. Every few seconds it puffs rosewater into the air.

'It's the perfume of the Prophet,' Reza says.

We weave through corridors, the chador around my face giving me tunnel vision so that I lose my sense of direction. We stop in a wide corridor – there are few people here but I can hear a murmur of voices. They ebb and flow like the tide, but the intensity of the sound never wavers.

'We are outside the shrine – do you want to go in?' Reza asks.

'But I can't,' I squeak, caught by surprise.

'Yes, I think you can. I know what is in your heart. Go.'

I know that if I go I am on my own. There are separate entrances to the shrine itself for men and women, so Reza will not be able to shepherd me through this experience.

'I'll meet you out here in 15 minutes,' he says, heading for the men's entrance and not giving me any time to think up more excuses.

The long anteroom I step into is so crowded with praying women it is difficult to find space on the carpet to place my feet. Others are sitting in clusters, reading the Koran or talking quietly. I am unsure which way to go. Understandably, Reza's knowledge of the women's section is a little sketchy. But I can hear that insistent whisper of voices to my left and so, picking my way through the crowd, I turn to follow it.

I step through two massive silver doors and am brought to a standstill, literally dazzled, blinded by the light. The interior of the shrine is completely covered in tiny mirrored tiles that glitter in niches, cascade from stucco stalactites and magnify the light emitted from a shimmering chandelier suspended above the Imam's tomb.

Directly ahead is a partition that separates the men from the women and slightly to the right the women's portion of the gold-latticed bars of the tomb itself. Or at least I can see glimpses of it. An undulating mass of black chador-clad women is clinging to the bars, praying, weeping, and kissing the metal.

A woman appears in front of me, wielding a multicoloured duster.

'Where are you from?' she asks in English.

I reply in Farsi (Iran's national language, which is also known as Persian). She smiles.

'Moslem?' I smile.

'Where is your husband?'

I wave vaguely in the direction of what might be New Zealand or simply the corridor. She reaches out and takes me by the elbow. I've come to a halt right where dozens of women are trying to move towards the tomb and another stream of pilgrims are returning to the prayer hall. Is she going to frogmarch me out through the praying ranks of the faithful? Waving her duster (which is the shrine attendants' highly visible badge of office) she leads me to the side, against the curtained glass barrier.

'You will be good here,' she says. 'Welcome.'

I close my eyes. Now that my reeling visual senses are quietened it is the emotional impact of the shrine that washes over me. Prayers of hope and pleading, murmurs of joy and awe, muffled sounds of weeping and whispered secrets. The atmosphere is as charged and overwhelming as the deluge of silvery sparkling light is awe-inspiring.

From the men's section a man's voice rises above the hum of several hundred others, singing in Farsi. Spontaneously, the crowd – men and women – join in, the sound reverberating around the mirrored space, drawing all of us up into the dome, closer to heaven. A shiver races up my neck.

A writer is supposed to observe, to take mental notes. I try but when I close my eyes now, I can't see architectural details – only silver and white light and the sense of adoration and loss that seep into the senses.

I retrace my steps, only to be halted by another duster-waving guardian.

'You are from?' she asks.

I reply and tell her the shrine is very beautiful. She extends a hand and strokes my cheek. There are tears on it.

Reza is waiting outside.

'How was it?'

'I don't know what to say. It was one of the most moving experiences of my life. I was caught by surprise.'

'Perfect,' he says.

As we walk back to retrieve our shoes the perfume machine gives a small sigh and a cloud of rosewater fills the air.

The next day we go back to the shrine again – it is the heart of Mashhad and draws its pilgrims like a magnet.

This time we explore the shrine to Gohar Shad, daughter-in-law of Timur, the 14th-century conqueror of vast tracts of Central Asia, modern-day Iran, the Middle East, Turkey and the

Caucasus. The shrine's exquisite decorations of floral tiles, stucco stalactites date back to the 15th century. The complex is much busier than the night before and the flow of people through the courtyards is increasing. There's a crackle over the loudspeakers and suddenly the *azan* – the call to prayer – fills the air. It is close to midday.

'Shall we go to the main courtyard?' Reza asks.

There is barely any open space in the Enqelab Courtyard. Shrine volunteers are directing women to one area, men to another, families to another section. At an open grill giving a view of the Imam's tomb itself, supplicants are clinging to the metal and praying.

'Many sick people go there,' Reza explains, 'and there have been many cures.'

Thousands of people are already sitting together, chatting. Others sit in islands of solitude reading, or meditating, prayer beads slipping through their fingers.

We go into an adjacent courtyard that is a little less crowded. Reza is looking thoughtful as the *azan* echoes around the domes with their exuberant arabesques of colour.

'Do you want to pray?' I ask him.

Reza looks at me. When I first met him we confessed to each other that we both had doubts about organised religion, whether Islam or Christianity. And to Reza one's spirituality was something deeply personal – not to be discussed lightly as part of a tour leader's lectures. Until our pilgrimage I'd been unsure just what Reza believed and how deeply held his beliefs were.

'What do you think?' he says, 'Would you mind? I don't want to leave you alone with all these people? But I think the saying is "When in Rome ...".'

I tell him I will be fine, and he should go. Prayers are about to begin so to avoid any more discussion I sit down in an archway at the back of the courtyard.

In front of me women are picking their way cross the carpets and mats spread on the flagstones to find a few available centimetres of space. Shoes are scattered around the perimeter – it's an eclectic collection of footwear: from worn slippers to ankle boots with stiletto heels. There's an expectant, almost festive air.

A young woman appears behind me, bends down and asks me in Farsi if I have a cell phone. I reply no, but when she launches into a long explanation I look blank. I'm only on chapter four of elementary Persian. Another woman beside me turns to help and fishes out a phone from somewhere under her chador. She then looks enquiringly at me. I say hello and she immediately shuffles closer.

Her name is Fatima, she says and her father is a mullah in Mashhad. Her black chador frames a long very pale face and solemn eyes. Two months ago she'd married an architect. A student, she likes to come to the shrine, especially for midday prayers. She points at my chador and asks how I am managing. By now prayers have started and there is a collective rustle as those in the courtyard bend forward: *'Beshmallahe rahmane rahim …'*

Fatima stays seated beside me. She wants to know more about my religion and I want to know what she thinks of *hijab*.

'It is good,' she says, 'I feel safe when I am wearing my chador.'

Another ripple moves through the people at prayer as they stand up. The Moslem prayer marries movement and rhythm with worship. Elderly women clutch at daughters' and granddaughters' arms as they struggle to their feet and then a few seconds later, they are creakily easing themselves back on their knees on the carpet.

The prayer ends – the last words a collective sigh among thousands that hangs in the air, wrapping itself around the domes of turquoise blue and weaving among the gilded minarets that glint like lightning flashes in the midday sun. My friend stands up to leave.

'I think one day you will become a Moslem,' she says, smiling at me as she gathers her chador under her chin.

Reza appears. 'Are you all right? Who were you talking to?'

I tell him about Fatima.

'So you've been talking to a daughter of the religious hierarchy. I wonder why she wasn't praying?' he says, 'Did you ask?'

I admit I'd not thought of that.

'Maybe today you were more interesting than praying,' Reza concludes.

We've flowed with the tide of the faithful out of a different entrance. Reza decrees we must go to the toilets. I tell him I don't need to go.

'Actually, we're going because I want you to see how luxurious they are.'

The toilets are underground and reached by escalators. A woman of about 50 is hesitating at the top, despite the pleadings of her daughters who are already halfway down. I take her elbow and we descend together. It's a few seconds before she turns to look up at me. Astonishment at finding herself on the arm of a Westerner replaces her earlier look of terror. Reunited at the bottom with her family she begins an animated conversation. Reza, always interested in Iranians' reaction to my presence, is listening avidly, grinning.

'She is telling her family that she got such a shock to see blue eyes under the chador and that you have been very kind,' he translates.

The women's toilets are a vast echoing chamber of white marble. More fascinating to me than the fittings, however, is the sight of so many uncovered heads as women of all ages comb, brush and re-tie ponytails and buns. So conditioned am I after only a few days in Iran that I am almost too embarrassed to look. Deciding that I, too, could probably do with repairing what I'd nickname *hijab* hair (a head of hair pressed completely flat and lifeless under a layer of scarf and chador), I remove both and rummage in my bag for my hairbrush. The hum of female chatter ceases. I'd been planning a thorough grooming session and then careful rearrangement of *hijab,* but the intense scrutiny is too much. I bundle my hair back under cover and retreat.

Beyond the shrine perimeter shopkeepers are busy making money from the pilgrims the way they've been doing for centuries. My nose tells me we've reached the perfume sellers' bazaar long before we see the small shops lined with myriad glass bottles filled with a rainbow hue of liquids.

Reza steers me past the shops until we reach a stubbly-faced, grey-haired man standing on the footpath. His perfume stall is on wheels – the cabinet lid is open to provide a shelf for his display and to reveal a small worktable containing empty bottles, stoppers and syringes. Reza points at a bottle and the man dips in the syringe, fills a small bottle and squirts the remainder over Reza's jacket. He then sprays a final flourish over me.

'This is the perfume of Imam Reza's shrine,' Reza explains, identifying many of the other perfumes as being associated with different holy sites. The perfumes are intense, intoxicating and speak to me more of sensuality than spirituality.

They are a great example of the Persian conundrum – the

drowning of the senses in architectural splendour, in haunting music, heady perfume – one wing of the Persians' beloved nightingale. On the other wing – the masking of the black chador, the expression of emotions kept behind closed doors, the imperative to at least outwardly conform.

Reza buys several perfumes, testing them all first, and the salesman opens up a series of drawers in his mobile perfumerie to take out half a dozen tiny cardboard boxes with floral designs. Each small bottle is laid in a box and covered with a layer of protective sponge.

While Mashhad does not lack souvenirs it certainly seems to lack places to find a cup of tea – a strange dilemma in a nation of avid tea drinkers. After numerous enquiries among the shopkeepers we are directed down a narrow alleyway, past windows full of antique brassware to an unprepossessing shopfront.

Inside the walls of a long narrow room are lined with bench seats. Set on tables in front of the seats are dozens of *qalyans* gurgling musically. The smokers, all men, look up and on seeing me the pipes fall silent.

'I can't come in here,' I hiss at Reza. 'There are no women.'

'We're going to the family area,' he replies leading me to the right and in the direction of the kitchen where we take our seats at an empty table, screened from the main body of smokers by a fish tank.

From my seat I can watch the tea-maker swinging teapots under a bubbling stainless steel samovar and then pouring out long streams of amber liquid into glasses. Iranians never, if they can help it, drink tea in opaque cups – tea is to be enjoyed not just for its taste, but also for its colour. It's for this reason that *qalyans* have glass bases. Iranians like to be able to see the water bubbling. It's another example of an appeal to the senses – the sound of water and the rhythm of a poem, the perfume of a rose, the feel of a silk carpet underfoot, the taste of fresh pistachios. All this in a country brimming with sensuality but where dancing is prohibited and public displays of affection are officially frowned on.

Beside the tea-maker a young man with a face beaded with drops of sweat tends a fiery furnace used to heat charcoal to glowing incandescence. When the fire is burning to his satisfaction he turns to a sink to rinse out the water-filled glass *qalyan* bases. Once they are washed and refilled, he attaches the top section that contains the tobacco covered by a layer of tinfoil on which are placed three or four red-hot pieces of charcoal.

Contrary to widely held beliefs in the West, *qalyans* are not, at least in public teahouses in Iran, stuffed full of hashish. Drugs are illegal in Iran. But smoking tobacco in the *qalyan* is a widespread and popular pastime, for women as well as men.

Beside us a third man with a deeply lined face, wearing an old blue blazer with gold buttons, is chopping up blocks of tobacco, separating the dry leaves and letting them flutter into a bowl.

The tea-maker lets two cups of tea clatter onto our formica-topped table as he sweeps past on his way to the serious smokers carrying in his other hand four glasses balanced on saucers.

Already on the table is a small lidded bowl containing sugar lumps. There are no teaspoons because in Iran sugar is not stirred into the tea. Instead traditional tea drinkers dip the sugar lump briefly into the hot liquid to soften it, then clamp it between their front teeth. Sipping one's tea through the sugar, without forgetfully crunching it up, is something of an art.

Our *qalyan* with orange-flavoured tobacco arrives. Before coming to Iran I'd never so much as had more than one puff of a normal cigarette, but somewhat guiltily I've taken to *qalyan* smoking like a professional. But only with flavoured tobacco. There are dozens of flavours, with orange, apple, cappuccino, strawberry, banana and mint among the most popular and both Reza, who was also a non-smoker, and I are working our way through them to decide on our favourite.

Teahouses frequented by fashionable Iranian youth and/or tourists sometimes go light on the tobacco and don't heat the charcoal properly, making for a less-than-memorable *qalyan* experience. But the Mashhad teahouse has a discerning clientele. Reza briefly disappears behind a cloud of smoke as he exhales (a thick pall of smoke indicates that the charcoal has been properly heated). After one puff each we're both feeling a bit giddy.

The door swings open and a tall distinguished-looking man with a bushy moustache breezes in, accompanied by a dumpy woman in a headscarf. Taking a seat at the end of our table, the woman studies me with interest as her husband drops a large plastic bag of sugar lumps on a bench and then inspects the charcoal brazier. Coming over to us he asks Reza where I am from. Reza, well versed in all my particulars, provides details.

'He is the owner,' Reza tells me, when there's a pause in the questioning while the proprietor relays all the information to his wife. 'He is an Azeri Turk, that is from Iran's Azerbaijan province. He says welcome to Mashhad and he hopes you like his teahouse.'

Reza then asks the owner if he has heard of New Zealand. He has, but is a little vague as to its location. We show him a postcard that features a map of the world with New Zealand circled in red. Reza then offers the card to the man cutting up tobacco, who takes a brief look before telling Reza he already knows where New Zealand is.

'They have had a woman prime minister, they have a governor-general who represents the Queen of England and no constitution,' he says. Reza translates all this with a look of amazement.

'I like documentaries on television,' the man says, not pausing in his work.

We are plied with numerous cups of tea for which the owner at first refuses to accept payment. Reza keeps proffering the money until after the third time the owner finally relents.

This is the Iranian custom of *tarof* in action, an extreme form of politeness that involves repeatedly refusing a gift or payment. It can be very confusing for foreigners who tend, after maybe the second refusal in a shop or taxi to wander off, amazed at the locals' generosity. They can therefore be a little bewildered to find someone running after them demanding money.

Out in the street, awash with tea and slightly light-headed from the *qalyan*, we hunt for a taxi. We are going to visit one of Iran's largest and best-preserved caravanserais.

I can't remember when I first heard the word caravanserai, but it immediately embedded itself in my traveller's soul the way the name Timbuktu does for others. As mentioned earlier, caravanserais are the ancestors of the modern motor inn – oases of security, comfort and opportunities for socialising along the often hazardous and arduous silk routes that linked China with Europe from the second century AD until the early 20th century.

Once there must have been thousands of these walled compounds dotted along the various branches of the silk route. Most have disappeared, but in Iran, thanks largely to Shah

Abbas's decree to build 999 of them, a remarkable number remain – some in ruins, others restored as historical monuments, still more entering a new century of use as hotels and museums.

Mashhad lies on the silk route that swung south from Central Asia and the region is dotted with caravanserais in various stages of disrepair and repair. Although I'd been anxious to visit Mashhad's shrine, I'd also been a little worried that if the theme for our journey was going to be the silk routes of Iran, embarking on a pilgrimage could be viewed as something of a literary detour. Reza, however, is unperturbed.

'The silk routes were not simply for trade – pilgrims used them too, so what we have been doing in Mashhad, visiting the shrine and praying in the mosques, is exactly what thousands of travellers along the silk routes would have done over many centuries. We are following a very old tradition.'

When we arrive at the Rubat caravanserai a couple of hours' drive northeast of Mashhad, there seem to be children popping out of the stonework in all directions. I'm trying to visualise the camels tied up to the stone mangers in the stables, striving to imagine the call to prayer from the caravanserai's own mosque, but instead all I see are small dusty bodies swarming through the water troughs and scrabbling noisily over the walls.

As we are the only visitors and there is just one small cluster of buildings outside the caravanserai, I am mystified where all the children have come from.

'They are all the children of the caretaker,' Reza explains after a conversation with the oldest girl, who has a bare-bottomed baby perched on one hip. 'It seems their father has two wives – one out here and one in the village. I think there are about twelve children in all.'

Clearly the man's caretaking duties do not take up all his time.

'Come and see where the caravan leader stayed,' Reza says, leading me towards the arched entranceway. Caravanserais had just one entrance, which made it easier to defend as well as monitor the comings and goings.

A tumble of broken stairs curves upwards in the gloom. We climb up into a room above the arch. This was always reserved for the caravan leader – a place befitting the status of someone who was responsible for the safe passage of dozens of people, hundreds of camels and cargoes of untold wealth across some of the world's most inhospitable terrain.

We look down into the central courtyard where two of the caretaker's brood are kicking an empty can around the remains of the caravanserai's well.

'The camels would be brought into the courtyard and unloaded in the middle – sometimes there is a raised platform for that – we'll see some in other caravanserai,' Reza says. 'Then the camels would be taken to the stables which often were outside the caravanserai building itself. The caravans always had a mullah with them so he'd probably go to pray at the mosque. And did you know,' adds Reza, warming to his topic, 'that the caravans also had an astronomer with them? Because they travelled mostly at night during the hotter months of the year between spring and early autumn; they needed him to navigate using the stars.'

'It's interesting, isn't it, that in English we talk about camels being ships of the desert, because that's not the only analogy with the sea. There's the navigator and then, of course, there are the lighthouses.'

I look at him. He's regarding me with a slight smile, clearly willing me to ask him more. Reza loves everything to do with the architecture of Iran, especially mosques, theological schools and historic houses. And although he works part time as a tourist guide, he has a strong academic bent. Over the years he has studied English literature and linguistics, historical linguistics and has a Masters degree in ancient Iranian languages, enabling him to translate the decorative calligraphy that is a feature of many Persian buildings. He's also devoted to Persian poetry.

And when he's not translating the angular *kufic* on a mosque, discussing the poetry of Robert Frost and reading Hafez aloud in English and Persian, he is dedicated to tracking down the best examples of Persian cuisine. No one can track down the most delicious saffron ice cream or the tastiest walnut and pomegranate stew like Reza.

Meanwhile, he is waiting for me to quiz him about the lighthouses in the desert.

'You've seen the lighthouses, you know,' he says.

I'm being put to the test.

'Do you mean the minarets?'

'Yes, exactly,' he says approvingly. 'People think of minarets as being simply the place for the muezzin to call the faithful to prayer, but one of their most important roles when the silk routes were in extensive use was to guide the caravans. At night a fire could be lit at the top of a minaret, which the caravan navigator would see and thus be assured he was going in the correct direction.'

We return to Mashhad as night falls. The shrine is bathed in light and the crowds are still pouring through the entrance gates. I knew we'd be joining them – the illuminated courtyards and minarets will draw us in like unresisting moths.

Mashhad has been the beginning and end of thousands of travellers' journeys over many centuries. For me it is and always will be a spiritual springboard from which to launch into the soul of Iran and its people. But in the case of this particular journey, our travels actually begin in the more prosaic surroundings of an apartment building in central Tehran.

POTATO SALAD IN THE DESERT

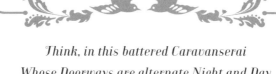

Tehran to Shahrood

Think, in this battered Caravanserai
Whose Doorways are alternate Night and Day
How Sultan after Sultan with his Pomp
Abode his Hour or two, and went his way.

Omar Khayyam, 11th-12th century Persian poet

When the caravan leaders of old awoke, ready to set forth along the silk route, they had the assurance of knowing that their camels were almost certainly in the caravanserai's stable, loaded and ready to go.

We, on the other hand, have just received a telephone call to say our transport is stuck in traffic. But given the starting point of our journey towards Mashhad is Tehran, being caught in the city's clogged arteries is almost inevitable.

'People often ask me what is rush hour in Tehran,' Reza says, as we pile up our luggage for our journey beside his apartment door.

'I tell them it starts at 7 am and finishes about midnight.'

He has just been talking to our driver, who is somewhere out there on the streets, marooned in the daily gridlock caused by its 12 million inhabitants and their two million vehicles.

While we don't have the luxury of a train of camels to accommodate our luggage, we do have a van, so there is no need to pack particularly lightly. It's just as well because the mound of gear is growing rapidly.

Reza's family, like that of most Iranians, is close-knit and everyone is helping. Sedighe, his widowed mother, is pouring walnuts from the family's summer house at Damavand into a plastic bag; Nastaran, his sister, brings us glasses of tea and brother Mojtaba is searching through the household's vast library looking for a book from Reza's collection, a battered but valuable guide to Iran's caravanserai.

Recently retired from teaching, Sedighe now devotes much of her time to steering her household of adult children through the complexities of modern Iranian life. Each morning she gets up long before everyone else to tidy the kitchen and prepare breakfast. As her husband died some years ago, Reza, as the eldest son, is head of the household, but as in most Iranian families, wives and mothers wield much influence.

His sister, Nastaran, usually abbreviated to Nasik, has long, wavy chestnut hair that frames her delicate face with its pale, perfect skin. In her early twenties, she combines working in a travel agency with studying for a degree in psychology. Around the house she wears jeans and T-shirts, talks on the phone, texts her friends, argues sometimes with her mother and her brothers like any other young woman her age and is doted on by everyone.

Younger brother Motjaba or Mojik is studying to be a tour guide, having just finished his compulsory military service. He is unfailingly kind, gentlemanly and is always unobtrusively there when the rest of the family needs him. Which is why he's now systematically sorting through a cupboard trying to find that book. Reza knows it's here somewhere, but it's proving elusive. I'm not really surprised – there are shelves of books everywhere and the overflow of Reza's collection is stored in a metal filing cabinet on the verandah.

We are travelling with our own 'library' gleaned from this collection – all the essentials for travel in Iran – guide books in English and Farsi, my Persian language books and dictionary, academic papers on everything from Sufism to archaeology. Perhaps the most important, though, are the books of poetry: Hafez, Omar, Sadi, Jala-u-Din (Rumi) and Attar. Iranians from all walks of life love their poets; bus drivers to academics, shopkeepers to farmers – all appear to be capable of quoting favourite lines of verse at the drop of a hat.

I'm intrigued that although there are three large bedrooms in the apartment everyone seems to store things in different rooms. The wardrobes in the room shared by Reza and Mojik contain not only clothes and more books, but sets of glasses and plates and bags of nuts and dried fruits. I sleep in Nasik's room, which is also home to the freezer and the ironing board. I like this arrangement because of the warm feeling of communal living involved – people drift into each other's room to find things and to talk. In the faint light of a Tehran dawn I sense rather than see a figure tiptoeing past my bed to grab the iron or lean into the freezer to find bread – I feel absorbed into the routine and into the family.

Reza is confidant and advisor to all and, of course, the apple of his mother's eye. Frequent travel, sometimes involving only a few hours' turnaround, means his life is sometimes less than well organised. Everyone in the household recognises this, especially now, and pitches in to help him pack, find clothes from the washing pile or search for his missing mobile phone while he sits at his desk, suddenly lost in thought.

'What are you doing?' I ask him. 'The driver will be here soon.'

'I am thinking,' says Reza unperturbed, 'about our journey and where we will stop today.'

I suspect the thought of having to pack for the umpteenth time in a few months is more the problem. I put a jumble of shirts on the desk and tell him to sort out what's coming and what's to be bundled back into the wardrobe.

The Mirkhalaf household is a comfortable fusion of Persian, Islamic and the international. Unlike some families who eat all their meals while seated on the floor, Reza's family has a dining table that is used for most meals. When everyone comes in from wherever it is they've spent their day, they tend to flop into armchairs or couches rather than directly onto the floor.

Appropriately, the apartment's floors are a patchwork of Persian carpets: the swirling intricate blues and creams of the urban rugs, nomadic rugs in shades of red, ochre, orange and browns. The dining and living room actually features an elegant parquet floor, but like most Iranians Sedighe likes to have every centimetre covered with rugs.

Footwear worn outside the house never comes into contact with these beautiful works of art, which involves a complex – at least to my eyes – shoe ritual. On coming home, everyone takes off their shoes outside the front door and then mostly pads around the house in their socks. But just inside the door to the bathroom are several sets of plastic slip-on shoes that must only be worn in this room. More sets of bright yellow sandals are located by the kitchen door and similarly must only be used in the kitchen. It takes a few hours for me to get into the routine – take shoes off outside the apartment door (someone regularly goes into the stairwell, gathers up the shoes and carefully places them on a shoe rack just inside the door, the overflow on neatly folded newspaper on the floor), go to the bathroom (slip feet into plastic shoes), leave bathroom (remembering to leave shoes behind), go into living room, put sandals on to go into kitchen to watch dinner being prepared, return to living room (take off kitchen shoes), avoiding tripping over the spare sandals on the way.

The fluidity of Iranian family life means that while Western-style pop music (via satellite) is singing to itself in the living room, someone could well be saying their prayers in their bedroom, a small prayer rug spread on the floor, a set of prayer beads in hand and the *mohr* (a small tablet containing clay from the sacred city of Kerbala) placed on the rug where their forehead will touch it. The contact with this symbolic piece of earth is a sign of humility and also brings the person praying blessings from the sacred site). There is nothing either overt or covert about prayer. It is simply a part of life.

The doorbell rings – our driver has arrived. Before we open the front door though, we three women have to find our manteau and scarves and then there is a mass scramble for the right shoes as we hop around in our socks and drag the bags into the hall.

Sedighe brings a large copy of the Koran to the door and holds it above our heads. Reza and I pass underneath it – following in the footsteps of pilgrims and travellers who for centuries have carried out the same ritual to ensure a safe journey. I shake hands with Mojik and am then enveloped in an embrace by his mother who kisses me on both cheeks. 'Look after my son, it is a long journey,' she tells me, and then tells Reza to look after me, too. Nasik kisses me. 'I will miss you,' she says. I only met her for the first time two days ago, but I know she means it. She wraps my hand around a small gift – an early Valentine's Day present of a pink bear-shaped candle with an 'I love you' message on its tummy.

Down in the street, having miraculously found a car park, the driver (also called Reza and whom from now on I'll call Reza B to avoid confusion) is waiting outside the van. In his mid-forties, he's smartly turned out in a grey check sports jacket and dark trousers, but it's his moustache that commands the greatest attention. Gleaming black and luxurious, it caresses both his cheeks in gentle curves.

We say a somewhat formal *sob bekheihr* (good morning) in Farsi, after which Reza B indicates the van and asks me if I am happy with it. I admire the shiny green paintwork of what is to be our transport for the best part of the next four weeks, then he slides the back door open with a flourish so that I can admire the interior – and his wife, Ferengis, who immediately gets out to kiss me. Reza B had asked if Ferengis could accompany us as far as Mashhad so she could go on pilgrimage to the shrine. Not knowing any better I'd anticipated travelling in the company of a black-clad, religious woman who'd spend the entire two-day trip with her head buried in the Koran. I'd already decided, somewhat pessimistically, that she'd probably disapprove of me.

However, the woman who has just kissed me on the cheek is wearing an elegant black jacquard *manteau* and smart black pumps. Dyed blonde hair peeps out from under her lacy headscarf and, like many Iranian women, she is wearing a lot of make-up. I guess her to be about ten years older than her husband. She immediately lights up a cigarette, coughs, and laughs heartily and somewhat throatily, as Reza B twirls his moustache for me. Reza and I look somewhat scruffy beside them.

We load the van (with Reza B groaning theatrically as he hauls the 'library' onto the back seat) and for one blissful minute drive down a street devoid of traffic before being engulfed in a tide of cars, from gleaming 4WDs and glossy Mercedes to bruised and battered Paikans (the Iranian version of a Hillman Hunter).

It takes at least an hour to thread our way out of central Tehran and onto the highway that leads east to Mashhad. Eight lanes of traffic fight to escape the city where once single files of camels plied the trail that led to the steppes of Central Asia and on to China.

As we clear the featureless concrete-box jungle on the outskirts of Tehran, the Alborz mountains emerge on our left from the brown haze that often envelops one of the most polluted cities in the world. It is February, so snow coats even the lower flanks of the range that rises to its highest point in the form of 5671-metre Mt Damavand, an inactive volcano and Iran's highest mountain.

Ferengis and I are conversing in a mix of my scant Farsi and her even more limited English. This will be her seventh trip to the holy city of Mashhad. Iranians all want to go the shrine of Imam Reza at least once, but if they can go again and again, so much the better.

'I go because Imam Reza was a great man,' she says. 'I always feel relaxed there. It has a special atmosphere.'

The traffic thins out a little as the road begins to wind through deeply incised hills striped in layers of pink and violet. There is not a vestige of plant life on them, but the first few tufts of spring grass are emerging by the roadside where we have just come to a stop.

I assume we've developed some kind of mechanical fault, but it turns out to be the first of our journey's many tea breaks. Iranians fuel their travels by partaking of frequent cups of tea and an almost constant array of snacks, with a midday break for an enormous lunch.

In the back of the van are capacious flasks of hot water and a mobile café. Along with the drinks are fresh dates, pistachios and Reza's mum's walnuts. We drink our tea as juggernauts thunder past, making the van shake and threatening to send our headscarves blowing into the hills.

It's cloudless and cool as the van begins to climb through the low Abovan Pass. The sun gleams on the snow that covers the undulating hills and lies in piles beside the road. It's a sign that winter is not quite ready to give way to spring here in northern Iran.

Beyond the pass and across an uneven stretch of boulder-strewn ground studded with scraggly shrubs are two square buildings with watchtowers at each corner. Reza directs our driver to go off road and we bump our way across to our first caravanserai of the journey.

To our right is a fourth-century AD Sassanian caravanserai made of layers of rough stone, and to the right one of Shah Abbas's Safavid 17th-century versions built of small bricks.

Why, I wonder aloud, did they build a second caravanserai when there was an earlier one still standing and presumably still habitable? It was probably a simple matter of demand outpacing supply for room, Reza explains.

'Necessity is the mother of rebuilding,' he says, as we shake the 400-year-old double wooden doors that loom over us. They are padlocked shut. Not a good start. But I am determined not to be thwarted and we begin to work our way around the building's perimeter.

Most caravanserai outer walls consist of a series of shallow alcoves with pointed archways. These are not merely decorative or structural (the hollow spaces reduce the weight of the outer walls), but acted as refuges for late arrivals. If the inner rooms of the caravanserai were full, the alcoves at least offered some shelter from the elements (if not from bandits).

At the back of one alcove someone has hacked a hole through the brickwork. We clamber over the broken bricks and drop into the central courtyard. Snow lies thickly in the shadows, its surface pitted with the footprints of small animals and birds. The only sound is the crunch of our feet through the snow.

Alcoves also line the inner walls of the rectangular courtyard. Halfway along each side is a much taller, deeper alcove called an *ivan*. In the courtyard's four corners are arched entranceways into the inner corridors, on each side of which are more alcoves. These would probably have been the first to be snapped up by travellers as they would have been much warmer in winter than those exposed to the elements and completely protected from the sun in summer.

Reza leads the way into one of the corridors, with me following behind hoping somewhat unchivalrously that he'd scare away any snakes before I got there. It is extremely dark until my eyes adjust from the bright clear desert light outside. But once I become accustomed I discover it is not nearly as gloomy as I'd expected.

Caravanserai architects had found a simple solution to the problem of providing natural light to these inner corridors without sacrificing the security of the solid outer walls, winter warmth and shade in summer. The roof above the corridors consists of a series of small domes and every second or third dome has a square aperture at the top. From here light floods down, illuminating the nearby alcoves. There is only a small pyramid of snow under some of them. I notice the domes are black with soot, 400-year-old soot.

At the back of each alcove is a fireplace with a chimney built into the wall.

'In most caravanserais people cooked for themselves, although occasionally there might have been someone available to cater for them. That's why there are so many fireplaces.'

Reza's voice is slightly muffled as he peers up one of the chimneys.

We gaze down the corridor. In the snow-blanketed silence it is not difficult to picture the flicker of cooking fires dancing on the alcove walls, to hear the sound of meat sizzling, the smell of bread baking, the bellow of a camel being unloaded in the courtyard and the murmur of voices speaking a babble of languages.

Although caravanserai designs have a number of common elements, such as the central courtyard, having only one entrance/exit gate and the provision of individual sleeping and living spaces for guests, each one is also as distinctive as a fingerprint. It was almost as if the architects had responded to the lonely expanses around them and, freed of conventions and constrictions, had unfettered their imaginations.

'As you can see, symmetry is very important in Islamic architecture, including caravanserais,' Reza says as we emerge from the corridor to explore the other side of the padlocked main door.

'If you stand here in the centre near the well you can see that if you run a line through the middle of the caravanserai from the main door, the two sides are identical.'

The deep main entrance was covered with a dome of herringbone brickwork under which a number of archways led to small rooms and to the roof. This was the domain of the caravan leader who was always assigned the best room above the gate. Frustratingly, the stairs to the roof had been padlocked.

If I'd been a caravan leader I'd have opted for an extra night at the next caravanserai along the route to Mashhad. Qusheh, another 17th-century building, has formidable guard towers in each corner and fortuitously the staircases to the gallery and caravan leader's quarters are unblocked.

Reza and I climb the stairs to emerge into a room with five archways overlooking the gate and the arid landscape beyond. Patchy grass glows slightly orange in the sun – on the horizon a mountain ridge rears up sharply against a cloudless sky.

We look down to see Reza B and Ferengis unpacking lunch.

They've set out a picnic on a small tribal rug in an alcove built into the outer wall of the gateway. Thin sheets of Persian bread the size of a tabloid newspaper page lie folded in a plastic bag, and Reza B is busy slicing up cucumbers and tomatoes. Ferengis produces a bowl of potato salad that we spoon into pieces of bread.

I can't have been eating enough, for both Rezas start handing me rolled-up pieces of bread with a selection of fillings and insisting I eat them. Food is treated very seriously in Iran and plying guests with mountains of food is an essential part of their innate sense of hospitality.

The caravanserai has held us in suspended animation – it is after 3 pm and the winter sun is already slipping behind the walls of the Tarikaneh mosque in Damghan while we wait for the caretaker guard with the keys to be unearthed.

A young man in green army fatigues eventually arrives at a jog and lets us into the courtyard of what is probably the oldest surviving mosque in Iran. It was constructed in about AD 760, little more than a hundred years after the Arabs conquered Persia bringing the new religion of Islam with them.

On three sides of the courtyard are arcades of baked brick, while on the fourth is a deep portico of columns, in the centre of which is the *mihrab* – the niche facing Mecca.

Reza is deeply engrossed taking photographs but I am distracted by the sound of three small boys, clutching notebooks and arguing loudly among the columns.

As we head towards the gateway, the trio follow us. They stop Reza to ask about me – foreign visitors are rare in Damghan.

Once their curiosity is satisfied Reza asks his own questions.

'They are doing a school project on the mosque but they are having problems,' Reza says. 'Do you mind …?'

One of the boys hands over his exercise book and Reza begins to draw a plan of the mosque. The three stand, rapt, and then unconsciously lower themselves to sit on the courtyard floor as their new teacher keeps talking. Reza is now in full cry – even the guard has left his ticket booth to listen. I wonder if the youngsters will become bored, but instead they start firing questions at Reza who by now has also crouched down to draw more diagrams.

Behind the group, late afternoon sunshine is casting shadows across the intricate brickwork of a 10th-century minaret that dominates the skyline beside the mosque. A thousand years ago builders had painstakingly used the bricks to form geometric patterns and the words in angular calligraphy that spelled out verses from the Koran.

Reza finishes his impromptu lecture and his three young

students thank him solemnly. The sunset call to prayer is beginning as we walk through the courtyard of the nearby Friday mosque, in search of two 11th-century tomb towers. Reza B is in the courtyard, carefully washing his arms and hands in preparation for joining the prayers.

The towers are circular, with conical tops – they look like stubby rockets. Here, too, the top sections are adorned with decorative brickwork. We climb a wall for a better view and look down on the local rubbish tip – a sea of plastic bags and rotting vegetation laps around the base of one of the towers that has been standing since just before the Norman conquest of Britain in 1066.

As we walk back towards the van, a motorcycle roars up behind us. The rider glances briefly at us, and then seeing me, turns back again for another look.

'For him you are the tourist attraction, not the towers,' Reza says.

Now staring at me over his shoulder, the motorcyclist continues to ride at speed towards a pile of rubble in the road. Just in time he turns around, sees the hazard and swerves wildly. He misses the stones by centimetres but instead nearly wipes out the display of oranges and apples outside a small fruit shop wedged between two crumbling, uninhabited ruins. Built of rough bricks held together by globs of mortar that had oozed down the walls before solidifying, the mere sight of this shop would be enough to make the craftsmen who built the tomb towers spin in their graves.

Damghan was once known as Hecatompylos during the Parthian dynasty that followed the collapse of Alexander the Great's Selucid empire.

'We know very little about the Parthians, which is very mysterious because they created the longest dynasty in Iranian history. They ruled this land from 161 BC to AD 224,' Reza explains. 'They were probably an Indo-European people who originated from the eastern side of the Caspian Sea – they never had a centre of power or capital because they remained nomadic warriors.'

Back in Parthian times, Damghan was an important staging post on the journey between Central Asia and the Mediterranean.

Business is not so brisk these days. The fruiterer calls out to us as we pass and points to his boxes of oranges. His shop is freezing cold and he is wearing a beanie and mittens. As soon as he has put the fruit into a bag for us he tucks his hands under his armpits to keep them warm.

It is dark when we arrive in Shahrood. We are spending the night with Reza's uncle and aunt but they are still on the road, returning from a pilgrimage to Mashhad.

We eat dinner in a tourist inn while we wait for them. Reza has to coerce the waiter into finding the cook as it is an hour before the restaurant usually opens. However, Reza convinces him that four early customers are better than possibly none at all later.

As we pull up outside the wall of Uncle Hamid and Auntie Fariba's house, Reza gives me some advice.

'My aunt is very religious so you may need to keep your head scarf on this evening. And unlike many Iranians, my uncle has decided to return to living in a traditional house rather than a modern one. Do you think you will be OK?'

The headscarf was not a problem, but I begin to worry just how traditional the bathroom and toilet arrangements might be. Born with a hip deformity that has now turned arthritic I find Asian-style toilets can be a challenge depending on how my hip is feeling at the time. Unwilling to have an in-depth discussion with Reza on the subject, I try to keep my worries to myself. I'd mastered the no-toilet-paper regime, but squatting for any length of time (and one drinks a lot of tea in Iran) can be torture if not downright impossible at times, necessitating some complex and time-consuming contortions.

I realise that night that I'd not hidden my fears, or my prolonged trips to the toilet, very well. This is the first of many occasions on which I'd open the bathroom door to find Reza nearby feigning interest in a flower, a stretch of wall, or sometimes merely the sky.

'Is everything all right?' he'd ask.

The family's house is built around a traditional Persian courtyard that contains fruit trees, a grapevine and small pond. There is a *takt* (a throne or square platform covered with carpets and bolsters) on which to sit when drinking tea and at each of several doors into the house is the usual jumble of footwear.

A vast Persian carpet covers the entire living-room floor and although there's a television in the corner, there are no seats other than cushioned niches set into the walls. A gas heater hisses in the corner.

Hamid, a serious-looking man, ushers us into the room. He studied as an interior designer, then became an archaeological restorer at the National Museum of Iran in Tehran. Later, he founded a museum in Shahrood and before his retirement was the region's Cultural Heritage and Tourism Organisation director with a special interest in archaeology, anthropology and ethnography. And to top all that, he is also an expert on calligraphy work on clay and has led several archaeological excavations.

Fariba, Reza's aunt, appears from the kitchen, a white-sprigged chador pulled over a long dress and a headscarf tied around her round face with its ready smile. She is the director of a vocational training centre in Shahrood. Once again I'd let dangerous preconceptions creep into my assessment of Iranian women – I'd assumed a woman who was a devout and regular pilgrim would almost certainly be a stay-at-home wife. I was annoyed at myself. I'd not have made the same assumption at home, so why had I done it here?

Reza's connections with Shahrood stretch back further than his uncle in that his great-grandfather worked as an architect here and some of the buildings he designed were still in use, including the town's museum.

'During the war with Iraq, we came here as a family when I was about ten years old to escape the Scud missiles that were falling on Tehran,' Reza says.

'I can remember one of the missiles falling before we left for Shahrood; it came down near our house and made the windows shake. We spent a month here in my great-grandfather's house, which had a big garden. I have very happy memories of it.'

Fariba tells Reza that I should take off my headscarf. I decline. They insist. I decline again, but am overruled a third time.

'This is your home tonight so we want you to feel comfortable,' his uncle says. I retreat to another room to revive my flattened, lifeless hair – if it is to be exposed I want it to look respectable.

Hamid and Fariba's two sons are introduced. I struggle a little to believe they are brothers: Hamed is thin, almost gaunt, with a full black beard, his brother Wahid is rather rotund and clean-shaven. While Wahid happily practises his English on me his older brother is more reserved, and seems reluctant to look at me. I suspect it is my lack of a head covering and wish I could put my headscarf back on.

Reza begins to tell his uncle about our exploration of Iran's caravanserais and there is a flurry of activity as maps and textbooks are dug out and spread out on the carpet. While we eat pistachios, walnuts, oranges and a box of chocolates I've brought with me, Hamid points out not-to-be-missed caravanserais.

The conversation is now in rapid Farsi and I've long been left behind, but I am aware that suddenly Reza is looking especially animated and his uncle has disappeared before returning bearing another book.

'I never knew this before,' Reza says, 'but my uncle has made a study of graffiti on caravanserai walls. Old graffiti, very old – some of it was probably written four hundred years ago. He has found the transcripts for us.'

Over a period of many months Hamid had scrambled through the caravanserais in northeastern Iran, often working by just the light of a torch, to peer at walls and staircases for signs of ancient graffiti.

'So many of the caravanserais are in bad condition and many are still being vandalised and others are being restored and cleaned, so I knew if I did not do this soon some of this history would be gone for ever,' he says. 'I found two hundred and fifty-five pieces of graffiti written between the seventeenth and nineteenth centuries.'

While we sip tea, Reza begins to translate the graffiti, every now and then making small exclamations of delight.

'Listen to this:

What kind of serai is this world
We are just guests here
So, don't be proud

Because we are guests,
In both worlds
Only God is immortal
Apart from that everything is mortal.'

Someone, maybe unable to sleep as he lay in the caravanserai
while a desert wind howled outside or the bricks sizzled in the
midday sun, had been mulling over life and death, and had
inscribed his poem into the stones.

How far was the writer from home, I wonder? Had loneliness,
or homesickness, or fear of the journey that lay ahead inspired him?

The fleeting nature of life seemed to preoccupy many of the
writers. One was to the point on the subject: '*I don't stay but my*
writing does.'

Another was more pragmatic:
'*Tell me what I have acquired*
Under this dust
Only vanity
Although I have left this
Graffiti in black ink.'

We continue to leaf through Hamid's collection of writing
(including an intriguing silk route version of Kilroy's 'I was here',
written by an Ashraf Anasar Begum 'an inhabitant of Azamibad'
(a *begum* is a Moslem woman of rank) and the photographs of
barely discernible writing that he'd found in shadowed recesses and
along crumbling staircases. Reza nudges me.

'My god, this is a real poet, let me translate very carefully:
Because I was parted from you
I built houses everywhere
And I created the mud of those houses
With the blood of my heart.'

SUNSET WITH THE POETS

Shahrood to Mashhad

And in the temple of mine inmost soul,
Behold the Friend; Incomparable Love.
He who would know the secret of both worlds,
Will find the secret of them both, is Love.

Attar, 12th–13th century Persian poet
from Neyshabur, near Mashhad

Our living room of last evening, which became my bedroom overnight (I find sleeping on the floor surprisingly comfortable), serves as our breakfast room this morning.

I had hoped to be able to awaken early enough to use the bathroom (complete with Western-style toilet) before the rest of the family was up and worrying if I was either too hot or cold, needed toilet paper, had enough towels, hot water, or other essentials.

It was not their kindness I wanted to escape, but the nagging worry that I might be perceived as a demanding and pampered Westerner.

But pre-dawn prayers had given at least one person a flying start. The light is on in the bathroom, and the gas heater is roaring (natural gas is sold at almost giveaway prices in Iran thus worrying about heating bills doesn't seem to be an Iranian preoccupation as it is at home). I've no sooner stepped into the sauna-like conditions than I hear Reza's voice outside telling me he's been sent across the courtyard with another towel.

Breakfast is a leisurely meal for the whole family: dates, butter, cream, and fried eggs and the ubiquitous Persian bread bought fresh from the neighbourhood bakery.

I am surprised to see Reza's uncle and aunt getting ready to leave the house with us.

'Oh, I forgot to tell you,' Reza says. 'The girls at my aunt's institute have been asked to come in early so you can see their pottery before we leave for Mashhad.'

Six of us pile into Uncle Hamid and Auntie Fariba's small Peugeot. Unlike at home, where it is now illegal to have more passengers than seatbelts, regulations are a little more relaxed in Iran. It seems perfectly natural to have one of Reza's cousins all but sitting on his knee in the front passenger seat and three of us wedged tightly in the back. We also have several pieces of our luggage in with us because we are meeting Reza B at Auntie Fariba's Institute.

The Iranian Vocation and Technical Educational Organisation is a near-new two-storeyed structure with light streaming through the high windows of the pottery studios. About eight girls wearing white lab coats and simple black wimple-style headscarves are already at work. They don't appear at all resentful that I've caused them to have to get out of bed an hour earlier than usual.

The girls are making vases, candle-holders and plaques from local clay and in many cases are following designs created by the multi-talented Uncle Hamid. Using tiny spatula-type tools, the girls working on plaques are carefully cutting out curling pieces of clay to create swirling calligraphy and abstract designs reminiscent of decorations found on mosques and minarets.

They like being at the institute, they tell me, and hope when they are qualified to be able to go back to their villages and neighbouring towns and make a living from their pottery.

'I want to be a potter for some time before I get married,' one of the girls tells me firmly.

Reza's aunt is clearly a much-respected role model. When we go to say goodbye to her she is seated behind a huge and immaculately tidy desk while Wahid kneels beside her, carrying out repairs to her computer.

Reunited with Reza B and Ferengis, we leave Shahrood for the 300-kilometre drive to Mashhad. We break our journey, much the way a caravan could have done 400 years ago, at the Miami caravanserai.

The branch of the silk route that ran between Mashhad and Tehran had been a particularly well-used one as it skirted the great inhospitable deserts to the south. Its popularity attracted unwelcome attention. We climb up on to the roof and are struck by the sturdiness of the watchtowers in each corner – protection from bandits was a crucial function of the building, hence its sole massive double door and windowless outer walls.

Nowadays the town of Miami has crept up to the caravanserai walls and to one side of the main door a fruit and nut vendor has set up an al fresco stall. Two wizened old men in black beanies, both leaning their chins on wooden walking sticks, sit beside him, occasionally scooping handfuls of walnuts from the sacks between them.

Although many caravanserais have quietly turned to rubble, a select few are being restored, either by the Iranian government's Cultural Heritage and Tourism Organisation or by private investors in partnership with the organisation.

Miandasht caravanserai is one of the lucky ones. It's a vast 18,000 sqm complex consisting of a rare Qajar (19th century) and two Safavid (16th–17th century) caravanserais, all linked by tall arched gateways. It would have been capable of housing hundreds of travellers. Outside its fortified walls are stables that would have once held their camels. Its popularity was due to its prime location – Miandasht was a silk-route crossroads as well as a place for pilgrims to stay as they travelled to and from Mashhad. From Miandasht one could take a route around the end of the Alborz mountains direct to the Caspian Sea and from there head for Turkey, the Caucasus and even Russia, or stay to the south of the mountains and press on for Rey (near modern-day Tehran) and south to Iraq.

The architects had lavished much decorative detail on the building, as befitted its status. A round lantern dome sheds light into the entrance foyer and in the centre of the courtyards are underground cisterns, their roofs doubling as unloading platforms for the camels.

The sound of thumping generators and rattling concrete mixers emanates from the Qajar courtyard, which a large sign in Farsi announces is out of bounds to visitors. Instead we disappear into the silent corridors of one of the Safavid buildings. The raised alcoves are in deep shadow, but we can still make out the wooden tethering rods that had been set into their bases. Camels were once brought in here, tied up and the valuable goods they carried unloaded directly onto their masters' platforms.

The caravanserai is set in the middle of an immense plain ringed by distant mountains. Where the two meet, the land shimmers in the light and white mist seems to be wreathed around the base of the mountains, but on a second glance the mist has flowed out across the plain transforming into a glistening salt lake. From a distance it is impossible to tell what is mirage and what is reality.

Reza and I are sitting in the back seat shelling walnuts while the green van consumes the kilometres. Reza B throws a plastic bag of seeds over to us. About the length of a pumpkin seed, they are thinner and striped silver and black. I take a few, put them in my mouth, crunch them up, swallow – and promptly choke.

Reza's cry of 'You don't eat them whole!' comes a moment too late.

Patiently, as if to a rather backward four-year-old child, he then shows me how the seed should be placed vertically between one's top teeth, split delicately, the tiny kernel inside extracted and the seed casing spat out discreetly.

'It's very simple,' Reza says, watching with bemusement as I inelegantly spit out mangled and soggy seeds, their insides indistinguishable in the mess.

Reza B is watching in his rear vision mirror and has a question for me.

'Reza says don't you eat seeds like this in New Zealand?' I say no and he goes into a long soliloquy, which Reza once more translates.

'He wants to know what do you eat when you are on a long journey when you don't have seeds, pistachios and fresh dates?'

I cringe at the thought of telling them both that I'd grown up on a travelling diet that consisted largely of Mackintosh's toffees, pineapple lumps and the occasional ice cream.

Luckily I am saved from answering by Reza B's cellphone bursting into life. This is no ordinary ring tone however. He'd downloaded a chant used by devoted Shia Moslems especially at *Moharram*, a time when they mourn the death of the third imam Hussein who was killed at Kerbala (in modern-day Iraq).

During the annual *Moharram* processions, particularly devout men and boys parade through towns, beating their chests to this chant as a sign of their grief at the death of Hussein.

As soon as the phone bursts into song, both Rezas rhythmically tap their chests over their hearts with the palms of their right hands, none too seriously echoing the annual rite.

The previously featureless plain on our right is suddenly studded with black dots which, as we approach, morph into a herd of wild camels. We stop to watch them as they graze among the wiry grass. Baby camels gaze at us with mock alarm before bouncing off towards their mothers.

This prompts more questions from Reza B. He is surprised to know that where I come from there are no wild camels. But he's deeply impressed when Reza tells him we can lay claim to 40 million sheep.

Reza B digests this for some kilometres and then announces he thinks he'd like to become a Kiwi shepherd.

I conjure up a picture of Reza B with his luxuriant moustache striding through the tussocks of the South Island high country, his cellphone broadcasting the *Moharram* chant to his team of bewildered dogs. Both parties would probably adapt quite well, I decide, but I suspect he would soon be investigating how he might import vital supplies, such as the edible seeds of which he is so fond.

We eat lunch among a handful of diners in an echoing marble-floored hotel dining room in Sabzevar that can seat several hundred people. The multi-storeyed hotel is the tallest building by far in the town.

As we drive out of town the outline of three curiously shaped buildings appear silhouetted in the late afternoon sun. They look like three inverted funnels, their circular walls stepped gradually from base to top. The only aperture is an arched doorway set at ground level on the northern, shady side.

These are icehouses, this trio now long disused and, unlike some in Iran, not restored, so they are slowly blending back into the landscape. Icehouses (*yakhchal* in Farsi, meaning ice pit) are found in few other places in the world.

Persian engineers seemed to have cracked the method for keeping ice frozen in the pitiless heat of the Iranian plateau summers in about 400 BC. In winter shallow ponds, with high walls on the sunny side, were filled with water. When this had frozen, the ice was chipped out and transferred into the icehouse. What can be seen above ground is only a portion of the entire structure – much of it lies underground. Some icehouses can be up to 20 metres high and their underground section can be 6 metres deep.

Ice stored here could be kept frozen all summer thanks to the combination of the thick walls (2 metres at the base) and the building's shape (cooling winds could spiral down the exterior) would keep the ice frozen for the summer (this was especially crucial anywhere where Persian royalty was staying as *faludeh,* or Persian ice cream, was a favourite of the upper classes). The single door would be insulated with a blanket of dry grass.

The Zafaraniyeh icehouse walls are crumbling badly but we can still make out some of the ingredients in the unique construction material. Icehouses were usually built of a mixture of sand, clay, egg white, lime, ash and goat hair. When we lean against the doorway of one of the icehouse we are met by the sight of mounds of decaying rubbish and a sea of plastic bags.

'Bloody plastic bags,' Reza says, as I baulk at the scene. 'The problem in Iran is that with so much oil it is so cheap to make plastic and now we are drowning in it.'

Zafaraniyeh's caravanserai is going the same way as its icehouses. Its main entrance is padlocked but we climb in through a gaping wound in the side, taking a wide berth around a mangy black dog tied up inside. What it is protecting we can't discern – there are piles of rubble in all the corridors and the ground is strewn with rubbish, including a number of disposable nappies.

When we climb out, a group of women is gathering up their washing from beside a narrow irrigation channel that separates the caravanserai from their village with its mass of domed roofs. When they see Reza they draw their chadors further around their faces and turn their backs to us.

By now the sun is hovering low in the sky and Reza B has left the van to come to tell us to hurry up. We arrive at Neyshabur, 114 km from Mashhad, just as the *azan* – the call to prayer – for sunset prayers starts.

The nondescript arid plain we have been driving across is suddenly transformed with the appearance of trees, lush grass and rose beds. Neyshabur is the resting place of two great poets, one a household name in the West, the other virtually unknown. Water has been lavished on the gardens surrounding their tombs to create the Persian idea of a touch of paradise on earth.

We walk alongside the long narrow pool towards the mausoleum of Farid od-Din Attar, a Sufi poet who died in about 1220. Rumi, a fellow Sufi poet who is today widely read in the West, regarded Attar as the 'Lord of All Sufis'.

'Rumi once said that Attar had visited the seven cities of love while we were still lost in the alleys of the first city,' observes Reza.

It's possible Attar died at the time as the Mongol invasion when the entire city's population was put to the sword by the army of Ghengis Khan. Their arrival was the death knell for a city that was briefly, in the 11th century, one of the most important intellectual centres for Sunni Islam. It did, however, remain an important staging point along the silk road that connected the Iranian plateau with Central Asia.

Attar's tomb is a blue confection comprising a single tiled dome set on a deep circular drum that in turn rests on an octagonal building decorated with mosaic work. Attar's most famous work, *The Conference of the Birds*, is one that I always struggle to read. But as the sun sets through the pine trees in the garden surrounding his tomb we read English and Farsi versions of his short poem *Looking for your own Face*, which ends rather enigmatically: 'What you most want, what you travel around wishing to find, lose yourself as lovers lose themselves, and you'll be that.'

Night is about to fall with a bang so there is no more time to reflect on Attar. We have to run out the gate, and into the almost-moving van; Reza B is in fast-getaway mode. He drives a few kilometres through a forest of pines to a large car park. While we were the only visitors to Attar's tomb we are not alone at the grave of Omar Khayyam. I am, however, the only foreign tourist. As we walk to the entrance to his tomb, a man in an old suit coat starts playing a lilting melody on a small wooden flute. Another tows a scruffy, dispirited horse and tries to persuade Reza that he's sure that I'd much rather go for a ride than visit the tomb. Reza B meanwhile is trying to brush off the attentions of a third vendor trying to sell him a range of fluorescent hair ties.

Thankfully, the vendors are not allowed inside the enclosed garden that surrounds Omar Khayyam's tomb. Although it is now past sunset, the fountains along the central pool are still playing and a loudspeaker is broadcasting his *Rubiyat*.

Khayyam's tomb is set under a tall circle of elongated diamonds that ends in a small dome. It's said to resemble an upside-down wine cup. Wine, somewhat incongruously now – given Iran's 'dry' status – is a constant theme that flows though Khayyam's poetry.

To me the shape seems to resemble arms stretched protectively over the grave.

It is apt that even Khayyam's tomb can be open to interpretation because the meaning of his poetry has been debated for centuries, including the intriguing issue of whether he actually believed in life after death (a core belief in Islam).

Iranians' reverence for their poets is always evident in the rituals that accompany a pilgrimage to their tombs. Ahead of us, visitors approach the tomb, and then bend low to touch it, speaking softly.

'Maybe they are saying the start of the sura (the key words in the daily prayer routine): "*Besmellahe, rahmane rahim*" – in the name of God, the most merciful the most beneficient, and then perhaps some lines of Khayyam,' Reza explains as we sit down on a stone bench nearby to watch.

The lights come on, flooding over Khayyam's tomb and creating a tracery of shadows among the trees in the garden. There is no one talking to Khayyam now so it is time for my own pilgrimage.

Omar Khayyam had been a feature of my childhood because it was one of my father's favourite books. He had once given a slim, green volume of the *Rubiyat* to my mother as a birthday present, but would often read it himself. I'd occasionally find it placed seemingly randomly in one of our many bookcases, sometimes wedged between books on animal husbandry or Churchill's history of World War II.

It was not until I was in my twenties that I realised that the *Rubiyat* was about the only piece of fictional writing my father ever read. And it was only after his death that I realised I'd never asked him why. This sense of regret only deepened when I began to read Khayyam properly for myself – what had drawn my rather undemonstrative and often very prosaic father to Persian poetry?

My fingertips touching the tomb, I tell Dad this visit is for him and that I'm saying 'hello' to Khayyam from him. I am no more the wiser about Dad's interest in Khayyam, but I am sure he's pleased I'm paying homage. As the loudspeakers crackle out a Persian song I imagine I can hear a 'Well done, old stick' amongst the music.

When I sit down beside Reza again, and blow my nose, he passes me a book of poetry.

'I think your father would like it if we read some Khayyam out loud.'

Under Khayyam's floodlit wine cup we read:

'Awake! For morning in the Bowl of Night
Has flung the Stone that puts the Stars to Flight
And Lo! The Hunter of the East has caught
The Sultan's Turret in a Noose of Light.'

I've choked up and can't read any more so Reza decrees it is time for a cup of tea – Iranians seem to have the same faith in the restorative properties of tea as the English.

Despite the fact that it is late winter and night has fallen it is still warm enough to sit outside where we can see Khayyam's tomb through the trees. There are other latecomers – beside us sit two teenage girls with their parents. Both girls are eating ice cream, while one is texting on her phone.

I pour out the tea and Reza drops sugar lumps into both cups, reciting in Farsi as he does so. The family nearby turns, smiles and applauds. He then translates for me:

'Ah, fill the Cup – what boots it to repeat
How time is slipping underneath our Feet:
Unborn tomorrow, and dead yesterday,
Why fret about them if today be sweet.'

On the title page of my father's gift of Khayyam to my mother he'd written the page and stanza numbers to these same four lines of poetry.

Reza B, however, is feeling less poetic when we finally return to the van. Just as the caravans of old had often travelled at night so, too, do thousands of Iran's fleet of trucks. Mashhad might be Iran's most holy city but it's also the country's second-largest and as such is a major industrial and business centre as well as attracting 20 million pilgrims a year. Reza B knows the road will be clogged with trucks and buses.

We drive through the darkness, sandwiched at times between juggernauts, some of which bear Turkmen and Uzbek licence plates. Occasionally we are overtaken by a bus, its curtained windows revealing glimpses of slumbering pilgrims.

Reza has chosen a cheap, pilgrims' apartment hotel for us all to stay in, but he's not been there before and neither has the other Reza. As we hit the city's outskirts we ring the hotel for directions. The trucks and buses melt away as we thread our way into the city's heart, but the streets are gridlocked with cars. It is after I've spotted the same fountain in the centre of a roundabout for the third time that I know we are lost.

It doesn't help that we are compounding the city's traffic woes by stopping on street corners while Reza winds down the window and asks passers-by for help. A long, and I thought fruitful, conversation follows at the first of these stops.

'That's sounds hopeful,' I say.

'No, he had no idea where the hotel is,' Reza replies.

Apparently most of the conversation was a string of Persian pleasantries and polite wishes for our health and safety. We could hardly blame the man – there are hundreds of hotels in Mashhad to cater for the influx of pilgrims, with new ones being opened every few months.

After our fourth pass along one of the main roads leading directly to the Imam Reza shrine Reza rings the hotel again. This time, maybe sensing a booking about to slip away, the manager sends a minion on a motorbike out to the nearest major intersection to lead us to the right place.

It's no wonder we couldn't find the hotel ourselves situated as it is among a labyrinth of narrow alleyways alongside which many of the old buildings are being demolished and new apartment blocks, grown old before their time due to hasty and shoddy building techniques, have risen from the rubble, almost overnight.

'If this had been a few centuries ago we'd never have had this problem,' Reza says as we try to tidy the back seat of the van of pistachio shells, seeds and fruit peelings before Reza B sees it. 'If there'd been a minaret with a fire burning at the top, we'd have had no trouble at all.'

WHERE THE SUN RISES
Mashhad to Yazd

We should play games in the rain
We should write, talk, sow morning-glory seeds in the rain
Life is a series of successive drenchings
Life is taking a dip in the basin of This Moment.

Sohrab Sepehri, 20th century Persian poet

This morning we say goodbye to Ferengis as she must return to
Tehran. We, however, are heading south to Tabas on the edge of
the Dasht-e Kavir, Iran's largest desert, one of the most arid places
on the planet and one of the most sparsely populated regions in
the country. The region of Khorasan is the realm of white space
on the map of Iran and its name translates to 'where the sun rises',
but few Iranians from beyond its boundaries would have seen
dawn breaking in the east here, and only a handful of foreigners.

While in Mashhad, Ferengis spent many hours in the Imam
Reza shrine, but also found time to shop diligently for the family;
she's got numerous plastic carrier bags full of saffron and sugar
swizzle sticks that she'll have to nurse through the 14-hour bus

trip to Tehran. When Ferengis and I say a tearful goodbye she says something in Farsi to Reza and then orders him to translate for me.

'Ferengis says you are not a tourist, you are now a *Mashhadi* – a pilgrim like her,' he says.

The brilliant blue sky that features during our first few days of travel is replaced today with overcast pearly grey. Mountain ranges fade into a blue haze to our left. Little more than 100 kilometres away three countries meet: Iran, Turkmenistan and Afghanistan.

A rubbly wasteland of ochre rock stretches away from both sides of the highway. Reza B is deep in conversation with the soft toy in the shape of a kiwi bird that I'd given him when we left Tehran.

'He's grumpy today – look at the way he's glaring at me,' Reza B says, tickling the kiwi under its diminutive beak. 'I think it was cold in the van last night.'

Reza is at the back of the van, ferreting among the books in the library. He returns with my Persian textbook and notebook.

'Today we start your Persian lessons,' he says, launching into the dialogue at the start of chapter one before I can draw breath.

Snow-dusted mountains that had been hacked and rent apart by eons of geological tumult close around us as we begin conjugating my first Persian verb.

'*Man khorshal hastam, to khorshal hasti* … (I am happy, you are happy …),' Reza intones.

I follow suit. Reza B takes his hands off the wheel as we speed down the road using his arms to conduct all three of us through the rest of the verb table.

The lesson is interrupted by our arrival in the village of Robat-e-Safed, named after its caravanserai.

'There are some interesting theories about the word *robat*,' Reza explains. 'One is that it is an Arabic word for caravanserai, but another is that it comes from the Persian word *rabt:* to connect. The Arabs took many Persian words and adopted them after they conquered Persia.'

Reza's explanation reminds me of an earlier conversation we'd had when I, in a blonde moment, had called the Persian Gulf the Arabian Gulf. Reza, normally the most equable of personalities, had bristled with indignation. Despite my attempts to retract what I'd said by saying I really did know it was the Persian Gulf and that it had been a mere slip of the tongue on my part, it was too late.

'Just recently some cranky Arabs have renamed it the Arabian Gulf but it has been called the Persian Gulf from at least Achaemenid times and that's two and a half thousand years ago. Then it was the Sinus Persicus or Persian Sea. Now some Westerners are calling it the Gulf to be politically correct but it's *not* correct.'

There's a complicated relationship between the Iranians and the Arab world. It was the Arabs who introduced Islam to Persia in the late seventh century AD, but the Persians later carved out their own path in the Islamic world by following the Shia line rather than the Sunni. The first language of Iran – Farsi or Persian – is an intrinsic part of national identity for the majority of Iranians, but it is written in Arabic script.

To many Iranians the Arabs of the Arabian Peninsula are simply nomads with sand in their shoes who happened to get lucky with the discovery of oil. No amount of wealth can ever, to the Persian mind, compensate for a lack of an illustrious and sophisticated heritage. It's an on-going frustration for many Iranians that so many ill-informed Westerners call them Arabs.

Robat's caravanserai is in a depressing state of near-ruin. But very strangely one of the first things we see is a badminton court that has been marked out in the courtyard; a moth-eaten net sags between two posts. To get into the courtyard proper we must edge our way past two dogs with matted hair – possibly of Saluki heritage – that are chained to a post on a mound of rubble.

I'm aware that I haven't seen many dogs in Iran. Interestingly, they are widely regarded by Iranians as being unclean; I've noticed Reza always gives any dogs we see a wide berth. I certainly don't need much encouragement to leave these two – with their bared teeth – well alone.

Beyond Robat, veils of rain hang between the distant mountains and the road, wafting closer as we drive south. I can smell the moisture in the air, but it remains tantalisingly just out of reach. However, the water suspended in the sky turns a usually harsh landscape into a soft watercolour world.

On Reza's suggestion that we stop to meditate for a while, we pull up at the side of the road. We walk towards the hills across a plain strewn with rock shards and small struggling plants. After a short distance Reza chooses a small ridge and gracefully sits down cross-legged. I follow, inelegantly.

We sit as the emptiness wraps around us. Reza has his eyes closed but my mind, never easy to still, wonders what Reza B might be doing. I look around and see he has the back of the van open and is preparing morning tea. Reza opens his eyes.

'You're not concentrating.'

I put the thought of fresh dates out of my mind and turn back to look at the hills. I shut out the view and my head seems to echo with the absence of noise.

The whining of a truck engine breaks the spell. The sound intensifies and then, when the truck approaches our van, which is the only man-made object for hundreds of kilometres and clearly stationary, the driver blasts his horn. I assume this is in case Reza B suddenly takes it into his head to leap into its path.

Reza's eyes snap open. 'Tea, I think.'

The road takes us ever closer to the Afghan border. There has been some rain here and the plain on our left is carpeted in green. Even the mountains along the border look flushed with vegetation.

I stare into the hills, wondering what is going on behind them. Ever since I'd lived in Pakistan more than 20 years earlier, Afghanistan has fascinated me. I'd stood in the Khyber Pass and gazed into its mountains, seen its boundaries from the Uzbek border – and now from Iran. One day I'll get there.

As we pass through a small nondescript town with a concrete box of a police checkpoint Reza spots a ruined icehouse in the fields beyond. Without being asked, Reza B turns the van down a side road so we can investigate and as we make our way down the pot-holed track we see an entire town, albeit abandoned, of adobe arches, tunnels and houses over a small ridge.

It is beautiful in its ruin and I am out of the van, camera in hand, almost as soon as we stop.

'Just be a little careful with the camera – we are close to the border,' Reza says.

But as far as I can see there's no one else for miles and I am just about to plunge into a crumbling covered alleyway when we spot a military-looking ute bouncing down the road towards us.

'Put your camera away and look respectable,' Reza instructs.

'I always look respectable,' I reply.

'More respectable,' he says firmly.

I pull my headscarf further forward until it is almost in my eyes. 'Now walk back to the van.'

There are times when even I can see the point of obeying instructions and being discreet. I return to the van, trying to find a balance between casualness and decorum.

From under my scarf I glimpse two young armed men climb out of the ute – one in camouflage blue and the other in khaki. They engage in discussion with the two Rezas, with occasional gestures at me.

Reza returns to the van and asks me for my passport, but won't catch my eye or answer my question about what's happening.

Meanwhile, things are becoming rather more animated outside. The two soldiers are still leafing through my passport, but Reza is pointing at the ruins. The passport is returned, then everyone looks intently at the old village followed by a round of hand-shaking.

The two soldiers return to their ute, passing by me in the process and I just can't help myself; I break decorum and wave at them. They wave back and grin.

'They saw us go past and wondered who we were,' reports Reza. 'They didn't think it could be a tourist because no one comes here. No one except for smugglers, that is,' he adds.

Apparently the abandoned buildings, so close to the Afghan border, were under suspicion of being used by drug runners and other criminal types.

'They told me they'd been here for a year so far but have never visited the village. I told them the houses were very beautiful and they should explore them. They said they would,' Reza says.

Only an enthusiast like Reza could turn the discussion from my possible impact on national security to the beauty of adobe ruins. But, as usual, his passion for Iran's past proves to be contagious.

At Gonabad we stop at the town's ethnographical museum. The curator is astonished to see us – and a little nonplussed. This is definitely the off-season in an area that even in peak times only receives a very sparse number of overseas tourists. He is having lunch into the bargain.

But, Reza, ever persuasive, manages to get him to open up the museum. Many of the small arched rooms around the courtyard have been converted into re-creations of local village life, complete with wax models in traditional dress.

In one room a family sits on the floor removing the precious anthers from the saffron crocus. A huge metal tray piled with purple flowers is in their midst, along with a small plate of the extremely valuable orange-red anthers.

It is the local version of a grain-mill that fascinates me most. An enormous beam has been set in the crook of a Y-shaped tree trunk. Attached to the high end of the beam is a vertical post that points down toward a cylindrical stone jar. It's a two-man operation in that one man positions himself at the lower end of the beam in order to pivot it up and down, while another straddles the high end, adding weight to the post when it crashes into the grain.

Although it is a beautifully constructed display, I can't help wondering who on earth will ever come to see it.

From Gonabad we leave the main highway for a minor road that will take us to Tabas. Iran's two vast deserts lie on either side of us, the Dasht-e Kavir desert to our right and to the left, the Dasht-e Lut.

We have one last stop to make before nightfall. Reza wants to check out the restoration of a *madrasseh* (theological school) in Ferdows. The newly cleaned brickwork glows pale yellow in the winter sun that has emerged from the cloud. It is an impressive building that must have once housed dozens of students and their teachers.

Madrassehs are today an integral part of Islamic society and function rather like an Oxford or Cambridge college in that students study in small groups with their tutors and, in most cases, live on campus. Most traditional *madrassehs* are of a similar design – usually two storeys of small rooms that serve as both teaching space and living areas set around a courtyard. Where this *madrasseh* in Ferdows departs from the conventional layout is that rather than the central space being on one level, its steps lead down to a sunken pool and garden area.

Theological debate was and is an important part of Shia theological training and it's easy for me to imagine students of yesteryear sitting around the pool, protected from the desert sun by the steep walls on all sides, earnestly discussing the religious issues of the day.

Among the ruins of an old village outside the *madrasseh* are the remains of an icehouse and the crumbling entrances to several underground reservoirs.

'Has anyone excavated these places?' I ask. Layer upon layer of village life must have been building up here for centuries.

'Probably not,' says Reza. 'Iran has so many archaeological sites and there simply is not enough money to study them all.'

We are still hours away from Tabas, where we plan to stay the night, and to slow us down further it is snowing on the 3000-m Robat-e-Sang pass. As the snowflakes drop onto the windscreen, Reza B moves the kiwi from its perch and puts it beside him.

'If he gets cold again he will be bad-tempered again tomorrow.'

The snow brings a crisp definition to the mountain folds, the fresh white contrasting with the tawny foothills that are scarred with vertical runnels where sometime in the past water must have cascaded.

As the sun sets we pull up outside a small lonely mosque. The entranceway and even the minarets are decorated in a rather garish shade of green and shiny white tiles. A few men in working clothes drift in as the loudspeaker on one of the minarets crackles into life with the early evening call to prayer.

Reza B decides it's time for a cup of tea, but there is much consternation on his and our part when he discovers the pump pot of hot water has developed a crack. There is water in the bottom of the van, but none for the cups.

While he mops up, Reza gallops across to a small teahouse set into the wall of the mosque complex and appears a few minutes later clutching a battered stainless steel teapot full of water. We drink our tea quickly as the air temperature begins to plummet.

The mountain range behind Tabas is a formidable black cut-out shape against a sky of deep apricot when we finally descend through a small pass towards the oasis town.

'What a perfect silhouette,' I say.

Reza pricks up his ears. He is always on the lookout for words to extend his English vocabulary.

We practise the pronunciation for some time, and then insert the words into sentences.

Meanwhile, Reza B, who did not appear to have been listening, suddenly asks Reza to enquire of me what shapes I could see along the silhouette.

'A sleeping dragon with a long tail,' I say, 'and an old man with a very short nose.'

Reza B seems happy with my answer, then points at a very distinctive pointed cone to the east and says something to Reza in

Farsi. I force him to translate.

'He says he does not have your imagination, but that mountain is very easy,' Reza says, looking a little embarrassed.

Reza had researched the Tabas accommodation scene before we left Tehran and had read about a teachers' hostel that lets out rooms cheaply during the college holidays. But as he doesn't know where it is we spend some time driving around the dark streets of Tabas, making repeat circumnavigations of several of the town's roundabouts, until we find a lone man at the roadside who points us in the right direction.

We turn into the gate of an anonymous-looking three-storey building and Reza hops out of the van and disappears inside to check.

I watch him lean over a counter in the foyer. After a few seconds a man struggles into view on the other side – clearly he'd been having a nap having quite reasonably decided that no guests were likely to arrive at 9 pm on a mid-winter's night. Reza signals to us that we are indeed at the right place and Reza B and I traipse in with our bags.

'Apparently there is a big neon sign on the roof,' Reza says. 'This man does not know how we missed it.'

Upstairs there are rooms galore from which to choose and before long I'm installed in one offering four beds and an immaculate bathroom. The two Rezas move in next door, where Reza B immediately collapses onto the bed and turns on the TV. His evening routine is set in stone – he never eats dinner (preferring instead to consume a massive lunch) and usually watches television until he falls asleep, leaving Reza to switch off the latest instalment of his favourite Iranian soap opera.

The two of us then venture out on foot into the dark and

apparently totally deserted streets of Tabas to look for something to eat. Only a few metres from the hotel we come across an Iranian-style fast-food shop, which Reza calls a sandwich bar, in which a number of men are slouched on padded wrought-iron chairs watching a soapie on the huge wall-mounted television set. Until I walk in, that is. Blonde-haired tourists in the middle of winter in Tabas are clearly a rare sight.

A huge domestic drama erupts on the television but the histrionics of an overwrought matron and her beautiful daughter go completely unheeded as everyone stares at me. Reza suggests I sit at a table with my back to the audience and we order the equivalent of an Iranian subway and a local cola.

While we eat, a regular stream of customers begins to pull up outside, mostly young couples on small motorbikes. They invariably head up the stairs to a mezzanine floor where they sit, heads close together, over fast food.

After our dinner we walk back to the hostel, which now that we can see it in the right perspective, is clearly one of the tallest buildings in the neighbourhood and is indeed topped with the brilliant green and red neon sign referred to earlier by the caretaker.

On our return to the hostel Reza suggests we set up the laptop on the dining table that stretches about 10 metres down the length of the wide corridor and view the day's photos. I can't find a plug in the hall so suggest, as I have four desks and plenty of space in my room, that we look at the photographs there. The room is also several degrees warmer.

'No, we certainly can't do that,' says Reza, looking horrified.

'But there's no one else here and anyway, we can leave the door wide open.'

He refuses point blank. Every now and then the strictures of life in an Islamic republic totally infuriate me and this is one of those times. With bad grace I stomp around looking for an extension cord all the while muttering to myself, then set up the computer on the table immediately outside my room.

'Shall I sit on the other side of the table?' I say sarcastically, immediately feeling ashamed of myself. 'I'm sorry. It just gets a bit much sometimes.'

'I understand, but that is our reality in Iran,' Reza says. He looks hurt.

That makes me feel worse.

Before leaving the oasis town of Tabas in the morning for the eight-hour desert drive to Yazd, we stop at the Bagh-e-Goshan, a walled garden in the midst of the city.

It's always disorienting to arrive in a new place at night, and my previous evening's impressions of Tabas as a place of rolling tumbleweeds and a lone sandwich bar have to be hastily revised.

The streets are lined with palm trees and even though it is early there are plenty of people about, most of them making their first visit of the day to the bakery to take home the huge sheets of flat bread for breakfast.

The Bagh-e-Goshan is undergoing extensive renovation so we have to negotiate our way around piles of building materials to the ticket booth.

'There is something special I want you to see here,' Reza says, walking quickly along a pathway lined with more palms and flowering oleander. We stop outside an empty metal cage that, although recently hosed out, smells rather strongly of guano.

'Oh, no, where are they?' he exclaims, turning on his heel and heading down a path stretching along one side of a long channel of flowing water studded with small fountains.

Catching a flash of white behind some shrubs he darts down a side path. I follow him, mystified. There in front of us are three giant pelicans basking in the morning sun, lazily clacking their huge beaks which makes the baggy pouches that hang beneath them wobble.

The pelicans, intent on warming up after a cold night, ignore us but I pelt Reza with questions; where the birds have come from, for starters ...

A local ruler Amir Hassan Khan had created the Bagh-e-Goshan in the 18th century. Although renowned throughout Iran for its palms, citrus trees and pomegranates, it is the pelicans that everyone loves to visit. No one seems to know when or how the pelicans came to be in Tabas, but after a colossal earthquake in 1978 that killed 80 per cent of Tabas's citizens outright, they disappeared only to reappear some time afterwards.

By the time we return to the central axis of the garden, the fountains in the main pool have been turned on and jets of water are arching over the central pool. The air is moist and small rainbows flicker in the morning sunlight that filters greenly through the palms. We are in an emerald oasis within an oasis.

As our journey across the edge of the Dasht-e Lut follows another of Persia's silk routes we come across caravanserais in various states of repair at frequent intervals. One such is the Kalmard caravanserai that, in a place almost devoid of man-made structures and dominated by barren, ragged mountains, can be seen for kilometres in either direction.

It looks typically abandoned as we push open the magnificent weather-beaten double doors that still swing inwards on their original wooden pivots. The creak of the gates is loud in the silence, but as they stop moving we can hear running footsteps somewhere ahead.

We step out of the gloom of the entrance tunnel into the courtyard and a movement to one side make us turn to see a slightly built woman in a long skirt and headscarf. She has her arm protectively around a small boy clad in a grubby red jacket several sizes too big for him and ripped black track pants that come halfway up his calves.

Reza slowly walks over to her and begins to talk, translating for me as he goes.

An Afghan refugee, she is alone as her husband has gone away to work, leaving her and her son in the abandoned building. Before leaving he'd built a wall across the front of one of the niches to make a dark, one-roomed alcove to house his family. A few skinny goats live in one of the larger corner rooms. Washing hangs across another niche.

'She speaks the most perfect Persian,' Reza marvels. 'Afghans are known to speak some of the purest Farsi.'

The small boy follows us as we explore the other rooms of what was once a five-star travellers' inn. Each of the niches has four wooden coat hooks – something we've not seen anywhere else. Then we come across a rarity in a caravanserai – an inside toilet facility.

When we climb the stairs to the roof we almost step into the teacups belonging to a group of three men, one of whom is wielding a clipboard, another a tape measure and the third, and youngest, a thermos.

Once we've all got over our surprise the most senior of them explains they are a survey party from the Cultural Heritage and Tourism Organisation, which has plans to restore the caravanserai.

'What will happen to the Afghan woman and her child?' I ask.

He tells us that eventually she'll have to move. I look over the parapet at the rubbly desert and the striated mountains. The road stretches far into the distance in both directions, disappearing into a shimmering mirage. Where was there to go?

It is a heavily fortified caravanserai – pairs of arrow slits are set into the parapet, between them a vertical chute that we guess could be used either by archers or to pour hot liquids down on attackers.

We are peering over the parapet at the view when Reza suddenly asks for my camera. Pointing it down the road we've just come from he zooms out the telephoto lens.

'Can you see that black smudge in the middle of the road far away? Look through here and see what it is,' he instructs.

Using the telephoto lens as I would a pair of binoculars, I look in the direction he is pointing and see an old man with a wispy beard, wearing a kilted gown and walking with the aid of a tall stick coming steadily down the road towards us. We'd passed that way only 30 minutes ago and certainly hadn't seen him – where had he materialised from?

By the time we come down the stairs the traveller is coming through the caravanserai doors. Seen close up, his face is wrinkled and burnt by the sun and his belongings are in a swag tied over one shoulder. Reza, ever curious and encouraged by me, asks where he came from and where he is going. He doesn't answer, instead shuffles over to a niche and sits down. He accepts a mug of water from the woman, but will not speak. We have to leave with that particular mystery unsolved.

Still following the caravan route we continue south through a landscape where salt has been sucked to the surface on such a scale that it looks as if it has just finished snowing. Another impressive caravanserai with round towers at each corner looms up beside us. The only way in is through a collapsed section of the wall; more perils lurk inside because this building seems to have an underground level, the roof of which has subsided in places.

We are picking our way carefully among the mounds of building material and rubble in one of the upper rooms when I almost trip over a donkey. It is very dead, but perfectly mummified in the arid atmosphere and still tied to one of the original camel tether rails set into the wall.

'The poor thing – someone must have forgotten about it and it's died of starvation,' I say, backing hastily away.

'No, no,' Reza assures me. 'I'm sure it died of natural causes but the owner for some reason hasn't shifted it.'

It is a good try on his part, but I don't believe him.

Behind the caravanserai is the ruined entrance to a water reservoir and the remains of an adobe fortress built around a small rock outcrop. Saltbush, with its ghostly silver-grey crabbed branches, clings to life among the sand and gravels.

A sapphire-blue sky hangs like a dome over us. All is utterly silent; remote, almost frighteningly vast and devastatingly beautiful in its starkness.

I want to stay longer, but Reza B is honking his horn – he's already seen enough caravanserai to last a lifetime and decides it is time we were moving. But it is he who stops the van a few kilometres down the road to admire a herd of wild camels, including babies, grazing nearby.

'Look, these are camels,' he says slowly in Farsi. Reza leaps in with his favourite 'substitution drill'.

'I have two apples, I have two camels. Jill has two camels, Ahmad has two camels ...'

Outside the language laboratory the mountains close in – jagged, slashed with fault lines, their feet hidden by a deluge of scree.

It looks like a road to nowhere. But for hundreds of years travellers, their camels and precious cargoes followed this route – it would have been a frightening, arduous journey, no matter what the season. And little wonder that the caravanserai along the way were so well protected – this would have been prime bandit territory.

When we stop at the next caravanserai, however, it is more akin to a barnyard than a link with the past. In the courtyard are two grumpy camels tied to old tyres and the side *ivans* have been blocked up with more tyres to create pens for a couple of donkeys and a small flock of sheep. When we climb up to the roof and look down through a collapsed dome a herd of goats gazes nervously back up at us.

Somehow, the amateur renovations, shoddy additional brick walls and manure everywhere make this a much more forlorn sight than even the most lonely ruined caravanserai. To make matters worse, someone has authorised the building of a mosque right beside the walls, and this looms above us in a less than elegant way. Its walls are covered with badly applied tiles that make it look more like a rather large public toilet with a dome of stained concrete plonked on top.

'Reza,' I ask, trying to be diplomatic. 'How can a country that once produced the mosques of Isfahan produce something like this?'

Reza stares at the building gloomily.

'I know, bloody modern shoddy building. I am ashamed.'

Once again we've spent too long digging up the past in the caravanserai because the sun is starting to set as we arrive at Kharanagh, an abandoned hillside village the foundations of which date back to pre-Islamic times about 1400 years ago.

Until 40 years ago this had been a small but thriving agricultural town and Reza and I leave Reza B contemplating his watch to wander into one of the arched tunnels that runs through the village. It's fascinating to note that the roofs of the houses or small shops form the floor of the level above; when it was still inhabited Kharanagh must have had a wonderfully organic, communal feeling about it. We climb up several levels, stumble on the old village bakery with its gaping wall ovens and end up on a terrace beside a small minaret that is catching the late sun.

Soot still clings to the walls and chimney places in some of the houses and graffiti has been etched into the smoky bricks. There is a mix of Farsi and English – initials inside hearts seem common to both. From an archway suspended over a sheer drop is a view down to terraced fields of green. It's the first sign of agriculture we've seen all day. In the distance an aqueduct crosses a small river and beyond that, set into the banks, is a series of caves created by local farmers as shelters for their sheep.

As we return to the van the roar of an engine breaks the silence and an elderly man riding an old Russian motorbike appears, the petrol tank of his machine draped with dozens of freshly dug carrots and a shovel balanced across the handle bars. He stops beside a small channel of fast-moving water running past the outer walls of the village, piles the carrots on the shovel and rinses them off in the water. Then he signals us to come over and holds out a bunch of the vegetables invitingly. The Rezas dutifully refuse them three times as custom dictates, and then take a few.

When we rejoin the main Tabas-Yazd highway shortly after, we find ourselves swallowed up in a line of heavy, labouring trucks. There is little chance to overtake because the stream is just as constant in the other direction; this is the main highway leading to Pakistan and Afghanistan and still follows one of the ancient caravan routes.

The sun has almost sunk below the rim of mountains when Reza B turns the van off the highway and bumps us over the sand to Zeynodin, one of only four or five round caravanserai in the whole country, and unusually it has been lovingly converted into a boutique hotel. A small door set into the massive wooden gateway opens and the hotel manager steps out to greet us, leading us into a circular vestibule draped with local carpets.

Twelve arched *ivans* face the inner courtyard in the centre of which is a platform that would have once been used for unloading camels. Some of the archways lead to simple bedrooms with high brick walls and carpets on the floor.

The dining room is also off the courtyard. The pièce de résistance here is one of the most ornate samovars I've seen in Iran. But before I can inspect it more closely Reza glances at the sky and hurries me up the stairs in the vestibule to the roof.

The sun is setting over the desert. The mountains that rim the small basin in which we are situated are difficult to see in the darkness and a single star hangs suspended over our heads. The road is still bumper-to-bumper with trucks. The air rings with the hum and whine of engines and their lights form an almost unbroken chain of white and red in both directions just as the road itself forms a continuum with the trading routes of old.

An icy wind sweeps off the mountains making us retreat into the small teahouse that has been created in a niche off the dining room. The floor is covered in a thick layer of hand-knotted carpets in tones of rich red and deep blues. The brick walls, now cleaned of their soot, are bathed in golden light from intricate brass fittings. A tray of tea and a *qalyan* are placed in front of a sea of cushions and bolsters set against the curved wall ready for us.

We sit and inhale – orange-flavoured tobacco and the ghosts of past travellers. Their spirits, after withstanding centuries of snow, biting cold, blistering heat, bandits and exhaustion, are all around us.

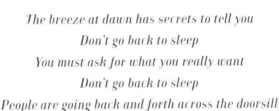

POMEGRANATES IN THE DESERT

Yazd to Kerman

The breeze at dawn has secrets to tell you
Don't go back to sleep
You must ask for what you really want
Don't go back to sleep
People are going back and forth across the doorsill
Where the two worlds touch
The door is round and open
Don't go back to sleep.

Jelaluddin Balkhi (Rumi), 13th century Persian poet

I wake in the night conscious that here in the room in which I am sleeping hundreds of people have slept before me: men, women, traders and holy men, wise men and simple souls, men of honour and miscreants.

If I'd been resting here 300 years ago, would I have been thinking very different thoughts? Or in the shivering hours before dawn do we all ponder the same questions, the same thoughts of love and the future and, most importantly for me at this moment, that off-putting need to stagger outside in the freezing air to the loo across the courtyard …

Reza and I had agreed to meet in the courtyard before sunrise at which point we planned to climb up to the roof so we could watch dawn over the desert and the caravanserai. But when I open the creaking door of my room there is no one in sight. The only eyes watching me are those of the desiccated fox skull that the renovators had found under a flagstone nearby and affixed to the wall above my door.

The cold is biting and, although I am determined not to miss the sunrise, I am not going to suffer alone. I cross the courtyard to the Rezas' door and bang on it. A sleep-heavy voice assures me he is coming.

A minute or two later he emerges, looking less than alert, and we climb the high steps to the roof. The low parapet affords no protection from a pre-dawn wind that flows down from the mountains. Every time I take off a glove to use my camera my hand goes numb.

But when the glowing orange sun edges above the mountains in the east, I stop moaning about the cold and my lack of sleep and watch the colours of morning wash over the adobe walls of the stable that stands just outside the caravanserai door.

The shadows intensify across the sensuous curves of the ancient building's rounded corners. The monochrome of the desert comes alive and the piercing lights of the omnipresent trucks are dulled.

After breakfast Akbar, the moustached manager, unlocks the stable doors to reveal three baby camels warming up in the early morning sun against the far wall.

'We think tourists will expect to see camels here. They cost five hundred US dollars each so I hope we are right,' he says. A small smoky grey donkey is keeping them company.

Reza B talks to the handful of other staff who all want to know where in Iran he comes from.

'I come from Azerbaijan,' he begins.

'What is that like?'

'Well, he answers, 'there is western and eastern Azerbaijan. In my western Azerbaijan the nights are full of stars.'

Although we are staying in Yazd that night we drive straight through the city and out to the small village of Taft.

Yazd, and some of the surrounding villages, such as Taft, is one of the last remaining strongholds of the Zoroastrian religion that is thought to have only about 200,000 adherents worldwide. Most of them are in Iran but there is also a community in India, specifically in Mumbai, where they are known as Parsees.

Before the advent of Islam, Zoroastrianism was effectively the national religion of Persia – and despite the country's modern-day status as an Islamic republic, the religion is firmly embedded in the nation's consciousness and woven into its sense of identity. Zoroastrianism dates back to about 550 BC when it is believed that its founder, Zoroaster (also known as Zarathushtra and Zarathustra) was born. No one is exactly sure where this took place but it may have been in northeastern Afghanistan perhaps or modern-day Turkmenistan. Regarded as one of the world's oldest monotheistic religions, its adherents believe in a saviour born of a virgin and that the world will end with a battle between good and evil and a final judgement.

Zoroastrians are mistakenly called fire-worshippers. They certainly do venerate fire, but only as a symbol of God the creator's wisdom and energy. Good thoughts, good deeds and good words are the key ingredients of their faith, along with a belief in free will. Traditionally Zoroastrians do not believe in conversion. You have to be born a Zoroastrian – each faith will lead one to God.

The village of Taft is also known for its pomegranates and on its outskirts, in the centre of a traffic roundabout, is a massive metal sculpture of a fruit basket piled high with gilt and ruby-red pomegranates.

We stop at the entrance to an unsealed alleyway bounded by high earth walls in the heart of Taft, and Reza and I set off down the path leaving Reza B to enjoy a snooze in the van. Apart from looping electricity and telephone lines it's a timeless scene. We stop frequently to peer through the cracks of the wooden gates set into the walls – last year's leaves and a few mummified fruits hanging in the suspended animation of late winter cling to orchards of apples, apricot and pomegranates.

We reach a T-junction and see in the wall in front of us a small niche black with soot that has a trail of candle grease snaking down to the ground.

'In the evenings someone comes out and lights a candle – it's a sign of the Zoroastrian faith, but also a way to light the darkness through the streets,' Reza explains.

We turn right and follow the lane until Reza stops outside a tall set of metal gates inside of which is the village fire temple, the focus of Zoroastrian worship and where communal prayers and other ceremonies are held. He gently pushes the gate open and we step into a tiny courtyard where two or three trees stand among the long grass and the thorny branches of a few rose bushes edge the path.

A simple rectangular building stands in front of us featuring a steep set of steps leading up to a plain metal door. A woman, bent double and with her back to us as she sweeps the concrete with a twig broom, is on the steps. Hearing our voices, she turns round and carefully makes her way down the stairs toward us.

Wearing a long green skirt and an orange and red scarf that comes down almost to her waist – quite different from those of all the other women I've met so far – she's tiny, only coming up to Reza's chest.

Encircled as her wrinkled but delicately flushed face is with her scarf, she looks just like a carefully preserved apple wrapped in colourful tissue paper. She smiles sweetly at Reza and launches into a rapid conversation in Farsi that I can't follow.

He identifies her as Tahmineh and tells me that she remembers him bringing his mother here to visit her a few months ago.

Tahmineh invites us to visit the temple and we take off our shoes and go up the steps. Fire temples, despite their rather exotic name, tend to be rather utilitarian inside. The fire burns in a small room in the centre, with windows set in the walls so the flames can be seen from all sides by worshippers and visitors such as ourselves.

In one corner of the room is a small bookshelf crammed with copies of the Zoroastrian scriptures, the Avestas, and various commentaries on it and the religion in general. Framed black-and-white photos of temple benefactors hang on the walls.

Tahmineh has been the custodian of the fire for 20 years. The fires in Zoroastrian fire temples must never be allowed to go out so she has been stoking it twice a day for two decades.

We contemplate the glowing embers and small flickering flames and then return to the steps to gather up our shoes. Tahmineh asks Reza if we'll stay for tea. He accepts and we sit in the sun while she disappears into a small room under the staircase.

When the door creaks open Reza jumps up to help her carry a

small tray of glasses, a teapot, a bowl of sugar and a coloured cardboard box tied up with string. Inside the box are diamond-shaped biscuits comprising paper-thin layers of crisp wafer.

'They're called *yokheh* – a speciality of Kermanshah province. She says she's been keeping them for a special occasion.'

Yokheh are tricky to eat neatly, not just because they are covered in a fine layer of powdered sugar but when you take a bite shards of wafer explode everywhere. They're delicious, though, and when Tahmineh offers the box again we can't resist. As we drop crumbs all over the freshly swept steps she tells us there are about 20 Zoroastrian families left in the village. Because agriculture in the area is flourishing, the village is thriving. There are even enough Zoroastrian youngsters to justify a religious school and a priest comes from Yazd every few weeks to conduct ceremonies accordingly.

As we gather up the tea things, Tahmineh asks Reza if he can help her identify the worth of a bank note she has in her possession. She disappears inside again and returns with a US dollar note. Reza explains what it is as she has no idea and offers to change it for her; he hands over double the exchange rate in Iranian rials.

Tahmineh escorts us to the gate and then tries to press on us a bag of pomegranates, which Reza refuses to accept. She pushes them back at him and once again he refuses.

'I'm not *taroffing*,' he says in an aside to me. 'I think they are the last of her winter supply. There are seven of them in the bag and I know they are very expensive at this time of year.'

I join in the battle but Tahmineh is not having any of it. When Reza hands them back again she simply puts them on the ground. It's a pomegranate stand-off.

The three of us contemplate the bag for a while before Reza picks them up.

'I think we'll have to take them now, but I feel terrible, especially as we have nothing on us to give in return.' I lean over, kiss her on the cheek and thank her.

'She says to take the pomegranates and go and eat them together.'

'Well, we would, wouldn't we,' I reply, a bit mystified.

Reza blushes.

'I'll explain later,' he says, as we say goodbye to Tahmineh and make our way back through the lanes.

Reza is still fretting about not having a gift for her when we get back to the van. However, inspiration strikes and he dips into my stash of polished paua (abalone) shell pieces, which I travel with, and quickly grabs a handful before he dashes back through the village with them along with a box of teabags from our picnic supplies.

'I feel better now,' he says on his return. 'But look – even then she insisted on giving me three apples in exchange!'

Thankfully, Reza decides to call it quits at this point. Just as well or he could spend all day to-ing and fro-ing with an increasingly desperate range of gifts.

From Taft we drive to another traditional Zoroastrian village, but unlike Taft, Cham has a forlorn feel about it. Adobe walls are crumbling into the surrounding fields that look largely untended. It's doubly poignant because the backdrop to the village is so magnificent – the massive snow-covered Shir Kuh (Lion Mountain), which at 4075 metres is the highest point of Iran's central mountain range.

Cham's main street is deserted but inside the fire temple compound, once again we find an elderly woman who has just finished tending the sacred flame. More unusually, this flame is in a small enclosure in the courtyard. Two withered pomegranates dangle from a piece of string tied to a tree that almost fills the courtyard.

The woman tells Reza that she and her husband are now the only permanent residents in the village. Their own experiences mirror those of many elderly rural people in Iran – one child lives in Yazd, the other in Virginia in the United States.

'There isn't enough water for agriculture here so everyone but us has left,' she explains.

Later, as we explore the village looking for good vantage points of the mountains, we see her again, this time sitting on a rickety chair outside her house, a wheelbarrow full of pomegranates in front of her, sorting out the good fruit from those that have rotted over the winter. Her husband appears, small and bent and loaded down with a sack of fodder and just as I'm starting to wonder who or what the fodder is intended for I become aware of some plaintive bleating coming from behind the shoulder-height wall that encircles one of the village's domed water reservoirs. Turning round and looking over the wall I find at least 20 pairs of eyes staring earnestly back at me. The couple's small flock of sheep is sheltered here and clearly they know their shepherd's on his way with their lunch.

Back at the van Reza B has ready a plastic plate covered in what looks like a pile of glistening rubies, but are actually the seeds from several of the pomegranates; the flavour is sharp and delicious. Pomegranates are thought to have originated in Iran and this region is especially famous for them. The exotic fruit pops up in myths and traditions of many nationalities including the ancient Greeks, Jews, Georgians and Armenians, along with the Persians. Even in modern-day Iran during the ceremony of the longest night (a celebration that actually has its origins in Zoroastrianism) people offer one another pomegranates.

Meanwhile, Reza accidentally drops a seed and Reza B tut-tuts at him, telling us that pomegranates are a gift of God and to drop even one seed is bad luck. This seems like a good time to ask him about the meaning behind Tahmineh's suggestion that the two of us should eat pomegranates together.

'Some people call them a heavenly fruit,' he responds. 'Prophet Mohammad said that one seed in every pomegranate comes from Paradise, which is why we have to be careful not to drop any.'

As for us eating them together, he coughs discreetly before telling me that they are an integral part of Iranian wedding celebrations – and a sign of fertility.

Reza B grins, his moustache bristling with mischief. He heaps up my spoon, holds it out to me and declares, in Farsi: *'Reza anar mixorade, Jill anar mixorade, ma anar mixorim.'* (Reza is eating pomegranates, Jill is eating pomegranates, we are eating pomegranates.) Reza looks at his watch.

'It is time we went to our hotel for lunch.'

After a series of somewhat spartan, if reasonably clean, hotels, I'm looking forward immensely to our Yazd hotel. Moshir-al-Mamalek, which was once a stable complex complete with its own Persian garden, captivated me on my first visit to Iran and I can't wait to see it again.

Like many traditional Iranian buildings, the Moshir presents only blank walls to the world, and even a glance in the doorway set in the angle of two intersecting outer walls reveals nothing more than a tiny circular lobby. But walk through the serpentine corridor – another typical Persian architectural feature – that leads from the lobby towards the dining room and the hotel then reveals itself.

A small interior fountain and pool are at one end of the dining room, in which all the chairs are covered in the Yazd speciality of silk brocade. Two macaws, one red and one yellow, are often to be found sitting on a wooden perch in the middle of this pool. A channel runs from the pool to outside where the water cascades into another channel that runs the length of the property. Small fountains spaced at regular intervals bubble and gurgle.

Most of the rooms are on the left, partly screened from the garden by a row of willows. Stairways that twist and turn lead to the rooms, each of which has a barrel-vaulted ceiling and panels of stained glass that the light causes to spread jewelled patterns across the tiled floors.

On the other side of the channel are *takts*, where one can sit on hand-knotted carpets and sip tea. Until recently it was also possible to smoke *qalyan* here, but sadly for us, this is no longer allowed.

As it's winter, most of the *takts* are stacked under shelter but a few are in use, sheltered by a large marquee. We vow to drink tea there later, no matter how cold it is.

Yazd is a treasure trove of traditional desert architecture and its old town of winding lanes and adobe walls is one of my favourite places. But this time Reza is taking me to see the biggest and best-preserved icehouse in all of Iran, which I hadn't known anything about on my previous visits. It stands near the centre of the city and at street level you would never know it was there. Even Reza takes a few minutes to find the small doorway that opens into a side alley, but once we're in we are delayed slightly by my glimpsing through a dark doorway what look like huge crystal geodes sparkling in the gloom. It's one of Yazd's speciality industries – the production of rock sugar. Golden platters of crystals are stacked on a wooden shelf to one side of the room and I only work out what they are when I hear a cracking sound and look to see a man belting one of the large circular crystal masses with a mallet. Hunks fly everywhere but I recognise the shards to be the same as the oddly shaped lumps of sugar crystal that I've enjoyed at various Iranian teahouses.

Outside the shop three men are trying to heave a plastic barrel of sugar syrup off the back of a small pick-up truck onto the pavement. As they take the weight of the barrel there's a collective cry of 'Ya Ali', which translates as 'Ali, help us!'

When we emerge from the first flight of stairs inside the icehouse, I discover that the 15th-century icehouse has been converted into a *zurkaneh*, meaning a house of strength, a meeting place for men who take part in a discipline that combines power lifting, gymnastics, Islamic chants and spiritual dance. Their exercise routines take place in a circular pit surrounded by tiered spectator seating and the rounded interior of the icehouse makes it an almost perfect venue. As it's early afternoon (most sessions take place in the evenings after work and school), there is just one young man, watched by his wife and baby, practising his routines.

We stop to observe for a few moments and Reza suggests I try lifting up the skittle-shaped wooden weights that participants toss into the air. Although some of the skittles only come up to my knees, others are nearly a metre in height and I can barely lift one even a centimetre up off the carpet. Dangling from a metal bar is a tangle of heavy chains that looks more like a medieval torture instrument than gym gear.

This is not the first *zurkaneh* session I've seen, although there is usually a number of participants rather than just one as is the case today; in any event I find them a typical expression of the complexity of the Persian mind because while the participants pray and chant, they are also rejoicing in their physical strength and endurance. On previous occasions I've noted that the men taking part wear tie-dyed cotton knickerbockers and T-shirts stretched tight across their muscular chests. It's an incredible sight – the gymnasts perform mass displays of press-ups, and take turns to toss various-sized wooden skittles high into the air. Then one by one each takes centre stage to twirl faster and faster like a whirling dervish, those who manage to stay on their feet longest getting the longest applause. Throughout the session the *zurkaneh* master, sitting on his elevated stage, chants, chimes a bell and beats out complicated rhythms on a giant drum. The strongest is then put to the test by being draped with the yoke of metal chains.

As one would expect there are always particular gymnasts with exceptional prowess in one or more of the exercises, but a special feature of the *zurkaneh* is the sense of comradeship in that the strong are applauded, while the weaker and more inexperienced are encouraged.

We leave the Yazd *zurkaneh* to clamber up the last set of stairs to emerge on a flat roof dotted with domes, rather as if the roof is suffering from an outbreak of acne. Above us five fluted towers rise up around the peak of the central domes.

'These are *badgirs* – wind towers – and Yazd has many of them. They form a natural air-conditioning system and are very effective.

We'll visit the tallest one in the world soon and then I'll explain how they work,' Reza says.

From our rooftop vantage point we look down on the plaza in front of the Amir Chakhmagh complex. Surmounted by two slim minarets is a three-storey façade of niches decorated with coloured tiles and calligraphy. It once served as a portal to a now-defunct bazaar but more importantly still serves as an extremely decorative grandstand or *Hosseini* from where an audience can view the Iranian version of a passion play. This cycle of dramas commemorating the martyrdom of the third Imam, Hossein, is re-enacted throughout Iran during *Moharram*.

'Let's climb it,' Reza dares me. 'I never go up there with tour groups because it can be a bit dangerous.'

We cross the square and puff our way up the steep winding staircase to the narrow platform that stretches between the minarets.

Yazd has preserved its traditional architecture and few modern structures can be seen from our 360-degree vantage point across the city. When Marco Polo visited during the 13th century he described it as a 'very fine and splendid city'.

We can see the icehouse towers, the minarets and portal of the Friday mosque, the tallest wind tower in the world rising up from its garden setting – and far in the distance and a little obscured by desert dust the Zoroastrian towers of silence.

'Let's go and see how the wind tower works,' Reza says.

The 33-metre-high *badgir* is the centrepiece of the Bagh-e Doulat Abad, a garden and pavilion built in the mid-18th century for a former ruler of Yazd, Karim Khan Zand. The garden is a typical Persian design of four garden plots divided in two by a long central pool. Two of the gardens contain pomegranate trees, and the others host a number of gnarled elderly grapevines. A tunnel of thin water jets forms a cool archway over the pool during the summer.

But the dominant feature of the garden is the pavilion that houses the wind tower, the windows of which contain some of the most exquisite stained glass in all of Iran. Two entire walls consist of these panels and when the sun is shining it is like standing inside a kaleidoscope.

However, it's the ancient air-conditioning technology that has drawn us here. From underneath a wind tower looks like a vertical chute, divided neatly in half. The tower itself is covered in angled shutters that draw in cool air, which is then forced down one side of the chute and over a pool set directly beneath it that cools the air even further. At the same time, warm air is forced up the other side of the chute.

When we are standing in the pavilion directly under the tower Reza uses a tissue to demonstrate the efficacy of the system. He throws the tissue into the air where it is caught by a surprisingly strong draught and shot skywards. When we stand at the other side, the gust of cold wind pouring down on us is decidedly chilly.

'You can see how effective and simple it is,' Reza says. 'Best of all it needs no electricity to work and creates no pollution. During the summer I went to stay with a friend of mine in a new house in Yazd that did not have a wind tower. The air conditioner was noisy and the house felt stuffy all the time. I think it is a tragedy that so few contemporary architects and builders are using this technique.'

By now it is late afternoon and the perfect time to visit the two towers of silence outside the city. The most obvious symbols of the Zoroastrian religion, they are also, perhaps, the most misunderstood.

Because Zoroastrians believe fire is sacred they do not cremate their dead. And their belief in the sanctity of the other elements of earth, water and air prevents them from using other conventional means of disposal.

For centuries past they have carried the remains of their loved ones to these so-called towers of silence, often a small hill, the top of which has been levelled and then encircled with a high wall. The body or bodies are laid in a small depression in the centre and left for the birds, vultures in particular, and the action of the sun. A priest is usually present for several days to pray over the body.

The Yazd towers of silence were once well outside the city, but an expanding population and related building boom has resulted in them now being on the city's outskirts. The proximity of vultures feeding on the bodies so close to residential housing presented obvious health problems and the practice was abandoned in the 1960s. Today most Zoroastrians in Yazd are buried in stone caskets in a graveyard at the base of the lonely towers.

It is still possible to follow the trails the bearers of the dead once took to the top of the towers. As the sun begins to set we scramble up a rock-strewn hillside devoid of any vegetation. A twilight wind blows, creating tiny dust devils and making eerie whistling noises around the wall above us.

At the top we duck through a low archway into the burial area. The wind is especially strong here, whipping my headscarf right over my face, then capriciously unwinding it until it is on the point of taking flight.

We walk over to the depression in the centre and knowing what is was once used for I can't help but look skywards. But these days there are no vultures. I notice that to one side a low wall has been built parallel to the outer parapet and Reza explains that it was the place where the priest would sleep and pray as the dead were never left alone.

Up here, enclosed by the stone walls and looked down on by a dusty blue sky streaked with peach and pink, I understand for the first time the reasoning behind the ceremony. It no longer seems barbaric; after all, like adherents of other religions, Zoroastrians believe the body is only the shell left after the spirit has been set free. Sadly for them however, the impact of 21st-century life, including urban sprawl and the disappearance of vultures caused by pollution and other pressures, has in most cases posed a real threat to one of their core traditions.

Back at our hotel it's started to drizzle. Not what one expects in a desert city, but we stick to our resolve and ask for tea to be served at a *takt* under the flapping canvas. We are joined by three Tehranis, a mother and her two adult children. The daughter, in her early 20s, has a small white plaster across her nose.

She is one of the nearly 70,000 Iranians (not all women) each year who have cosmetic surgery on their nose, earning the country the dubious honour of being known as the Nose Job Capital of the World.

Here it's considered a status symbol to have had a nose job, hence there is no embarrassment in being seen in public wearing the tell-tale plaster strip. When I first visited Iran I asked a young woman of my acquaintance why she'd had it done and she explained that she believed the typical Iranian nose is too big. However, she hadn't told her surgeon that; rather she'd told him that she'd had an accident as a child and now had trouble breathing. 'But really it was because I wanted to look more beautiful.'

It seems to me that the imperative for women to cover up all but their faces has in some ways backfired in that it's made many women, younger ones especially, become obsessed with their facial features and wear such heavy make-up. And it's my opinion that because their social interaction is more limited than in many other countries, there is perhaps almost too much time to lavish on personal appearance – and to worry about it.

The girl in the garden is too shy to speak much, but her older brother, who appears to be the head of the household, asks Reza many questions about his education and his job. He asks for Reza's business card and I wonder if he is sizing him up as a possible husband for his sister.

When the family leaves, Reza asks me if I thought the young woman was beautiful. I tell him that in my eyes she was indeed very attractive – and would have been so before her nose job.

Arranged marriages are not the norm in Iran today, but meeting potential spouses remains somewhat fraught as there are so many social constraints involved when attempting to mix with the opposite sex. Young Iranians are most likely to be attracted to a fellow student or worker, a member of their extended family, or someone they meet through family connections.

Although they go out on dates, there will be more vetting of each other's families at this stage than is usually the case in the West. Casual dating is uncommon; it is more likely that once a couple begins dating, the end result will be marriage.

A young woman is expected to be a virgin when she marries but in any event the opportunities for any kind of intimate behaviour is restricted because before marriage most young people live at home with their families. A night spent in a hotel, for example, would be impossible; not least because hotels in this country have the right to check on their Iranian guests' marital status.

I've become aware that during my travels the couples we see most openly holding hands and snuggling on benches are most likely newly-weds getting to know each other better *after* the ceremony.

The next day our drive to Kerman is taken up with intensive Persian lessons. During our essential morning tea stop Reza, who is helping dig out the tea things, exclaims: 'My god, look at this.' He pulls out the teapot we'd borrowed from the mosque teashop two days before.

'From a mosque, too,' Reza says, lightly banging his forehead with the heel of one hand.

We debate posting it back (none of us knows the address, however) and certainly driving there is not an option. We conclude with a decision to treat the teapot with great respect for the rest of the trip – and think about its future when we get back to Tehran.

The drive to Kerman is, by our standards, a short one so Reza decides we should choose our hotel and then go sightseeing. I'm amused to find he's using a Lonely Planet selection – budget category – as a guide.

'I find it very useful,' he says. 'But what exactly does dodgy plumbing mean by the way?'

I tell him it means I won't be staying there.

Reza decides, after our hotel splurge in Yazd, that we should economise for our two nights in Kerman. But after he visits and rejects several hotels I point out that although money is important, so too is our time. Reza wants to check out one more budget option but unfortunately it's hidden away in a neighbourhood with no street signs and by the time we find it all three of us are feeling frazzled.

A long low building, rather like a British Raj-style bungalow, the hotel appears to be run by two stern-faced young women, neither with a skerrick of hair showing, who lead us somewhat reluctantly to the far wing and throw open a couple of doors. My room looks adequate if somewhat basic, and soon afterwards Reza and I take a taxi into the centre of Kerman.

'Kerman has one of the best examples of a classic Islamic ensemble,' Reza tells me as we walk towards the Jama Masjid, the first of four components of the Ganj Ali Khan complex. The 14th-century mosque is decorated with candy-twist arches over the entrance portal and a confection of intricate blue and white glazed tiles covered with calligraphy and abstract designs.

'The mosque is the first component,' Reza says, diving through a side door of the mosque, up a set of steps then almost immediately plunging down more stairs. 'Here is the second – the *hammam* or bathhouse.'

'Imagine you have travelled in your caravan across the desert, like we have today. The minarets would guide you to the mosque for your evening prayers but also, very importantly, you would know that once you found the mosque you would be close to three other essential services: the caravanserai where you could spend the night and house your camels, the bazaar for your trading and buying of travel necessities and the *hammam* for a much-needed bath.'

I soon learned there was more to the *hammam* than just a matter of hygiene. Kerman's bathhouse has been converted into a museum complete with waxwork models to recreate the atmosphere that would have prevailed during the era of the great desert caravans.

A serpentine corridor brings us to the first major room, the *frigidarium*, a circular space with a small fountain and pool in the centre and a number of large arched alcoves each of which used to cater for men from different stations in life – for example, mullahs, merchants and workers – around the outer walls. Here they would take off their shoes, which they'd leave in special small niches set into the wall around the pool, then disrobe on their appropriate platforms. Before and after bathing they would relax, enjoy tea, smoke *qalyan* and, most important of all, catch up on all the gossip and local news.

More twisting corridors take us to the *tepidarium* where a large central pool is surrounded by raised platforms set in niches.

'The difference between a typical Persian *hammam* and, say, a Roman bath was that because water was always in short supply here, almost no *hammams* had pools in which people actually bathed. Water was too precious for that. Instead it would be ladled into jugs and taken to the platform where you would wash, or you could have a bathhouse attendant do it for you.'

Small cubicles were available for massages along with others where men would shave off their body hair. Brazilian waxes might be a novelty for Western men, but in the East having certain parts of the anatomy hairless is an essential part of Islamic culture.

'This is a perfect time to come to the *hamman*. Come and look at the walls behind the water reservoir,' Reza says, leading me to a room containing a deep tank of water. The western wall comprises thin sheets of translucent marble that glow in the setting sun. When Reza asks me to guess the purpose of this beautiful wall, I surmise that it exists simply because it is so good to look at.

'A good answer, but not so in this case. When someone was in the bathhouse there were no windows to the outside world so it was easy to lose track of time. But when the setting sun hit this wall the men in the bathhouse knew it was close to nightfall and therefore time to leave. They wouldn't want to stay once it was dark because of an ancient superstition about bathhouses being haunted by ghosts between sunset and sunrise.'

Next door to the bathhouse is an entrance to the vaulted brick-covered bazaar of Kerman. The lights are coming on in all the small shops and the main alleyway is thronged with shoppers. Copper, silver and steel gleam under the lights in the coppersmiths' bazaar, and the scent of saffron and frankincense wafts from stalls where spices and other powders, and even rosebuds, have been carefully fashioned into the shape of tall cones.

Kerman is the centre of cumin production and I'm amused when Reza tells me that the Iranians have an equivalent to our well-known English saying about taking coals to Newcastle; theirs is 'carrying cumin to Kerman'.

Iranian bazaars such as this one function just like a modern city mall: there are shops crammed with children's clothing, tiny stalls festooned with traditional gold jewellery, shops devoted specifically to electric samovars and melamine dinner sets, and stalls selling religious paraphernalia including prayer beads, evil-eye pendants and copies of the Koran.

Reza points at a set of arched wooden doors that open into the central bazaar. 'There's the third component of the Ganj Ali Khan complex – over there is the entrance to one of the caravanserais.'

He turns down another alleyway, smiles a greeting at a man standing behind a small desk and says to me: 'You're going to love this, I think.'

We are in another circular room, this one filled with chairs, tables and *takts*. The presence of a central pool and shoe alcoves is evidence that what is now a teahouse was once a *hammam*. Brass chandeliers provide a muted light, and the only sound is from the splash of water that cascades from a terracotta teapot fountain set in the centre of the pool and the quiet clink of tea glasses.

We order tea and lean back against the bolsters to admire the decorative brick-vaulted ceiling and the traditional teahouse painting on one wall. Teahouse paintings, which developed at a time when few people could read, depicted ancient stories and were used as props by the story-tellers who once frequented the teahouses of Persia.

Back at our cheap hotel Reza asks to check my bathroom.

'It smells,' he says. 'We're going to swap with you.'

I venture into the new bathroom where I am met by a massive cockroach that holds its ground and waves its antennae at me. I summon Reza. He strides in purposefully, armed with a metal wastepaper basket. I hear a decisive clang and Reza emerges to say that he thinks I will find the offending insect is now dead.

Next morning, when I go for my shower, the cockroach is sitting on the tiles immediately under the shower rose. I decide it's him or me so turn on the shower full power and hose him down the drain.

On our way out for the day Reza tells the staff that our rooms are unsatisfactory and we will require new ones for our second night. The two girls look nonplussed – they've already lost track of who is where.

It's very cold outside and starts to snow heavily as we drive into the mountains. We postpone our tea break until we reach the village of Rayen where Reza B produces *kolimpeh*, a Kerman specialty of shortcake biscuits filled with dates. The dates in this area are considered some of the best in Iran, which, according to Reza, means they are some of the best in the world.

We are travelling the highway that eventually leads to the Pakistan border at Zahedan. On the way the road passes through the devastated treasure of the Bam citadel, a world heritage-listed city that was completely destroyed by an earthquake in 1998.

But Reza knows of another smaller but exceptionally well-preserved citadel near Bam, one few Iranians and even fewer overseas visitors have seen.

Although the Argh-e Rayen citadel dates back to pre-Islamic times, it also contains buildings from the 11th century. Still inhabited until the middle of the 20th century, it was then abandoned for years, but is now in the process of being fully restored. We enter through a tall gateway, to one side of which a young man with bloodshot eyes is making traditional charcoal tongs using the most basic of blacksmithing equipment. He begs us to come back to see his finished products.

'I hardly see any tourists these days,' he tells Reza, somewhat forlornly.

We head for a terrace on the first floor above the gateway where the view is astonishing. A wall encases the entire city and in the right-hand far corner a multi-storeyed keep rises up from above the small houses that sit at its base. Made of adobe, the houses have soft sensuous curves that flow unbroken along the narrow streets as each structure shares common walls with its neighbours. Almost all the buildings are roofless, but recent work has restored most of the adobe walls to their original height and thickness.

Reza explains that there is a very distinct layout to the city, even if to my eyes it looks like a mudbrick maze. The tall building in the corner, protected by its own fortified walls within the city walls, was once the governor's house. The houses of ordinary citizens, a bazaar, shops and quarters for the governor's army were situated between the two sets of walls.

We wander through the alleyways towards the governor's mansion, accompanied at times by workmen pushing squeaking wheelbarrows full of clay ready for mixing with straw for more adobe reconstruction work. The governor's palace comprised personal living quarters, guest rooms and a banquet hall, all linked by serpentine corridors, which intersected at small vestibules lit by clerestories and decorated with small niches. This layout ensured absolute privacy in the rooms and courtyards that lay beyond.

Apart from the workers, we are the only visitors, so I don't need much persuading to stop at the blacksmiths and buy a set of tongs made of steel, brass and copper; the handle end is surmounted by a tiny owl.

We leave Rayen bound for one of the most famous gardens in Iran, Bagh-e Shazdeh, the Prince's Garden, but first there is the important matter of lunch. We pull up outside the Iranian equivalent of a truckers' café, Reza looking a little worried.

'Will you be OK in here?' he asks. 'I'm told they have the best kebabs in the area.'

It would be fair to say that the regular clientele of the kebab shop has not seen too many female tourists in their neck of the woods, but they are extremely polite and restrict their staring until they think neither I, nor the Rezas, are watching.

On the verandah of the shop a sweating cook is twirling at least 12 long kebabs at a time over a bed of hot coals at the same time ensuring that the essential accompaniment of halved grilled tomatoes doesn't catch fire. A young minion scurries between him and the tables restocking plates as fast as he can while, from the recesses of the restaurant, another youngster is also on the run as he drops huge ovals of freshly baked bread into the fast-emptying plastic baskets in front of the diners.

Watching Reza B eat, I can appreciate why he doesn't bother with an evening meal as his capacity for lamb, chicken, *shaslik* (minced kebabs), bread, salad, raw onions, pickled whole bulbs of garlic and yoghurt is prodigious.

After lunch, as a light drizzle falls on one of the driest parts of Iran, we drive to the Prince's Garden on the outskirts of Mahan.

A wet day in February is not the ideal time to see one of the most famous Persian gardens in the country, but we have the cascades and fountains all to ourselves. The garden was built in 1873 by one of the last of the Qajar dynasty princes, Abdul Hamid Mirza, and like most Persian gardens it has a strong symmetrical element. Tall poplars line the path to the entrance portal that is decorated with floral frescoes while the archway perfectly frames the cascade of waterfalls and pools set with fountains that climb the hill towards a small pavilion. The pools are bordered with gardens, edged with purple pansies, in which roses are just coming into bud. Plane trees and more poplars flank the path and behind them are gardens planted with cherries, figs, pomegranates and grapevines.

On our arrival at the pavilion, which houses a restaurant and teahouse, it's clear that the former is in a state of organised chaos. As he rushes past, a waiter tells Reza that a large party of Ministry of Culture and Heritage officials is due for lunch, but Reza is able to persuade the manager to allow us upstairs to see the stained-glass windows in the room that overlooks the cascade.

I'm surprised they agree because the entire upstairs floor is already laid out for the banquet. Salads and bowls of yoghurt are arranged at each place setting on the floor and bottles of fizzy drinks are clustered along the tablecloth. We tiptoe around the food to see the view and to photograph the jewel-like colours of the fan-shaped leadlight panels.

'Let's take some photos of the feast so it looks as if we are taking part,' Reza says suddenly, taking down a decorative *qalyan* from a mantelpiece as he speaks and arranging it in front of me. He then relocates some of the dishes of food, while I try to sit as elegantly as possible on the floor without upsetting the lunch arrangements.

Fortunately, before anyone catches us, we tidy up and go in search of the only person not taking part in the frantic preparations – the teahouse and *qalyan* man. He gives us a tray of tea and a *qalyan*, but asks us to sit out of sight of the VIPs when they arrive. We retreat up a small set of stairs with what feels like forbidden fruit because, despite its popularity throughout Iran, these days the authorities officially frown upon *qalyan*. Some teahouses will now only serve it out of sight of passers-by and in late 2007 there was an attempt by the government to ban it altogether (ostensibly on the grounds that some of the teahouses were less than hygienic) and as a result some of Iran's most atmospheric teahouses closed down, including many mentioned in this book. However, in early 2008, the rules were relaxed and much to the joy of many Iranians and visitors, some teahouses reopened. Another small triumph for people power, perhaps.

On our way back to Kerman we drive through the tree-lined streets of Mahan to the 15th-century Aramgah-e Shah Ne-matollah Vali, the tomb of Sufi dervish Shah Ne-matollah Vali.

Sufis are the mystics of Islam; they believe it is possible to be close to God on earth (as opposed to waiting until one is in heaven) and consider personal religious experience to be as vital as is having a spiritual master, such as Shah Ne-matollah Vali, to guide them. The word dervish (which derives from the Persian) has a similar meaning to that of master. Music, dance, trance, meditation and poetry are all part of the Sufi philosophy. Today it is estimated that there are at least two million Sufis in Iran, an estimate that may be causing the religious authorities some qualms given that in some quarters, Sufism is regarded as being something of a departure from mainstream Shia theology.

We enter the complex across an enclosed courtyard set with a pool of intersecting hexagons. Beyond this is a carpeted hall in which several people are praying, including some women – each of whom has covered herself up with a chador from the collection kept near the entrance for this purpose.

Although there is some mirror work typical of shrines around the Sufi's actual tomb, the walls in the central chamber are simply whitewashed and unadorned. However, through a very low doorway to one side is the Sufi's prayer chamber – a tiny barrel-roofed room which, although measuring not much more than 1 metre by 2 metres, is covered – wall and roof space alike – with calligraphy and paintings in vibrant reds and greens.

The elderly man who unlocks the chamber for us explains that many of the writings on the walls are poems by the Sufi's pupils. Set among them is a painting of a long sword – the double-edged sword of Imam Ali. Reza is fascinated by the poems and tells the man that one day, *inshallah* (if God wills it), he will return to transcribe them and translate them into English for visitors.

The magnificent Safavid-period dome built over the shrine is under renovation now, but the elderly caretaker unlocks the door at Reza's request so we can reach the roof to see it at close quarters and admire the two slender minarets.

The caretaker also shows us around a small museum containing Sufi relics, including the distinctively shaped Sufi alms bowls that look rather like wooden rugby balls. Sufis believe that accepting charity ensures they will stay humble.

'We have many treasures here,' he says to Reza, 'but why do not more tourists come to see them? Your friend must tell more people to come here.'

I promise to do my best.

Before we leave the complex we browse in the bookshop crammed with copies of the Koran, religious books for children, texts, music and, of course, Iranian poetry. Many of the most famous poets, including Rumi, Attar and Hafez, were Sufis.

Our next stop is Shiraz, home of one of Persia's best-loved poets, Hafez, so I decide it is high time I buy a set of his complete works. The two young female shop assistants select an array of editions for me to choose from.

'They are very surprised you know about Hafez,' says Reza.

I pick a beautiful English-Persian version with a gold spine and paintings of nightingales and flowers on the cover. Each page is edged with a floral border and contains both the Persian stanzas and English translations.

'Soon, in a few weeks, you will not need the English translation,' Reza says as he leafs through the book on our journey back to Kerman. It's snowing again.

I appreciate his optimism and faith in my Persian language capabilities, but I have my doubts. It seems a long way from being able to say: 'I would like tea, please' to translating 'Prudence and proper thoughts lie far from the dervish way; better to fill your breast with fire and your eye with tears.'

As we drive, with me reading the English words and Reza following with the Persian, Reza B utters sighs of contentment: 'Ah, Hafez ...'

One of the poems features a dialogue between a man and a woman:

He said: 'I will barricade your image from the road of my sights.'

She said: 'It is a thief and will come a different way.'

Reza B slowly shakes his head.

'He is long dead but his words still speak to me.'

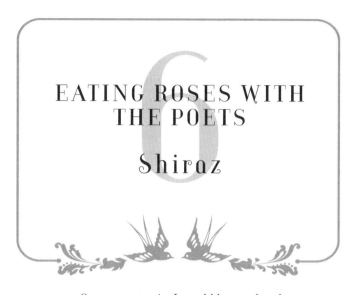

EATING ROSES WITH THE POETS

Shiraz

Open your tunic: I would lay my head
Upon your heart – ah! Deep within your side
Silence and shelter sweet I ever found;
Else must I seek them in the grave instead.
When Hafez sleeps indeed beneath the ground.
Visit his grave – it was for you he died.

Hafez, 14th century Persian poet

After our first breakfast of cold boiled eggs and stale bread in Kerman, the prospect of having the same again does not appeal and we decide to find breakfast on our way to Shiraz. A thick fog hangs over Kerman when we leave and it is still damp and chilly when Reza B stops outside a tiny and not-very-promising-looking café on the outskirts of the city.

Reza does his usual reconnoitre to check on the kitchen hygiene and returns to say it's acceptable and that the cook is now preparing scrambled eggs. But as there is nowhere to sit inside we'll eat in the van and so, while the eggs cook, we fold down seats to make a table, and Reza B makes tea.

A few minutes later the cook appears beside the van and hands in a large pan of eggs, which we scoop up with pieces of flat Persian bread as the windows of the van steam up around us.

At regular intervals there's a discreet tap on the door, which opens to reveals the cook with more eggs, bread and hot water for our teapot.

Later, as we draw near Sirjan, fields of dense and twiggy shrubs, their bark a ghostly white, each about a metre tall, appear on both sides of the road. This region is one of the prime areas in Iran for growing pistachios – if Iran had a national nut it would surely be the pistachio.

Just in case anyone has failed to notice the pistachios growing around the town, Sirjan's principal roundabout is graced by a sculpture featuring two slim hands forming a bowl to hold giant pistachios with their characteristic split shells.

By the time we arrive in Neyreez, just over halfway between Kerman and Shiraz, it's nearly midday on a Friday. Reza wants to visit the small mosque here, built in the 10th century and containing some beautiful stucco work around its *mihrab* and a stately cypress of uncertain age in the courtyard.

'It's not often we are in a mosque at prayer-time,' Reza says. 'Do you mind if we pray?' Although Islam calls on its followers to pray five times a day, it's the midday prayer on a Friday that is the most crucial. The two of them head towards a small arch that leads to the ablutions area and I move away to find somewhere to sit and wait.

'You can come with us and I'll show you what *vozu*, the washing ritual is all about,' Reza says.

We go through the archway into a second small courtyard

where there's a long trough with taps spaced along it. Both men take off their shoes and socks while Reza explains the procedure.

'First I will wash my face, like this.' Reza cups water in his right hand and then wipes his face.

'Now my arms.'

He scoops up water in his left hand and starting with his right elbow washes his arm down to the fingers. He repeats this procedure on his left arm, using water cupped in his right hand.

Somewhere in the mosque complex a girl's clear young voice rings out, singing the call to prayer. Water splashes in the trough as other men arrive to wash.

Using only the left-over moisture on his hands Reza then wipes his hair from the top of his head to his forehead using his right hand, and again not replenishing the water, wipes the top of his right foot with his left hand and then vice versa.

It's a very utilitarian courtyard and, with the exception of the *mihrab* and the tree, a relatively ordinary local mosque, but the entire experience of watching this intimate preparation for prayer moves me unexpectedly to tears. I'm thankful to have my headscarf handy to mop up.

Reza B disappears into the prayer hall that is used when it's either too cold or too hot in the courtyard or open *ivan*. However, after glancing at my red eyes, Reza announces he will pray in the *ivan* where I can sit with him away from the curious glances of the rest of the congregation.

Padding across to a niche in the *ivan*, Reza finds a *mohr* to use and begins to pray. I sit nearby, lulled by the timeless rhythm of the ritual: stand, bow, kneel, prostrate, stand, bow, kneel, prostrate.

Afterwards, as Reza puts on his shoes and socks, he asks me about my progress regarding learning the first sura of the prayer.

He'd written the transliterated Arabic words into my journal several days earlier.

I recite about half in Arabic: 'In the name of God the most merciful and benevolent, God be praised, the most benevolent, the most merciful; the Lord of the next world I praise you and only you and I ask you to help me.'

Reza smiles. 'We must find Reza B so you can demonstrate. You know these Arabic words are difficult even for us – I'm amazed.' I return to the van, hoping that I would not prove to be a one-hit-wonder.

It's kebab time. Along one of Neyreez's wide tree-lined streets we spot a white-coated man tending a brazier in which the charcoal glows with fiery incandescence. It's cold and gloomy inside the restaurant behind him however so we sit outside on the lone *takt* under a leafless plane tree. I stop eating long before my two companions who, seemingly worried that I might fade away if I don't keep eating, wrap up pieces of kebab in bread and hand it to me. I wonder if I can request a similar dining service at home, then decide I'd never get away with it.

Neyreez and the next town of Estahban are separated by the tail end of the Zagros mountain range that rises southwest of Tehran and stretches to the southeast almost the whole length of the country. It forms a formidable barrier between the Persian Gulf and the marshlands that separate Iran from Iraq, and central Iran.

Pinnacles and crags streaked with snow, their bases covered with scree, flank the road as it twists towards Estahban. We descend through a wide valley, the floor of which is planted with rows of trees growing against a backdrop of arid mesas

TOP LEFT: Reza in one of his favourite places in Iran, the Emam Khomeini Square in Isfahan. Behind him is the Sheikh Lotfallah mosque.

TOP RIGHT: Young students in Tarikaneh listen to Reza explaining the principles of mosque architecture.

BELOW: The Zarafaniyeh caravanserai no longer opens its doors to travellers but still presents a remarkably well-preserved façade to passers-by.

TOP LEFT: A rooftop view of the Kalmard caravanserai. Some of the archways have been bricked up to provide shelter for a family of Afghan refugees and their livestock. Heritage officials are on the roof checking out the caravanserai's suitability for renovation.

TOP RIGHT: A beautiful latticework skylight in a ruined caravanserai.

BELOW LEFT: A typical caravanserai interior showing a central unloading platform for camels. The soot on the walls probably dates back to the time when caravans still visited regularly.

BELOW RIGHT: The village of Kh'aranagh grew on foundations established about 1400 years ago. It was still inhabited until about 1970.

TOP LEFT: Tahmineh is the caretaker of Taft's Zoroastrian fire temple.
TOP RIGHT: One of the last residents of the village of Cham sorts pomegranates she has been storing over winter.
BELOW LEFT: Reza B preparing pomegranates for morning tea in Cham.
BELOW RIGHT: A zurkaneh (house of strength) session in full swing.

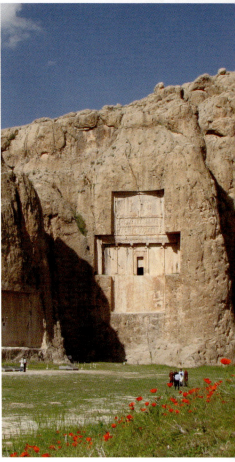

TOP LEFT: The minarets and upper section of the entrance portal of the Jama Masjid, the 14th-century Friday mosque in Kerman.

TOP RIGHT: The walls of the governor's house dominate the humbler adobe houses inside the Rayen citadel.

BELOW LEFT: A Shirazi breadmaker works to keep up with the lunchtime demand for fresh bread.

BELOW RIGHT: Poppies herald the arrival of spring beneath the cave tombs of the Achaemenid kings at Naqsh-e-Rostam.

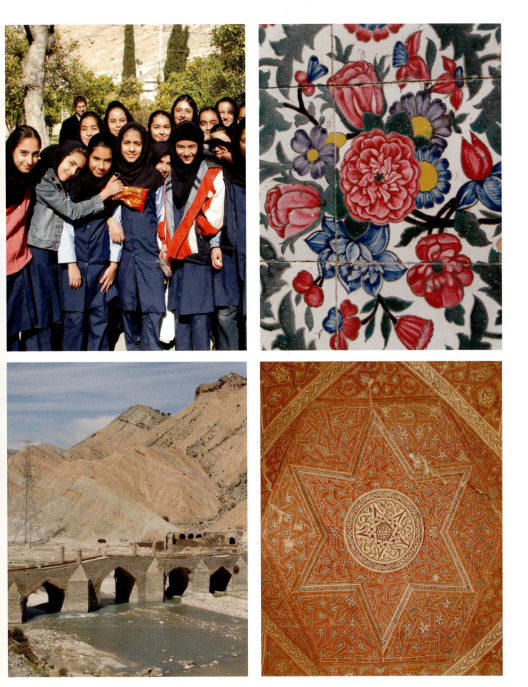

TOP LEFT: Students on an educational visit to Saadi's tomb in Shiraz, eager to have their photograph taken.

TOP RIGHT: Shiraz's Vakil mosque is a vibrant confection of floral wall tiles.

BELOW LEFT: A Sassanian bridge leads to the ruins of a caravanserai (on the far bank) used by travellers making the arduous journey between Shiraz and the Persian Gulf.

BELOW RIGHT: The ceilings in the galleries of the 14th-century Soltaniyeh mausoleum are adorned with decorative plasterwork that seems to echo the intricacies of a hand-knotted Persian carpet.

TOP LEFT: Zanjan's broom-sellers successfully entice us to buy one of their wares.
TOP RIGHT: Qaylan hosepipes festoon the ceiling of a shop in Tabriz's enormous bazaar.
BELOW LEFT: Kalisa-ye Tadi (the Church of Thaddeus) sits smothered in snow. Armenian Christians from throughout Iran make a pilgrimage here every year.
BELOW RIGHT: Party-dinner time Iranian-style in Bazargan, a town on the border with Turkey. The yellow on the platters is a sprinkling of saffron-coloured rice.

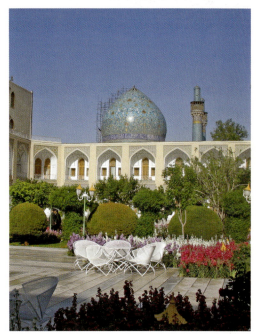

Top left: A tea-seller in the Tehran bazaar with the abacus he still uses in preference to an electronic calculator.

Top right: Nasik (Reza's sister) in a teahouse at the alpine resort of Darband high above Tehran.

Below left: A restored traditional Persian house in Kashan. The structure on the roof is a wind-tower, a natural air-conditioning device.

Below right: The courtyard of the Abassi hotel in Isfahan. This is probably Iran's most beautifully restored caravanserai from the era of Shah Abbas.

Top left: The spectacular dome interior of the Sheikh Lotfallah mosque in Isfahan.
Top right: The Azadegan teahouse is a treasure trove if you love lamps. The tables and the back wall are covered in typical Isfahani block-printing work.
Below left: Isfahan's Emam Khomeini Square. The Sheikh Lotfallah mosque is on the left, and in the centre is the Emam Mosque.
Below right: The gloriously decorated central courtyard of the Emam Mosque in Isfahan.

reminiscent of Arizona. We've left pistachio territory behind and have now entered the land of figs.

Reza requests a stop at a roadside stall where we inspect several varieties of dried fig displayed alongside baskets of sultanas and other dried fruit and nuts.

Both Rezas sample the fig and then get into conversation with the young man who, until our arrival, had been stretched out asleep behind the counter.

'The price of figs has gone up since last year and the size has gone down,' Reza observes.

The young man doesn't deny it, and instead commiserates.

'Yes, I know. This year we did not have enough water to produce big figs and there were not so many fruit ...' he shrugs.

While the Rezas select what looks like enough fruit, nuts and seeds to last us for a week (but which I know will probably only last until the following day) I wander round the back of the stall. Almost all of the trees are festooned with dangling tin cans to scare away the birds and on the ground a number of small stone shelters are dotted about. During the autumn harvest time, families of fig-pickers retreat inside these beehive-shaped huts to escape the midday heat.

We leave the sheltered valleys of figs and the road becomes long and straight once more. As we cross a vast basin tinged with the first signs of early spring grass, a massive structure with two crumbling domes supported by arches in various states of ruin appears in the distance.

We are looking at the remains of the Sarvasan Sassanian palace. The Sassanians, who were Zoroastrians and originated from the Fars province in which we are now travelling, ruled Persia between AD 224 and 637 and at the height of its power, the Sassanian's Second Persian Empire stretched across all the lands between Persia and the Indus River (now in modern-day Pakistan). It had even defeated the armies of the Roman empire in battle. They traded around the Persian Gulf and were early proponents of urban development and their rule only ended with the invasion of the Arabs and the introduction of the new religion of Islam.

Scaffolding covers the domes and parts of the wall of the palace and inside its walls a small group of men is working to strengthen and preserve the building that has dominated the plain for about 1500 years.

One of the workers, an elderly man with white stubble, wearing overalls and grey rubber gloves, sits on a section of scaffolding using a chisel to carefully tap the date into a panel of fresh cement.

Reza has come across him before as the man is a recognised expert in the preservation of ancient stone masonry and tells me that dating his work in this way serves as a record of the latest round of work.

'These stones talk to us,' he tells Reza. 'There are rules of archaeology, of course, but we also need to have very acute ears to listen to the walls, and the building itself, so that we can know what needs to be done.'

We pass under the giant domes and supporting exterior archways that have withstood more than a millennium of human contact and not infrequent earthquakes.

As we walk away from the palace to take photographs, I pick up shards of pottery, some decorated with blue geometric designs, others in shades of terracotta, which lie everywhere. I hand them to Reza for his comment, feeling sure he'll tell me they are part of an Iranian dinner set, circa 1950.

'Yes, they're probably Sassanian – and that's only what's on the surface. Imagine what might be under that mound over there,' he says, absently dropping my finds back onto the ground and pointing at a partially excavated low hill about 100 metres away.

'My pottery!' I exclaim.

'I think we should leave it here where it belongs,' Reza says.

It's going to be another after-dark hotel arrival as the sun is setting as we drive past the pellucid Maharlu Lake, 30 kilometres from Shiraz. As the desert landscapes of Iran so often seem to shimmer between mirage and reality I'm not sure this really is water until the road begins to run alongside the shoreline. But even then the lake looks strangely illusionary with its almost unnaturally still waters that reflect the pink- and apricot-streaked sky.

We stop beside a 6-metre-high mountain of salt crystals streaked with red to take some photographs. Almost immediately a small battered Paikan car pulls up beside our van and I wonder if we are trespassing. But after getting out of their car the three men ignore us, going straight to the boot of their vehicle and taking out a spade. Approaching the small mountain of salt one starts digging while the other two study the quality of the crystals. Cascades of salt roll down around them and we walk over to find out what they are doing. It transpires that the trio work at the nearby salt works which once supplied salt for table use all over Iran.

'But now potassium and magnesium are seeping into the lake and the salt is no good for human consumption. We can only sell it now to a local rubber factory,' one of them informs us.

Shiraz, the city of poets and nightingales (and once the home of the variety of wine that bears its name), is full of traffic and evening shoppers when we arrive. Thankfully, we've already chosen a hotel en route and the van has barely cooled down before we are back in it heading towards Reza's favourite hamburger bar.

It's not hard to find Hamburger 110 as it boasts two life-size neon palm trees outside its doors. And it's also evident as we squeeze inside that Reza is not alone in his preference for this place. It's heaving with people ordering hamburgers, hot dogs and pizzas. Behind a glass screen a man with a thick black moustache deftly and speedily constructs six pizzas simultaneously while the two men working the tills shout orders at him.

Oddly, the restaurant itself is across the alleyway. It, too, is packed and it takes some doing to find a spare table; once again I am the only non-Iranian present. Reza takes out a pen and using a table napkin to demonstrate, explains why the name Hamburger 110 has spiritual significance. In Arabic, the numbers 110 represent the saying *Ya Ali* (Oh Ali).

We are now much further south and close to the heat of the Persian Gulf so it's appreciably warmer next day as we walk towards one of the glories of Iran, Persepolis. Winter or not, if these ruins were located almost anywhere else in the world they would be thronged with visitors. Today, however, there are no tourists other than our small group and a few Iranians.

In the soft light of early morning the marble columns and archways are washed a delicate gold. Even two and a half millennia after the Achaemenid kings ruled their vast empire from here, the approach to their ceremonial palace is imposing.

Work began on Persepolis in 512 BC at the command of

Darius the Great. His successors, including Xerxes and Ataxerxes, augmented it over the next 150 years. Historians think that these great kings never actually lived here on a permanent basis – more likely it was a complex designed especially for the vitally important spring (*No Ruz*) celebrations.

Ancient records report that Persepolis took 50,000 people 15 years to build. The materials used reflected and symbolised the vastness and complexity of the Achaemenid empire brought harmoniously together – the deliberate intention of King Darius. It featured cedars from Lebanon, gold from India, lapis lazuli from modern-day Afghanistan, silver from the Iberian peninsula, and housed artisans, goldsmiths, weavers and sculptors from Egypt, India, Persia, Syria and Greece.

According to those early historians, King Darius' throne room inside the palace was decorated in purple and gold and the throne itself was made of ivory and cedar and studded with precious stones. Throughout the palace the floors and walls were covered with carpets and tapestries. The treasury was said to overflow with buckets piled with coins, gold and silver ingots, chests of gems and pearls, ceremonial armour, royal regalia from throughout the empire, silks, linens and wools. There were beautifully designed gardens, too, with cypresses, poplars and planes.

But in 330 BC Alexander the Great and his army arrived at Persepolis and the ceremonial city was sacked, looted, set on fire and the contents of the treasury taken away. (Interestingly, Iranians hardly ever refer to Alexander as 'Alexander the Great', as we do in the West. Rather they call him simply Alexander the Macedonian.) Today, although there is little evidence of the beauty and lavishness that made Persepolis one of the greatest cities on

Earth at the time, there is enough of the structure left to be able to imagine a little of the awe and wonder experienced by those who visited from far-off lands to pay homage to the kings of all lands.

Two gently sloping staircases lead up to the platform constructed all those centuries ago to heighten the natural grandeur of the site. The steps are shallow so that visitors in their long robes of the day could make a dignified entrance. Heraldic trumpets would have greeted them before they were led through the magnificent Gate of All Nations, the portals of which still stand today.

Massive winged bulls with human heads guard the gateway. Reza points up high to draw my attention to the cuneiform writing.

'Xerxes had this message written in Persian, Babylonian and Elamite – it starts off by saying, "I am Xerxes, Great King, King of kings, King of lands, King of many races ... son of Darius the King, the Achaemenid." Then it finishes, "Many other beautiful things were constructed in Persia. I constructed them and my father constructed them".'

Full of power and absolute confidence these words are so direct I can almost imagine Xerxes dictating them to the stonemason.

One of the most special features of Persepolis, possibly because it escaped the attentions of the Macedonians and remains largely intact, is the Apadana staircase that leads to a palace in which the kings would receive delegations from their empire.

The staircase contains panels of bas reliefs, one of which depicts 23 separate delegations bringing gifts to the king. Each nationality's facial characteristics, hairstyles and dress is so accurately portrayed that today it is possible to identify almost all of them: Elamites leading some rather reluctant lions, Parthians with snooty camels, Egyptians with a muscle-bound bull, Central Asians with a prancing horse and Ethiopians bearing an elephant's tusk.

Today the staircase has been roped off but it's easy to spot everyone's favourites; all the camels, for example, have shiny noses from being rubbed by so many people over so many years. One of the most enduring symbols of the Achaemenids is also to be found on the staircase – a lion sinking its teeth into the flanks of a bull. The Achaemenids were most probably Zoroastrians and the sculpture symbolises the triumph of spring over winter.

The staircase leads to a vast area that was once a palace featuring 36 columns, each 20 metres tall and topped with gryphons, bulls or lions. Today only a few are still standing and examples of the capitals lie at their base.

Sometimes the only way to grasp the former glories of a place such as Persepolis is to stop, lean against a piece of ancient stone, close one's eyes and listen to the sounds of the past – and thus we find a section of collapsed column against which we can rest.

After some silent contemplation I ask Reza if he thinks, as some historians do, that Alexander had not intended to set fire to Persepolis, but that its destruction had been accidental.

Reza almost bristles with indignation.

'No, of course it was deliberate! He destroyed one of the greatest cities on earth, a glory of the ancient world.'

Cleary 2500 years have not dulled the pain for Reza or many other Iranians. When it comes to invasions, this nation has a long memory – something modern-day sabre-rattlers could do well to remember.

Persepolis is awe-inspiring even in its ruin, but for me the most spectacular reminder of the might of the Achaemenids lies just four kilometres away at Naqsh-e Rostam.

When Reza first brought me here, several years ago, I was rendered speechless. In front of us, carved high up into the sheer cliffs were four cave tombs, each with a cross-shaped façade with a small entry to the funeral chamber set in the centre.

Here it is believed the bones of the kings, Darius I, Ataxerxes I, Xerxes I and Darius II, were stored after the traditional Zoroastrian sky burial had been completed. Today the chambers are out of reach and empty, but the scale of these tombs, and the sheer audacity of their site, is truly awe-inspiring. It has its own beauty too, especially in spring when the short emerald-green grass at the base of the tomb is studded with scarlet poppies.

We return to Shiraz to keep a vital appointment – experiencing sunset at Hafez's tomb along with several hundred Iranians.

Shams od-Din Muhammad (or Hafez, the name means 'he who knows the Koran by heart'), the most beloved of Persian poets, epitomises the duality of modern-day Iranian life. I find his poetry deeply spiritual rather than overtly Moslem and scholars and amateurs alike argue incessantly about whether Hafez's frequent references to wine, taverns, and love are simply symbols of more esoteric matters, or really are about wine, women and song. What this means, of course, is that Hafez can be read and enjoyed on many levels.

Hafez is much more to Iranians than simply a poet. Almost certainly every Iranian household today will have, along with a copy of the Koran, a copy of the *divan* (anthology) of Hafez. For centuries Iranians, young and old, have believed that if you open your copy of Hafez at random, the lines on which your eyes fall will hold the secrets of your future.

Here at the tomb are so many cars and buses outside the entrance to the complex that the traffic police on duty wave us further down the road. We join the flow of pedestrians turning in through the gate but are stopped by a small scruffy-looking man holding a green and yellow budgie and a little box full of cards.

'He wants you to seek your fortune from Hafez,' says Reza, reaching into his pocket for what I regard as his alarmingly thick wad of Iranian rial notes.

The man fans out the selection of cards and holds them in front of his bird. After a second or two of encouraging clucking sounds from its owner, the bird delicately tweaks one of the cards out of the pack and the man hands it to me. As we are blocking the gateway Reza suggests we divine my fortune inside.

We go through the narrow gateway into an enclosed rectangular garden with a long narrow pool in the centre ending at the base of a set of steps leading to a marble colonnade behind which is the tomb of Hafez. Born in Shiraz some time between 1317 and 1326, Hafez also died here in his hometown in 1389. In one of his poems he said of his birthplace: '... no land can ever vie with bright Shiraz in purity'.

Against the gentle backdrop of the fountains and a broadcast of Hafez's poetry set to music we climb the steps to the tomb on which some earlier visitors have placed three long-stemmed roses.

Everyone that approaches the tomb follows the same routine involving placing the fingertips of their right hand on the cool marble and reciting lines of his poetry.

Reza steps forward and begins reciting in Farsi, translating for me when he's finished. Others around the tomb smile appreciatively – poetry in Iran is very much a shared pleasure.

'Through love, bitter things seem sweet
Through love, bits of copper are made gold
Through love, dregs taste like pure wine
Through love, pains are as healing balms
Through love, thorns become roses.'

One thing is certain, there'll be no toasting of Hafez here despite the frequent references to wine in his poetry and, as mentioned earlier, the city's close connection to an ancient variety of wine. But there is tea. Befitting the poet's love of beauty and romance, the teahouse behind the tomb is one of the most magical in Iran, especially at night.

The tiny courtyard – with arched carpeted niches on two sides and its central space crowded with *takts* grouped around a small fountain – is almost always packed and we are lucky to find a corner niche unoccupied. We take off our shoes, settle ourselves against the bolsters and before long a tall man with a Persian-style tightly wrapped turban around his head and wearing baggy pantaloons and a sequined waistcoat strides over and greets Reza like a long-lost relative. He knows Reza through his regular tour group visits during the tourist season.

Reza orders tea and *qalyan*.

'Apple, but proper strength, not tourist strength,' he says. 'My friend has smoked many times before.'

I try not to look too dissolute.

As we wait for our tea to arrive we survey the teahouse clientele. A young couple who can't find proper seats perch on a low wall, a poetry book open between them. Closer to us a group of men who look like they have just come from work are smoking in earnest. When a latecomer arrives everyone shuffles closer together on the *takt* to make room. The new guest opens his briefcase, takes out a large box of chocolates and passes them around.

'I think it is his birthday,' Reza says, his ears flapping as he tries to pick up snippets of conversation.

Not far away is a young man on his own, smoking a *qalyan* with three plastic mouthpieces attached, one on top of the other. We're intrigued and Reza leans over to find out more. A long conversation follows.

'That was some explanation,' I say, when they've finished and Reza sits back against his bolster.

'Oh, we were discussing how busy it is in here tonight – even though it is winter – the building of new hotels in Shiraz, all kinds of things. By the way, he says *qalyan* is much stronger when you use three mouthpieces.'

A tray of tea, rock sugar, a small dish of fresh dates, and our *qalyan* arrive. Before he slots the plastic mouthpiece in place our waiter draws deeply on the end of the wooden mouthpiece, making the charcoal on top of the pipe glow red. He passes it to Reza to check.

Reza takes a long puff and exhales an impressive cloud of smoke followed by a small bout of coughing.

'It's quite strong,' he tells me, somewhat unnecessarily, passing over the mouthpiece. 'I feel a bit giddy already.'

As Reza reads Hafez aloud in Farsi we drink our way through three teapots of tea. Translation is not really necessary as the beauty of Persian poetry lies partly in the beautiful rhythms, the repetition of phrases and the lilt of the language; Persian is deeply melodic in its own right to the extent that even a set of building specifications read aloud in Farsi would sound irresistible.

Reza remembers to translate my fortune before we leave. On

the front of the card is a painting of four nightingales making good their escape from a gilded cage hanging in a tree. On the reverse are two passages in Persian – one a stanza or two from Hafez and the other an interpretation. 'You need to know there's some poetic licence with these,' Reza says, 'but in essence it says you will achieve all your goals in the near future.' It seems good fortune takes similar forms no matter what the language.

On our way back to the hotel, almost audibly sloshing with tea, we stop at the shrine of Shah-e-Cheragh, the mausoleum of the King of the Lamps, the brother of Imam Reza of Mashhad. At night the domes and gold-covered minarets are stunningly spotlit making them a beacon to pilgrims.

We are following in the footsteps of almost all Iranian visitors to Shiraz. 'First stop Hafez's tomb, and then to the shrine,' Reza says.

This shrine for Shia Moslems is among the most important in Iran, and although the Shiraz site is not quite on the same scale as that of Mashhad I still need to don my sprigged chador and enter the building through the women's door. The sparkling silver mirror work inside is dazzling and where illuminated by concealed lights it shines a luminous emerald green.

Although the atmosphere inside the tomb is as reverent and as emotionally charged as Mashhad on the outside, under the portico, there is more of a holiday atmosphere as entire families sit in circles on the carpets eating late-night suppers of hamburgers and fizzy drinks.

Our taxi back to the hotel is driven by a young man who, after a quick glance at me in the rear-vision mirror, asks Reza where I'm from.

This is normal procedure in Iran as it would be improper for a man to ask me directly, and Reza has become expert at reeling off my life history and the reasons for my being in Iran.

The ice broken, the taxi driver asks Reza what I think of Iran.

'She can tell you herself in Farsi,' Reza says, displaying the proprietary pride of a teacher whose pupil has just mastered the alphabet.

Usually, my standard response of 'I love Iran' is met with nothing but gratified smiles, but on this occasion the driver turns around and looks at me thoughtfully before asking if I really mean it.

He explains that he is an engineering student currently doing his military training in the Iranian Air Force.

'I love my country, too, but I am planning to emigrate to England because there are better job prospects there and the standards of living are higher.'

Two of his brothers are there already, both with established shops in London.

'I'll miss my home and family, though,' he says reflectively, as he drops us off outside the hotel. When Reza pays him the fare he point blank refuses to take it, even after the obligatory *taroffing*.

'You are a guest and I have enjoyed our conversation,' he says.

Next morning we make another important pilgrimage to the tomb of poet Musleh od-Din Saadi, born in Shiraz in 1189 and believed to have died in 1290, which would have made him over a hundred years old. Unlike Hafez he was a traveller, journeying through Iraq and Syria, and en route possibly even being captured by the Crusaders.

Saadi's tomb is housed in a blue-domed pavilion supported by tall, slim pillars that is set in a garden of palms, pencil cypress and citrus trees. Back when Saadi was alive this place was well outside the city and one of his favourite retreats where he wrote much of his poetry.

However, the enclosed tomb is noisy today, because it appears that parties of girls from several of Shiraz's schools have chosen to visit all at the same time.

Little girls in black wimples chatter excitedly, and when we sit down outside to admire the tomb I'm immediately swamped by dozens of older girls who want to say hello. When I speak to them in Farsi they dissolve into fits of giggles and it's only when their teacher calls them that they leave reluctantly. Reza and I descend a set of steps into a teahouse converted from a water reservoir. In the centre of the round underground room a railing surrounds a sheer drop into a deep pool of crystal-clear water in which dozens of fish are swimming.

Above us we hear the clamour of more students and then a rising tide of voices as a crowd of young boys comes tumbling down the stairs. Like boys everywhere, they make a beeline for the railing and lean over, bottoms-up, to look at the fish.

The teahouse proprietor scurries among them grabbing jackets at random and hauling them back from the brink. Eventually their teacher arrives and orders them upstairs, causing the proprietor to sigh with relief.

We move on to visit the Arg-e-Karim, a citadel built by Karim Khan who ruled Persia in the 18th century. In 1750 he made Shiraz his national capital and the *arg* his seat of power.

Considered a benevolent ruler and patron of arts, he was responsible for many of Shiraz's impressive buildings, including the citadel, mosques and its bazaar. His regent's mosque is an exquisite pearl of a building with tiles covered in pink roses and purple irises. Throughout his reign Karim Khan steadfastly refused to be called king, preferring to be called the regent or the servant of his people.

Inside the partly restored citadel the courtyard is planted with orange trees, covered at this time of year with large, ripe oranges. After walking through the Khan's bathhouse and his audience chamber we find an exhibition of black-and-white photographs taken in Shiraz in the late 19th and early 20th centuries. They are an extraordinary record of a society in transition: wide Western-style boulevards peopled with pedestrians in medieval dress, dodging some of the first cars in Iran. There's also a poignant shot of a group of women with bobbed hair and cloche hats, taken the day the first Shah banned the veil. Reza, who usually loves to study every exhibit in a museum, is standing, trying to look casual, in front of one of the few photos I haven't seen and suddenly announces it is time to leave the room. I try to look around him. 'Please don't look at this one,' he says. Which, of course, means I have to look, but I should have listened to him. It's of a 19th-century criminal tied to the mouth of a cannon and clearly the fuse is about to be lit. The image haunts me still.

Reza has the cure however. Among a row of shops facing the massive citadel walls is one of the most popular spots in Shiraz, a shop specialising in *faludeh* – a local ice-cream made of chilled starch strands, mixed with lemon juice and rosewater.

We buy two large pottles and sit on a tree stump outside to enjoy this tangy and refreshing treat. Near the ice-cream shop is a display of massive bottles of coloured liquids.

The owner, a whiskery older man, sees me looking at the bottles and beckons me inside. With Reza interpreting his words, he explains to me that he is a seller of juices as well as a range of distilled water flavoured with orange blossom, rose and mint respectively. Iranians believe such cordials to be excellent tonics and useful in the treatment of stomach problems and other conditions.

Reza then asks me if I'd like to try a speciality that even many people in Tehran have never heard of. It involves going into the Vakil bazaar to find it, which will not be a hardship for me because with its vaulted brick ceilings, glittering array of metalwork and jewellery, sumptuous carpets and shimmering, sparkling fabrics favoured by the nomads who still live in the mountainous areas outside Shiraz it is probably the most fascinating bazaar in Iran. Mounds of rose petals sit on trays at the entrance to the apothecaries' stalls and every now and then we must dodge the motorbikes that always seem to be roaring through the bazaar's lanes, narrowly missing unwary pedestrians.

The Shiraz bazaar attracts not only nomad women with their full flowing skirts and veils dangling with sequins and coins, but Middle Eastern tourists from the Gulf states. Women in swirling black chadors come round a corner towards us, their faces covered with extraordinary gilded metal masks that extend across the nose and top lip, giving the impression of a golden moustache.

We weave our way through the early evening crowds, twisting and turning through the bazaar's many side alleys until we come to a tiny stall with a couple of plastic seats and one small counter.

'This is a *sharbat* stall – I've ordered one made of the blossoms of Seville oranges and one made from pink roses,' Reza tells me as he explains that *sharbat* is a drink made of fruit or flower syrup mixed with water and a little sugar, best enjoyed icy cold. The word sherbet probably came to the English language from Persian via India.

As we drink our *sharbat* the shoppers ebb and flow down the alleyway and the call to prayer from the mosque next door drifts along the vaulted ceilings.

A NIGHT BESIDE
THE WORLD'S
HOTTEST REACTOR

The Persian Gulf

Behind us, there is only the weariness of history
Behind us, the memory of waves carries cold shells
of inertia on to the shore
Let's go out to the seashore
And cast our nets into the sea
To catch the water's freshness
Let's pick up a pebble
To feel the weight of being.

Sohrab Sepehri

We leave Shiraz with the Rezas in hysterics as a result of one of
my less-than-erudite observations made in the city centre.

Inspired perhaps by the fact that Shiraz has been much milder
than anywhere else on our journey so far I'd been looking for signs
of spring – and am delighted when we sweep into a roundabout
to see four trees covered with white blossom.

'Look, spring really has come to Shiraz. Life is returning to the
trees!' I cry. All that poetry has clearly affected me.

The two men look mystified. What, they ask, am I looking at?

I point at the blossom trees and while Reza B tries not to drive us off the road as he erupts into laughter, the other Reza, also hugely amused, tells me that if I look closely I'll find it is not blossom.

I look more closely at the trees. Made of metal and studded with delicate glass lights along the branches which obviously are designed to be illuminated at night, they are clearly artificial.

Unfortunately for me, these metal trees adorn many towns along the rest of our route and whenever we drive past one, Reza cannot resist.

'Spring has come to such and such a town,' he solemnly intones in a passable imitation of my Kiwi accent.

'It is truly remarkable how similar these trees are to those in the last town,' he adds, trying to look serious, but not completely succeeding.

We are travelling west through another tail-end range of the Zagros Mountains through Kazerun; some of the mountains look extraordinarily like loaves of bread with rounded tops dusted with snow. Others have sheer sides of striated rock that give way to tapered flanks. As we drive further east oak trees appear on the slopes – the first forests I've seen since arriving in Iran. They wear a haze of pale green and this time it really is a burst of spring growth.

The Zagros mountains form a natural barrier between the humid warmth along the Persian Gulf and the arid central deserts of Iran – the contrast between the two aspects is dramatic. As the van descends through the forests, the oaks are replaced with groves of citrus fruits and the roadside stalls overflow with blood oranges, tangerines and oranges. We stop and buy the customary mountain of fruit. Reza also succumbs to the pleading of a young boy in a ragged striped jersey and worn jeans to buy chewing gum. Reza resists the entire time he is inspecting then buying the fruit, but I can tell he'll give in eventually, even though he doesn't like chewing gum.

Just before we reach the plain that stretches all the way to the sea itself, the road snakes through a gorge carved out by a river that runs like a turquoise ribbon along the valley floor.

We stop at a lay-by for tea and Reza points down to an elegant stone bridge that spans the water. Adorned with two pairs of decorative pillars topped with stone carvings of Sassanian-style hats, the bridge has been here for about 1500 years. On the far bank are the ruins of a caravanserai.

'You see, we have not forgotten the silk routes. Some caravans came this way via Shiraz to the Persian Gulf so their goods could then be sent by sea, and vice versa. You have experienced something of the terrain across Iran so you can appreciate why being able to cut short the land journey in favour of going by sea was an advantage,' Reza explains, as he peels the first of our few dozen pieces of fruit.

When the caravans were traversing this route between Shiraz and Bushehr it would have taken them up to a week – we cover the same distance in about six hours.

'I have read accounts of some of those journeys – they spoke about the mountain roads, having to carry exhausted sheep and about donkeys falling off precipices,' Reza comments.

The road emerges from the gorge onto a narrow plain, green with date palms. Gritty sand lies between the road and the fringes of the palm groves but beyond the dates are the sea and the port of Bushehr. It's my first sight of the Persian Gulf from the Iranian side. Neither of the Rezas believes my previous sighting from Dubai counts.

When it comes into view at last, I'm not sure if at first my eyes are deceiving me. The sea is motionless, limpid and pearl-grey, seemingly suspended a little above the desert plain.

It is not the most picturesque of sights as these days the harbour area is surrounded by a mish-mash of oil tanks and cranes and several rusting ships lying seemingly permanently anchored in the bay.

As we drive further into the city itself a high steel mesh fence appears on our left, screening a vast construction project, a maze of towering metal and concrete.

'What are they building there?' I ask in all innocence.

Reza turns to look at me.

'Surely you know what that is?' And when it's clear that I have no idea he tells me that it is Iran's nuclear power station.

Snippets of a hundred news stories suddenly tumble through my mind. Somehow the actual location of probably the most contentious nuclear power plant on earth had passed me by amid the largely US-led furore about its existence.

The building of the two-reactor plant had originally been a joint German-Iranian project. The Germans, however, pulled out in 1979 after the Iranian revolution, apparently under some pressure from the US. At the time it was believed that about 50 per cent of one reactor had been completed, and 85 per cent of the other. During the Iran-Iraqi war the Iraqis bombed the plant; once in 1985 and again in 1988.

Work on the $800-million project got under way again in 1995 as a Russian-Iranian venture and the first reactor was completed in 2008. The plant was finally opened in August 2010. During the entire construction process the US consistently claimed that the Iranians would use the plant as cover to develop nuclear weapons while the Iranians have equally consistently denied doing so.

I stare through the wire mesh at the plant which, to be honest, to my eyes looks like any other immense industrial site. Even the sentry boxes along the boundary don't look that formidable, but no doubt there is more attention being paid to the Persian Gulf side of the complex and to the skies above.

And yet here I am being driven alongside it as I eat oranges in a green transit van.

'I don't suppose we could slow down a bit …' I hint.

Reza B looks resolutely ahead and keeps driving.

Not having been to Bushehr before, Reza is unable to recommend a hotel and so we drive around the city and stop passers-by for suggestions. We circle several times around one of the city's landmark roundabouts featuring a rather menacing-looking giant prawn before eventually Reza strikes oil when a local suggests we go to a new hotel near the old town.

One of the few multi-storeyed buildings on the edge of the old port, the hotel's ground-floor restaurant is packed, but the hotel manager tells us he has rooms to spare. And when he learns Reza is involved with the tourism industry, he quickly replaces the sets of keys he'd originally taken from the reception desk with a somewhat grander collection.

'I think you will like the suites,' he says showing me into a pale yellow suite complete with chandelier and two capacious couches with gilded legs and scrolled arm-rests. A slightly smaller but still very ornate chandelier looks down on the mosquito net-draped wrought-iron four-poster bed in the bedroom. The suite allotted to my companions is equally spacious although we all agree my lounge chandelier is the pick of the bunch.

The manager invites us to have lunch in his restaurant and refuses to take any money for rooms or meals.

'You are my first guest from New Zealand and maybe you will, *inshallah* (if God wills it) bring more tourists here in the future,' he says.

Although I admire his optimism I can see a few marketing complications such as the description in the itinerary: 'Tonight we stay in Bushehr, just a few minutes' drive from one of the most controversial nuclear power plants in the world. Here you won't have to worry about luminous dials on your watch ... everything glows in the dark ...'

Before the advent of its nuclear facility, Bushehr was better known as one of the more picturesque and historically intact of the towns along the Persian Gulf, and the city's past reflects the political complexities of the entire Gulf region. Its location on a small peninsula jutting into the Gulf saw it develop into a desirable trading port from as early as the seventh century. Nearly a thousand years later it became particularly strategically important when in 1759 the British East India Company made Bushehr its Persian Gulf headquarters; the British government later established its Residency for the control of the entire Persian Gulf here. Control see-sawed between Britain and Persia for decades and during World War I, the British even invaded Bushehr and surrounding area.

'Do you remember that impressive war memorial we saw in that small town on our way to Bushehr? It was to commemorate the town of Delwar, which defeated the British during that invasion. It remains a national symbol of bravery in the face of great odds,' Reza explains.

The role of the British on this northern coast of the Persian Gulf only ended when the Iranians nationalised the Anglo-Iranian Oil Company in 1951.

It's a fascinating history but as a New Zealander, who has spent almost all her life only a few kilometres from the sea, I am desperate for a paddle. But I know that Reza wants to visit some of Bushehr's unique traditional houses so I have to get in first, not least because once we disappear into the winding alleys of the old town, it will be dark by the time we emerge.

We drive through the port, passing kilometres of rocky breakwaters until I spot a tiny crescent of sand. Just off the beach, two men stand up in a long slim wooden boat, casting out their net. Far out to sea beyond them I can make out larger ships, black smudges really, immobile on the horizon.

I jump down onto the sand, a slightly bemused Reza following.

'Are bare feet un-Islamic?' I ask, already taking off my sneakers and socks.

'I think you will be all right,' Reza says.

'Well, come on, take your shoes off and come for a paddle,' I tell him.

Close up, the water is milky blue and the waves are flopping rather than crashing onto the sand, but it is still the sea. I look furtively up and down the shoreline, then roll up the bottoms of my trousers just a few inches. The water swirls warmly around my legs.

I don't want to push my luck or worse still get Reza into trouble, so in order to resist the temptation to fling myself bodily into the sea, I find a piece of driftwood and practise writing the Farsi alphabet and then our names in the sand. Reza joins me and we happily write until we become aware of a couple and their daughter standing on the footpath above and gazing down at us.

They don't look like members of the police so I wave. Without hesitation they clamber over the rocks and join us. After the usual round of polite greetings they begin a gentle interrogation of Reza: Where have I come from, why am I playing on the beach, how come I can write Arabic script?

Reza answers them and then asks his own questions. It transpires that the family is from Shiraz. They've seen many people from Shiraz come to Bushehr for their holidays, they told him, but they have never before seen a foreign tourist here – and certainly not one barefoot on the beach.

We set off to find Bushehr's unique historic houses. Over the centuries there has been some infilling of the old town and outside a modern concrete house Reza starts up a conversation with a man washing down his car.

He is a retired shrimp-boat captain who has spent more than 30 years at sea, mostly fishing between the Persian Gulf and Cape Town, and the wrinkles on his face remind me of a walnut. He tells us many men of the sea retire to Bushehr; being within sight and sound and smell of the port helps quell the restlessness that is part of their nature after spending so long on the ocean.

Somehow, despite his unfamiliarity with the town, Reza leads us between high-walled lanes to a rubble-filled square, on one side of which is a four-storey building. The lower part is a blank wall broken only by a set of double wooden doors that is firmly locked from the inside. Closed doors are not going to put him off, though, and he bangs on them until after a few minutes' wait the doors creak open theatrically to reveal a thin man in a stained singlet and baggy fatigues. His opening words clearly tell us that the house is not open for visitors but as usual Reza manages to charm him and he allows us to climb through the builders' rubble inside the doorway to have a look.

An Afghan from Mazar-e-Sharif who moved to Bushehr to escape the endless wars and turmoil in his home country, he speaks beautiful Persian and tells Reza that although he is paid much better here than in Afghanistan he still goes back and forth when he can to visit his family.

Apparently there are three men working on the house. The Afghan foreman says he's already been employed on the project for 12 months and he expects to be there for many more. After letting us in he goes back to work, asking only that should we ever meet the house owner we must not tell him we'd been allowed in. We agree; any encounter with the absentee owner seems unlikely.

The house is built around three sides of a central courtyard and the upper storeys are only one room wide. Rooms at the end of each arm of the 'U' feature floor-to-ceiling sash windows on three sides. Intricate panels of stained glass are interspersed with narrow double doors fitted with louvres.

'This design gives excellent ventilation, especially in this area with its high humidity. The stained glass filters out the harshest of the sunlight, which helps keep the rooms cooler, as do the shuttered doors,' Reza explains.

Curved stairwells with deep steps connect each floor. By the time we've scrambled up to the flat roof we can see how the top levels catch whatever breeze blows from the sea. To the south the Persian Gulf stretches shimmering and sparkling and on the town side we can see other traditional houses, in various states of repair, rising up from their more modern, but lower neighbours. Below us, a soccer game has started up on the wasteland outside the house.

When we descend to the ground floor the foreman is waiting to show us the reservoir set into the courtyard. It's more than 8 metres deep and once held the household's entire water supply. He then beckons us into a ground-floor room now converted into a workshop where, propped against the walls, are many window frames awaiting restoration. In the centre of the room is a workbench; a frame set into a clamp sits on top. The foreman explains that since he's been working on the restoration project he's taught himself how to restore the intricate stained-glass work. Each piece of coloured glass is set into a border of tiny pieces of wood that builds up into an interlocking geometric design. Almost all the work is done by hand.

He also shows us some unique Bushehr-style brass door-knockers that are shaped like hands with the fingers pointed towards the ground.

Not far away we discover the newly opened and little publicised Bushehr Anthropological Museum – many of the locals do not even know of it. Inside we come across two young female photography students who have been sent to the museum to take a series of photographs, but on meeting us decide it's much more fun to act as informal guides.

They point out a display featuring a large basket suspended from the ceiling.

'That is to keep bread in – it is in the museum but we have one at home,' one of them tells us. They take great amusement in clamping a series of headphones on me so I can listen to recordings of Bushehr's distinctive musical instruments that include oboe-like wind instruments and a range of drums.

They explain that because of Bushehr's trading heritage, many foreign words have been absorbed into the local Farsi – 'very' and 'tomato' from English, for example, 'aqua' from the Mediterranean, and a few Russian words. When Reza asks them to say some of the Russian words, they collapse into masses of giggles, holding each other's arms for support. 'We can't remember,' they gasp.

One of them looks at her watch, exclaims with horror – and they are gone. From an upstairs balcony we watch as they run down the street beside the sea, arm in arm, presumably trying to get back to class on time.

We leave the museum with the aim of wandering at random through the lanes. There is little sign of life in the streets, but we can hear snatches of conversation from behind the high walls and now and then the aroma of cooking rice wafts past our nostrils. Palm fronds hang over the walls along with tendrils of flowering bougainvillea. In the narrowest lanes, rickety ancient verandas protrude overhead, almost touching the equally ramshackle verandas on the other side.

As sunset approaches, doors start opening and householders begin to emerge. We follow them down to the seafront esplanade where the promenade is thronged with people eating ice creams and kebabs and sipping tea. We join the parade of extended families and what seems like representatives of every branch of Iran's armed forces, all off duty, except for the military police in their white puttees who are on the prowl for miscreants.

Among the crowds are young sailors and naval officers, army ratings and air force cadets. Civilians and military alike are finding seats along the sea wall to watch the sun sink into the Persian

Gulf. Young couples sit snuggled together on park benches.

'We'll never find a space,' I say, but then notice that no one is sitting on the large dry rocks piled up at the base of the promenade. We perch there as the sun, now an improbably large deep orange orb, slowly sets. Silhouetted against the dying light an array of ships sits like a collection of cardboard cut-outs between the molten sea and the deepening dark sky over the Arabian peninsula. A path of shimmering golden sea stretches from the horizon to our vantage point, lighting up the plump rats that are scampering around the rocks close to our feet, which explains why no one else is sitting with us.

(It was only the next day, when I checked my emails, that I found a number of somewhat panic-stricken messages from family and friends. 'I think you had better skip the Persian Gulf,' said one. 'In the news today it says the US is undertaking naval manoeuvres in the Gulf – it's not a safe place to be.' I have no idea if any of the ships we saw in the distance were of US origin – we, and the rest of the promenaders, including hundreds of military personnel, were too busy admiring the sunset and buying snacks to worry.)

We retreat to a concrete picnic table out of reach of the cavorting vermin. A little boy of about eight, with jet-black straight hair and melting large brown eyes, sidles up to us clutching a set of bathroom scales under one arm.

'He is an Afghan refugee and he wants to weigh us – for a small charge, of course,' Reza tells me after a brief conversation with the boy. I baulk at the thought of a public weigh-in. Once again I am proving a novelty item along the foreshore and if I stand on the scales it will be a sure-fire crowd-puller.

'You do it and I'll pay,' I say.

The boy puts the scales down on the ground and carefully wipes them with a very grubby handkerchief. Reza, trying to look very earnest, stands on them and we all look at the dial that resolutely sits on 0. The little boy clucks anxiously, asks Reza to get off the scales, and fiddles, fruitlessly, with the dial. He looks like he is going to cry.

Reza reaches out and touching him on the shoulder, hands him some rial notes with the other hand. A smile flits across the boy's face.

'He thought I might not pay him. I can't imagine someone doing that to him.'

I want to find out if he is on his own, but after thanking Reza he disappears into the crowd.

We eat dinner in a converted bathhouse beside the sea. The restaurant is crammed with sepia photos of Bushehr's heyday as an important port, but of most interest to us is the clientele, which includes a group of Russians trying to make the best of the Iranian brands of non-alcoholic beer. A passing waiter confirms that they are working on the nuclear power plant.

Beside us are six Asian men in suits being fêted by local officials. Each is presented with a bouquet of gladioli then a giant basket of fruit. There is much bowing and hand-shaking, but despite a lot of shameless ear-flapping on our part we are unable to work out what is going on.

We over-order dinner so Reza asks the waiter to make up several doggy bags to deal with the leftovers.

'We'll find some people to give the food to on our way back to the hotel,' he says.

As we drive past the promenade I remember the small boy and his broken scales and mention him to Reza.

'Just what I was thinking,' he says. He asks Reza B to stop the van and leaps out with the food and quickly merges into the crowds that are still enjoying the warm sea air. A group of young men is singing under an archway – strictly an illegal activity in Iran where public performances of music are still banned, hence one of their party is on the watch for any officials.

About 10 minutes later Reza returns, still clutching the bags of food.

'I can't find him so that might mean he has found somewhere warm to go for the night,' he reports.

Giving away the food proves more difficult that expected. Eventually we find a somewhat incredulous road-cleaner in a dark street near our hotel. 'Well, he wasn't a beggar, but I think he is the most deserving person we are going to find tonight,' Reza says.

I share the lift to my suite with two men. They are not Iranians but when I ask them where they are from, they choose to look purposefully blank. Maybe they're spies checking out the power station, I muse as the lift stutters upwards. Then, as we all stand staring at the lift safety notice, it occurs to me that they could be equally suspicious of me. When I get to my room and take off my headscarf I realise that spies, of whatever nationality, probably don't spend their evenings with their headscarves thickly festooned with leftover saffron rice from dinner. The street cleaner had clearly been short-changed.

I go to bed with the window open and the mosquito net wafting gently around my four-poster. There are no mosquitoes but if someone did decide to wipe out the nuclear plant overnight the net might stop the chandelier dropping on me. It will certainly be a picturesque setting to be found in; I wear my best nightie just in case.

THE PLAINS OF OIL AND DEATH

Khuzestan

He falls and gets up, falls again
Floundering on the sharp reed-ends
People come and find him dead, the ground
Wet with blood and written on every reed-top
The word Allah. This is the way one must
Listen to the reed flute. Be killed
In it and lie down in the blood.

Attar

We wave goodbye to the giant prawn long before most of Bushehr's residents are up and moving. As we head north, on a road running parallel with the Persian Gulf, our route once again takes us through extensive date palm groves.

Along the side of the road are stalls selling fresh dates and I notice that each stall also features a half-metre-tall piece of peeled palm set on a wooden table alongside the dates. The vendors stand in front of these pale cream stems, whittling at them with knives like contemplative sculptors and I presume it's a way to while away the time between customers.

I'm wrong. When we stop at one of these stalls to supplement the fruit already rolling around in the van and the plastic bags full of seeds and nuts I watch as the Rezas consult with the salesman. He cuts off several hunks of the palm and parcels it up along with the dates. I should have guessed – it is yet another Iranian travel snack and of course I'm keen to try it, anticipating that the flavour might be at least reminiscent of dates. However, I soon find that eating date palm is what I imagine chewing on a piece of balsa wood would be like.

Reza B, who is enthusiastically munching through his piece of palm, asks me what I think of it. I tell him, as best I can through a mouthful of tasteless stringy fibre, that I'll stick to the dates, thanks.

He replies in Farsi and Reza, laughing, translates.

'He has two new phrases for you to learn: "We are eating dates" and "We are eating trees".'

We are travelling in one of the most fertile regions of Iran and the roadside stalls selling boxes of sweet, moist dates are soon joined by stalls offering mountains of melons and boxes of huge tomatoes and cucumbers. Spring wheat and barley sprout in the fields.

But it is the wealth under the ground that makes this corner of Iran one of the most important in the country, both economically and strategically. As our road heads north towards a low range of hills I'm riveted by the sight of flaming orange-and-gold oil flares leaping skywards from the top of tall, slim chimneys. Trails of smoke from the flares drift even higher through the winter-blue sky. At ground level, kilometres of metal pipes snake through the gorges, undulating with the landscape.

Khuzestan is the largest oil-producing region in Iran. As the country is the second-largest of the oil-producing OPEC nations, with 10 per cent of the world's proven oil reserves, I am smack-bang in the middle of one of the most oil-rich areas on the globe.

More used to the concept of off-shore oil rigs, I'm fascinated by the landscape of perpetually burning gas, especially as many of the oil fields (there are about 27 in Khuzestan) are surrounded by lush green pastures. Fields of cucumbers, carrots and salad greens stretch right up to the chain-mesh fences that surround some of the extraction plants. It's such an extraordinary combination I want to photograph it, but Reza isn't keen.

'I don't think it would be a good idea … we don't want anyone to think you are a spy,' he explains.

Oil might be Iran's greatest source of wealth but with it has come more than a hundred years of intermittent strife, political upheaval and death.

In 1901 the British, via the Anglo-Persian Petroleum Company (which later evolved into British Petroleum or BP), were granted control of the Khuzestan oil fields for 60 years. By 1950, 85 per cent of the profits from these vast reserves was lining the pockets of foreign interests and so in that same year the Iranians put a stop to this happening by nationalising the entire oil industry.

But the troubles surrounding the Khuzestan oil fields were not over. By the 1970s Saddam Hussein, in neighbouring Iraq, had his eye on Iran's oil fields, along with the fertile lands that surrounded them. He claimed the region was historically part of Iraq, and in 1980 his soldiers poured over the border. This was the beginning of an eight-year war – a war that would end with about 500,000 Iranians dead and millions more displaced. Those events have left deep and painful scars on the country, especially as many of the weapons directed at them were supplied by the United States, other Western nations and the former USSR. As a result every town and city in Iran commemorates its 'martyrs' or war dead on huge billboards. Throughout the country young bearded faces with earnest expressions and eyes burning with patriotism look down on traffic roundabouts and city squares. The war is not forgotten and certainly not forgiven.

Personally I hold very strong objections to the death penalty and after the execution of Saddam Hussein, I commented to Reza that I found the circumstances surrounding his death to be extremely distasteful, although I hated what the man had done to his own people and especially to Iran. Reza, who has one of the most peaceful and sweetest of dispositions of any person I know, was not having any of it.

'He was an evil man, a despotic dictator and it was right that he should die. He brought misery to both countries.'

As we continue our drive north I notice that Reza B has become uncharacteristically thoughtful, then suddenly he starts a long, impassioned conversation with Reza.

When our driver pauses for breath, Reza tells me that Reza B had been a soldier in the war.

'He fought as a regular in the artillery against Iraq for the whole eight years of the war. He knows this region very well but the memories are not all good ones. This is the first time he has seen many of these places since the war ended.'

'I do not know why God let me live when so many men died,' Reza B says.

I reach forward from my seat and touch him on the shoulder.

'*Mashallah* (thank God), he did,' I say. Reza B sniffs.

When we cross the Karim River that runs past the city of Alvaz, only about 50 km from the Iraq border, Reza B points into the water.

'The Karim flows into the Shatt-al-Arab [the confluence of the Euphrates and Tigris rivers which form the border between Iran and Iraq], where some of the bloodiest battles of the war took place,' Reza B informs us.

'There were so many corpses here it attracted sharks from the Persian Gulf. When the war ended, we saw sharks swimming about a hundred kilometres upstream to Alvaz looking for more bodies.'

Near Alvaz we can see the hills between Iran and Iraq. Reza B has slipped into the role of tour guide as memories of the war engulf him. He stops the van of his own accord and points out a small stream weaving its way though undulating pastureland.

'My unit found a young Iraqi soldier here. We knew that if the local farmers found him they would kill him so we dressed him in one of our uniforms and let him escape. That is the way it is in war.'

Although it is more than 20 years since the war ended, evidence of that terrible time still litters the landscape – concrete bunkers and ammunition stores with gaping holes for windows and doors nestle among the low hills, and the land itself is pockmarked and scarred.

'During the war where we are standing now was only ten kilometres from the enemy.' He gets out of the van and looks around. 'It was about here that one of our mobile mess caravans overturned and killed one of our soldiers …'

I ask what the Basijis had been like. The Vahed-e Basij-e Mustazafin (Unit of Mobilisations of the Deprived) were volunteers, usually recruited from Iran's mosques, including boys under 18 – some as young as 12 – and women and men over 45. Some of the missions for which they volunteered meant almost certain death such as leading the way through minefields. They were recognisable because they wore a red or yellow headband, which proclaimed the greatness of God or Iran's leader, Imam Khomeini, and a large key hung around their neck – the key to paradise (Moslems believe that all martyrs go direct to paradise or heaven).

'There was great unity back then,' Reza B remembers. 'Volunteers or ordinary soldiers, we were all the same and rank was not important.'

As we drive further into the hills, eerie jets of flame suddenly appear above ridges of swirling, tortured rock strata. If it's a surreal landscape now, it must have been a vision of hell in war.

'This was once a minefield,' explains Reza B. 'One of our units was trapped right in the middle of it. We went to rescue them ...' His voice trails off as he unearths memories that Reza and I cannot, and probably would not want to, imagine.

We leave him, alone and thoughtful, in a car park beside one of Iran's 12 World Heritage sites and probably the least visited by foreigners. The Choqa Zanbil ziggurat, 60 kilometres north of Alvaz, is the largest well-preserved ziggurat (a tiered temple, rather like a truncated pyramid) in the world. We are still in the war zone but if the unfired bricks of Choqa Zanbil could speak they could tell of not one battle, but hundreds as this structure has stood here for more than 3000 years.

This ziggurat would once have boasted five storeys reaching to a height of about 60 metres. Now only 25 metres with just three tiers remaining, it is still an arresting sight rising up as it does in the midst of a remote plain.

Ironically this ziggurat, which vanished from sight for over 2500 years, was rediscovered by accident during Anglo-Persian Petroleum Company surveys.

It was built by the mysterious Elamites, who are considered to be Persia's first empire builders and whose realm extended from the Tigris Valley across modern-day Western Iran and down to the Persian Gulf. Contemporaries of the illustrious Mesopotamian civilisations in what is now Iraq, the Elamites built the temple of Choqa Zanbil as a place to worship their chief god Inshushinak. The five concentric towers were intended to replicate the feeling and grandeur of a mountain (as mountains were considered auspicious places for worship, the Elamites built artificial ones in those regions lacking a suitably high promontory). The actual temple was located at the very top of the towers.

Reza leads me to a large flat-topped stone at the base of the ziggurat.

'Experts think that animals would have been sacrificed on this stone and then the offerings would have been carried up to the temple by priests who would probably have been the only people, along with possibly the Elamite kings, with access to the temple. There may have been statues of the gods at the top as well.

'It's remarkable what the Elamites developed here – the first arches in Iran, the earliest examples of glazed tiles were here, they even developed decorative water cascades down the sides of the pyramid that also acted as drainage channels.'

We gaze up at a giant sundial set on the south-facing wall – no one is absolutely sure of its significance, but Reza's guess is that it was connected with the timings of ceremonies held in the temple.

Some of the bricks set in the walls and even in the pavements are covered with cuneiform writing, with its distinctive angular style, proclaiming the name of gods and Elamite kings.

Reza stops near one of the steep staircases set into the centre of each side of the ziggurat. In the pavement of bricks at its base is a deep footprint; probably made by a worker or even a child more than 3000 years ago.

It's almost impossible to even attempt to grasp the passage of time between a man forming this brick and me standing gazing at it more than three millennia later. But for me, the footprint is a kind of link. I can almost hear the sigh of exasperation from the builder as his brick was spoilt by that footprint, feel the ooze of clay between the toes, and I can't help but wonder about the person who left this one solitary tangible very human touch on this site devoted to unseen gods.

Reza wants to visit some of the ruins of the town that stands beside the ziggurat so we cross the road and climb the gentle slopes that have built up over the centuries around more ancient walls and archways.

A tinkling of bells alerts us to the presence of a flock of drab-coloured sheep among the mounds. A young man in a black leather jacket is leaning on a crook nearby, watching us.

He calls out and signals we should meet in the gully that separates us. He leaves a tan dog guarding his sheep.

The shepherd is a Lor, an ethnic group whose true origins are lost in the mists of time. However, they are thought to be an Arab-Persian mix with possibly some ancient Mede and Kassite thrown in for good measure.

'What is the significance of this place?' he asks Reza in halting Persian, pointing at the ziggurat in the distance.

'Why do they come here?' he says looking at me. 'What is its value?'

Reza looks mildly horrified that this local lad clearly has no idea about the ziggurat's importance and launches into an impromptu lecture to which the teenager listens intently. I have seen this before – Iranians of all walks of life appear to be genuinely interested in their country's history, positively thirsty for information to the extent that they often tag on to the back of tour groups to listen to Reza's explanations.

We hear the sound of our van start – Reza B is hinting it was time to leave. The shepherd says goodbye and returns to his flock.

'That is sad,' Reza says. 'I think he is quite an intelligent boy, but he's dropped out of school because his uncle needs him to help with their three hundred sheep.'

Some of the only other remnants of the Elamites lie in Susa, further to the north.

The capital of their empire for about 300 years, Susa is best known as the winter headquarters of the Achaemenid emperors. It was very handily placed, being about halfway between Babylon and Persepolis.

However, after Alexander the Great swept into Susa in 330 BC, followed by the depredations of subsequent rulers, little now remains of what was once a majestic city renowned as far away as Greece.

What is left sits perched on a hill and comprises the foundations of several palaces, a few pillars and some beautiful, almost intact, giant horses' heads made of stone. The small museum on the site contains bronze masks and fertility figurines found locally, but considering the expanse of history represented outside it is a somewhat sparse collection.

'If you are wondering where most of the artefacts that were found here have ended up,' Reza remarks, 'the answer is that the early twentieth-century Qajar king of the day made a deal with the French who did most of the excavations that everything that was not actually gold or silver could be taken out of the country.

So many precious things such as a fantastic glazed tile lion frieze and a bull's head capital are now in the Louvre rather than here. It was a very ignorant decision because of course it is not just gold and silver objects that are priceless.'

Ironically, the most eye-catching building at Susa now is a 19th-century castle built as a base for the French Archaeological Service during their excavations and which was inspired by the Bastille in Paris.

Khuzestan is ethnically less homogeneous than many other regions of Iran and is more influenced by Arab culture than almost any other part of the country. Although Arabs make up only about 5 per cent of the entire Iranian population, the proportion is about 85 per cent in Khuzestan. The region is also home to many Kurds, about five million of whom live in Iran, mostly in the west.

We are going to be spending the night in the town of Andimeshk with a family that typifies this ethnic diversity. Hojjat Shams had befriended Reza B during the war and when he was given leave from the front Reza often stayed with him. It was a brief respite from the terrors of war and the two men have remained friends ever since. Hojjat is half Kurd and half Lor and is in business (but what kind of business is never made clear to me) while Senober, his Kurdish wife, although trained as a natural science teacher is now at home looking after their three-year-old son, Ali.

Reza B tells us a Lor joke before we arrive, the Iranian equivalent of Irish jokes.

'A Lor gets on a bus. Everyone around him goes to sleep. The Lor walks up to the driver and asks, "Why are you still driving? Everyone is asleep!"'

Hojjat, Senober and Ali live in an apartment above a row of

shops. A staircase leads from street level to a small terrace off which opens a bathroom and a door to the main apartment that consists of a large open-plan living room and kitchen and a separate master bedroom.

Reza B takes my bag straight into the bedroom. I tell him I hate the idea of my hosts being thrown out of their bedroom for me.

'It is their honour and their duty to you as their guest,' Reza B says firmly.

'Where will everyone else sleep?' I ask. Reza waves his arm vaguely around the living room

'There is plenty of room.'

Senober produces refreshments for us – a bowl of fruit and glasses of tea which we consume sitting on a very new lounge suite. However, dinner – kebabs cooked by Hojjat in the courtyard – is served in traditional style, i.e. on a large plastic tablecloth spread over one of the two vast Tabriz-style carpets they'd been given as wedding presents.

After dinner, Ali is whisked into the bedroom and his jeans and T-shirt exchanged for a miniature version of traditional Kurdish dress comprising a pale grey jumpsuit with a black-striped cummerbund and on his head a tiny pillbox hat embroidered with black and white geometric designs. Little he might have been but he is already familiar with a number of dance moves that he demonstrates to us, his admiring audience.

On hearing that the Shams have guests numerous relatives call in for a chat. But surrounded by incomprehensible conversations and with my every move scrutinised by strangers, I am suddenly hit by waves of exhaustion – my vision is blurry and I'm dizzy with tiredness. The Rezas have become family – travelling with them represents normality, the warmth of the familiar – but at this moment I feel very alone and badly dislocated.

I excuse myself to tackle the local toileting arrangements; always a battle with my unco-operative hip. Feeling sorry for myself I weep briefly over the outside basin while cleaning my teeth. Back in the living room Ali has gone to sleep on a cushion and the men are lounging nearby absorbed in conversation. Senober is in the kitchen bottling enormous plastic jars of pickles.

'Hojjat can eat a jar of these in one day so then I have to keep making more,' she says as she hauls a huge pan of spiced vinegar from the stove. I ask if I can help but she is horrified by the thought.

'No, no, you are a guest!' she laughs.

I go to bed.

Next morning I feel ashamed that my mini-collapse last night might have been viewed as impolite. Determined to get a grip I venture out of the bedroom to find Senober asleep on the kitchen floor, Ali curled up beside her. I'm aghast. The three men start to stir from their mattresses on the living room floor.

While I'm washing my face in the courtyard Reza emerges.

'It's awful that Senober had to sleep on the kitchen floor while I slept in her bed. I understand about the importance of hospitality but that is too much,' I hiss at him.

Reza is upset.

'It is our custom, please don't worry about it,' he says, a little stiffly.

He turns away and goes back inside. I guess it is appropriate in this area where memories of war are so raw that I had stomped into a minefield of my own making. And I had certainly not emerged covered with glory.

As we say goodbye to the family Senober pushes up her sleeve and before I can stop her she unfastens a turquoise bracelet and puts it around my wrist. I feel ashamed once more that I had not insisted on keeping her company in the kitchen.

Today's drive will take us to Kermanshah, located in a bulge of Iranian territory that protrudes into nearby Iraq. Almost due west of us, only a few hundred kilometres away, is the deeply troubled and violent city of Baghdad. Although war now restricts trade between Iraq and Kermanshah it used to be a different story. For centuries Kermanshah had been a trading centre along the silk roads and was strategically placed on what was known as the Royal Road that linked the Achaemenid capital of Ecbatana (modern-day Hamadan where we will stay tonight) to Babylon.

The contrast between the chaos of Baghdad and the panorama of velvety green pastures and lonely but peaceful low hills of barren rock is a stark one.

With no scheduled stops planned Reza declares it time for some intensive Persian lessons and as the van hums along the road we sing rhymes designed to imprint Persian numbers on my mind. As usual, Reza B conducts, both hands off the wheel rather more than they should be.

Kermanshah is one of the biggest cities in western Iran with a population of about 700,000. When we reach the street leading to our central city hotel it appears that all 700,000 have brought their cars to town for the evening.

About eight lanes of traffic are gridlocked at the entrance to the street that leads to our hotel. An area beyond the street has been blocked off to provide parking and so while on the one hand there are several hundred cars trying to get into the street, on the other there is an equal number trying to get out. It is the traffic jam from hell, made worse by almost every driver's belief that if he honks his horn loudly enough, the sea of cars will part in Biblical fashion before them. Iranian drivers are usually refreshingly free of any inclination towards road rage, but this piece of motoring hell pushes a few drivers over the edge. Some cars are abandoned altogether while their occupants get out to argue with other drivers about who should move where.

Several passers-by thump the sides of our van, which makes Reza B's moustache bristle dangerously. After some minutes of going nowhere Reza gets out and threads his way through the chaos to find the hotel and maybe even a porter to help us. I find his optimism particularly endearing given there is barely room between the cars to fit one person, turned sideways.

Reza B and I contemplate the scene in silence until a man wearing a dark uniform with white belt and shoulder holster bangs on Reza's B window. Muttering quietly he opens it and a heated exchange follows.

Apparently we are in the parking queue and we have to move to the left to get into the lane that goes past the hotel. My newly acquired ability to count to 1000 in Farsi is no help at this point.

To the left of us is a sea of vehicles, just as stuck as we are. The policeman is now blowing his whistle stridently and gesticulating at Reza B. As the man has a gun, I resist the temptation to gesticulate back at him.

'Where does he expect us to go?' I ask.

The van suddenly lurches. A group of motorists, inspired not so much by goodwill as by the thought that if we are out of the way they'll be able to move, is physically lifting our van out of the wedge of vehicles. Nearby others are doing the same with the remaining cars in our path.

Car by car, the jigsaw of tightly locked vehicles is rearranged and miraculously we emerge in a narrow but clear stretch of road between two rows of angle-parked vehicles.

'We'll never find a park after all this,' I say. Reza B doesn't bother replying as he turns into a space occupied by Reza who has been repelling would-be invaders. A porter stands beside him.

After we offload, we go in search of dinner on foot. Outside the hotel the cacophony of shouting, blaring horns and penetrating police whistles is unabated and as we carefully thread our way through the shambles to a side road, I tell Reza I am on a one-night strike from kebabs and hamburgers. Luck is on my side because after only a few minutes' walk we find a pizza parlour with gleaming floors and tables that passes his hygiene standards.

The owner is so surprised to see a tourist at the counter that he bounces up from the till, asks me to take a seat and tells Reza he'll personally come over and consult on my choice of pizza toppings.

In due course a delicious pizza arrives and we tuck in. Our host makes frequent visits to our table to check on us, on one occasion begging Reza to tell me that he would happily have cooked me anything I wanted, including Chinese or Italian, but he was so surprised when we came in that he forgot to say so.

I assure him in my stumbling Farsi that his is the best pizza I've eaten for ages. But when we try to pay, Reza has to exceed the usual amount of *taroffing* before he will accept the money.

When we return to the hotel the street is all but deserted – our van is one of the few vehicles in sight.

Iranian winters might be harsh in most regions, but most homes and hotels are heated to the extent that I often find bedrooms in particular too warm. My Kermanshah hotel room is one of these and annoyingly it appears that the windows are fused shut and I can find no way to turn off the radiator. It is a long hot night, punctuated by the sounds of a constantly dripping tap in the bathroom and I am only too pleased when the pre-dawn call to prayer tells me it's time to get up.

Although Kermanshah's unheralded claim to fame is probably the world's worst traffic jams the city is better known for a nearby cliff of bas reliefs that were carved during the fourth century at the command of the Sassanian kings.

Carved into grottoes at the base of the dramatically barren and deeply gashed cliff, the sculptures at Taq-e-Bostan are first glimpsed from across an ornamental lake of milky blue water fringed with trees.

The massive figures represent the coronations of Sassanian kings Khosro II and Ardeshir II. The Zoroastrian god Ahura Mazda is also depicted as is the god Mithras who stands on a lotus flower, both sporting curling beards and luxuriant moustaches.

Two stone carved angels with draperies clinging to their legs float over one of the scenes and the walls around the bas relief of Khorsho are covered in wonderfully lively hunting scenes featuring elephants, horses, stags and wild boars.

While we are studying the sculptures a party of about 20 schoolgirls accompanied by a young woman teacher arrives. Aged about 12, the girls sit down on the shallow step in front of the grottoes while their teacher begins to describe the events carved into the walls more than 1500 years ago. The girls watch her with rapt attention – there is no giggling or fidgeting and even the arrival of a couple of custodians wielding huge twig brooms does not distract them. In their minds they are back in the time when their ancestors defeated the Roman Empire and when their long-dead kings received their crowns in person from the gods. However, it's time for us to go and we leave them to their lesson.

We're now travelling through along a fertile valley flanked by snow-covered mountain ranges to the village of Bisotun where we stop to visit Iran's equivalent of the Rosetta stone. After scrambling up a narrow track 60 metres above the road, we find, carved into a sheer rock face, the fabled words of the Achaemenian king Darius I, who in 520 BC ordered them to be carved here after he'd defeated a rival ruler and quelled some serious rebellion among eight other would-be kings. Alongside is a bas relief of Darius I with his foot on the body of the defeated king; the eight rebels are chained together nearby.

The inscription is written in ancient Persian cuneiform, a language that no one had been able to decipher until Englishman Henry Rawlinson cracked the ancient code in 1838. Alongside the tablet or panel are versions of the same text in Elamite and Babylonian that were carved at the same time.

When Rawlinson came here in the 19th century he was helped by two Kurdish children to lower himself and his young helpers down the cliff on ropes where they spent countless hours carefully transcribing the incomprehensible Persian cuneiform. Then, working with the Elamite and Babylonian texts (ancient languages that had been deciphered earlier) Rawlinson was able to translate the words for the first time. In doing so he also provided the key to understanding many other hitherto indecipherable inscriptions, making the ancient inscription something of an Iranian equivalent of the Rosetta stone.

Because of their immense archaeological value, these three

panels can now only be accessed close up by the privileged few, but I don't need to get any closer because Reza translates the script for me. He is one of only a few modern-day Iranians who has learned both old and middle Persian (a later version of the same language).

'It's a very informative story – especially as it is actually Darius who is speaking to us. He talks about the rebels and traitors and how he, Darius, had stopped the rioting in different parts of the empire.'

We turn around to look out across the valley. At the base of the cliff is a small lake created by a natural spring.

'Imagine looking at this when it was the royal road which also led to a Zoroastrian temple, a trading route – and from Islamic times it has been a pilgrimage trail to holy sites in Iraq,' Reza says. 'It was a very clever place to put this inscription. Anyone passing by would have stopped and seen the picture and read the words – and because it is in three different languages they would instantly have appreciated the might and power of the king.'

The snow on the mountain range to the south shimmers in the sunshine. The spring waters tumble from the lake and gurgle down a serpentine series of channels created to provide Persia's picnickers of today with plenty of choice spots. Reza murmurs words of ancient Persian as he uses the telephoto lens of my camera to zoom in on the inscriptions. Even after so long on the road, so many thousands of kilometres, Iran continues to astound me with its spectacular, albeit sometimes stark and uncompromising, landscapes. I realise, too, how privileged I am to have the country's essence uncovered for me by an exceptional Iranian like Reza, who chooses this very minute to announce that it is time for a cup of tea.

On the outskirts of Bisotun, as we head towards Hamadan, I spot a building of now very familiar design with its domed roof and lofty single gateway. This caravanserai would have been a popular spot back in its heyday, strategically located as it is on what was both a pilgrimage and trading route. But today there is no trade with Iraq and the few pilgrims who still persevere with the dangerous mission of crossing the border stay in hotels en route. The caravanserai has been converted into a cinema.

Travelling in the wake of kings and pilgrims, caravan camels and invaders, we follow the road to Hamadan. Another of Iran's ancient capitals, it has its share of attractions but we are there primarily to support Reza on a personal mission which involves collecting his master's degree in ancient Persian languages from the city's Bu Ali Sina University. He's been working on this degree for some years, fitting in his studying around tours, travelling the five hours between Hamadan and Tehran by public bus late at night and sleeping in temporary accommodation at the university. It wasn't possible for him to attend the graduation ceremony because he'd been away with a tour group when it took place.

The university is a modern complex set in a sprawling campus of trees and lawns on the outskirts of the city. We park outside the registry and Reza goes inside, only to return a short time later empty-handed.

'I have to have a special seal from the post office and that is now closed for the day. I can do nothing about it until tomorrow.'

We all feel the sense of anticlimax.

But Reza suggests what is for him at least the perfect antidote to disappointment.

'Let us go instead to see some very interesting ruins – and then I know where there is an excellent and very picturesque teahouse.'

A DEGREE OF CELEBRATION
Hamadan and Zanjan

If the boy is immersed in his craft to some extent ...
he will have esteem for it and will be all the more
motivated to excel in it and to explore all its secrets ...

Aviecenna 980–1037

Reza's university, Bu Ali Sina, is named after Hamadan's most famous son, Abu Ali Hussein ibn Abdallah ibn Sina, better known both in Iran and in the West as Aviecenna.

Not actually Persian by birth, Aviecenna was born near Bukhara in today's Uzbekistan. He was something of a child prodigy, having learned the entire Koran before he was 10 years old and then by the age of 18 it was said of him that he'd mastered maths, physics and logic. He became court physician in Bukhara, wrote *The Book of Remedy*, and the *Canon on Medicine*, and later became the physician to the ruler of Isfahan in Persia. He died in Hamadan in 1037.

The fame of Aviecenna's *Canon on Medicine* spread to the West where it was translated first into Latin and much later into

English. It was used in European schools of medicine up until the 17th century.

His philosophical views, however, were not universally well received and he was criticised by both Islamic and Western scholars. Despite this, Aviecenna is regarded as the father of modern philosophy and certainly of early medicine.

To me Aviecenna's shrine in Hamadan is yet another example of the duality of Iranian society. Even though his views on religion and spirituality do not sit comfortably with some modern-day scholars and clerics in Iran, his burial place is revered and well cared for. Above the grave itself is a soaring monument of 12 pillars surmounted by a small pyramid. Modelled on the Persian tomb tower, Gonbad-e-Kavus in Iran's eastern Caspian region, the world's tallest brick tower, it has a flanged cylinder capped with a conical roof. In the galleries surrounding the grave are copies of some of his writings, which as the text at the start of this chapter attests, would appear to contain at least in part some common sense.

We climb to the shrine's roof and as we look down on a park Reza points out the lawns and benches under the bare trees.

'I used to come here while I was at university for some fresh air and to study in the peace and quiet.'

Hamadan was once the capital of the Median and Achaemenid empires (when it was known as Hagmataneh – the place of gathering). Archaeologists are still uncovering reminders of this city, but as yet the fabled walls of gold and silver have not been found. The Medes, a confederation of tribes that are thought to have had Indo-European roots, built their chief city here in the seventh century BC.

In the process of excavating the remains of these empires, archaeologists have uncovered evidence of an even earlier civilisation that may date back beyond 1000 BC. No one knows who these people were, but according to what has been uncovered they appeared to have lived a communal lifestyle. We stand on an overhead walkway to view the newly excavated remains of small rooms entered from a central corridor and served by communal kitchens.

Around us are masses of mounds yet to be explored. More time and money will reveal what else lies under the detritus of centuries past.

A bitingly cold wind is sweeping across the excavations and by the time we've driven 12 kilometres to Ganjnnameh in the Alvand mountains that curve around the city, it's snowing gently.

It's so cold that when we reach our destination that the edges of the small stream, contained in a man-made channel, which flows from the mountains, is encrusted with ice. A path on one side leads uphill past a line of teahouses, most of which have their *takts* outside under awnings. Beside several of the shops are displays of pottles of gorgeously red preserved sour cherries alongside sheets of translucent fruit leather. These tart snacks are favourite winter treats.

'Children love them but most mothers tend to be suspicious about the lack hygiene involved in their preparation,' Reza says.

We walk past them, somewhat gingerly as the damp flagstones are starting to freeze. Reza points out what we've come to see – two panels of inscriptions carved into a rock face on the other side of the stream. To get to them we must cross a bridge covered with snow and ice and then make our way up a steep slope of snow.

The panels, written in Old Persian, Neo-Elamite and Neo-Babylonian were commissioned by two of the Achaemenid kings, Darius I and his son Xerxes, between 522 and 465 BC.

We slither across the bridge and stomp our own sets of steps into the snowy hillside in order to get closer to the carvings.

'Darius starts by praising the Great God, Ahura Mazda, who created this earth, who created yonder sky, and who created people and happiness for people,' Reza translates.

'He also says, "I am Darius, King of Kings, King of Many Lands".'

We stand in the falling snow hearing the echo down the ages of Darius' claim to power and then turn to descend the treacherous slope which, from this angle, seems to present a particularly direct route into the icy stream bed far below us.

'I know it's un-Islamic, but I'm going to have to hold on to your coat sleeve,' I tell Reza.

As we walk past the teahouses one of the proprietors is outside intent on priming a *qalyan*.

Reza and I look at each other.

'Let's sit outside in the tent,' he says.

I study him doubtfully through the snowflakes.

'Don't worry, you won't be cold – there is a special heating system.'

The air temperature must be well below zero as we take off our shoes and sit on the *takt*. In the middle of the *takt* is perched a very small blanket-covered low table.

Reza sits down cross-legged and lifts up an edge of the blanket and instructs me to look underneath to see the brazier of glowing charcoal.

'This is a *korsi* and it was once a traditional way of keeping warm in winter – even houses used to have them.'

After ordering tea and *qalyan* Reza goes off to invite our driver to join us, even though Reza B clearly disapproves of our smoking habit and tells us we are becoming addicts.

Despite the flurries of snow we see through the open side of the teahouse and the icy chill that sneaks in through the gaps in the canvas, it's remarkably warm thanks to the charcoal brazier that toasts our feet and hands.

Four teenage girls, rugged up in many layers of jerseys and jackets, are slipping and sliding their way up the hill outside when they catch sight of us. They walk on a few paces, form a giggling huddle, then retrace their steps and join us on the next *takt*. They direct a blaze of smiles at me, but seem too shy to speak.

'I think they have come in to have tea purely as an excuse to talk to you,' Reza observes. 'Maybe you should start the conversation.'

I smile at the girls and say hello in Farsi. This has the usual effect of making them collapse in fits of giggles. I'd stopped long ago being offended at this reaction after Reza explained that so few foreigners speak Farsi that the giggling is prompted by total surprise – and nothing to do with my appalling accent.

After identifying themselves as students from Hamadan, one of them asks my religion. I tell her New Zealand is a predominantly Christian country.

'Do you go to church?' another enquires.

I can't imagine too many casual conversations in the West taking such a direct and serious turn so quickly.

Three of them have simple short black veils over their hair and wear Western clothing but the fourth has her hair scraped back under a long chador and is dressed much more conservatively. However, although she is just as giggly as the others she does not want to be in a photograph with me or Reza.

Seemingly happy with their encounter, the girls drink their tea quickly and leave, only to return a few seconds later, nudging each other until the most outgoing speaks.

'We would like you to pray for us that we will find good husbands,' she says earnestly.

'Not like that man over there,' she says (pointing at the owner of the next-door teahouse), 'who has been trying to chat us up.'

This sends all four of them into hysterics but before they leave I promise I'll pray for them.

'You should perhaps also pray for help to stop the smoking, too,' says Reza B darkly.

Back in Hamadan Reza and I walk through the streets of the city that, despite the cold, is packed with early evening shoppers. Our destination is a bakery set in a triangle created by two converging roads and it is so small that the two of us seem to fill all the customer space. But three more people arrive after us, so we all stand tightly wedged, facing the same way, to avoid anyone falling backwards out the door.

'It is a very popular bakery because it sells *komaj*, sponge biscuits, which are a Hamadan speciality.'

Reza places his order and the baker packs our biscuits in a small cardboard box printed with pastoral scenes. He ties it up with string, finishing with a loop so we can carry it easily.

Our next stop is at one of the photographic shops that abound in Iran and which are full of modern processing equipment and banks of computers operated by competent young men and women. Surrounded as they are by all this state-of-the-art equipment I always find the sight of the women in uniform veils rather incongruous.

One of the girls takes my memory card and as she clicks away at her computer she quizzes Reza about me. In front of her on the screen, photographs from our last three or four days' travelling materialise. She calls over two other staff members and they peer intently at the screen, asking Reza about the location of some of the mosques and ancient buildings.

'We have chosen our favourite,' our assistant says. She turns around the screen so I can see – it is a photograph of me paddling in the Persian Gulf.

Next morning, the clouds look heavy with the promise of more snow and Reza thinks we should head out of town as soon as possible in case we get caught in the mountains. But this would mean postponing collecting his degree, which Reza B and I think is unacceptable.

Soon afterwards we arrive at Bu Ali Sina University where Reza B parks in a no-parking area beside the Registry while Reza goes inside to collect his degree. While he's away I leaf through my Persian books to work out how to say 'Congratulations on your degree' and then practise it under my breath.

We watch the doors open and close, open and close and then finally Reza emerges waving a furled piece of paper. With his other arm he punches the air.

Reza B leaps out of the van and goes to meet him on the steps, hugging him tightly and patting him on the back. At home I would do the same thing but here such a gesture could get us into trouble. When the men return to the van, Reza hands me his degree to admire and I labour through my Farsi phrase. He smiles and we peel oranges and open the box of *komaj* to celebrate.

'It's not exactly a grand graduation ceremony,' I point out, rather unnecessarily.

'It's perfect,' says Reza, the front of his jumper covered in crumbs.

Reza is an untidy traveller – the van floor is always littered with pistachio shells, seed husks and curling dried bits of peel that I'm constantly brushing out the door before Reza B sees them. A few days earlier I'd asked Reza B to teach me how to say 'Reza is very messy' and buoyed by my earlier success I say it now.

Caught by surprise Reza chokes on his biscuit, splutters and has to be thumped on the back by Reza B. My Farsi is proving hazardous.

We take a minor road north to Zanjan so that we can visit a building that boasts the third-largest dome in the world. But thanks to the snow we make slow progress up the Asadaband Pass. Previous falls are banked up on both sides of the road and the entire landscape is blanketed white. In fact, the air temperature is so low that our windscreen wipers keep freezing up, rendering them useless in the snowstorm so that Reza B has to stop every few minutes, bash the ice off the wipers and sweep the snow off with his bare hands.

Centuries ago, the approach to the mausoleum at Soltaniyeh must have been impressive, but today a nondescript village of adobe walls emblazoned with painted advertising slogans laps at its boundary. The blue dome is almost completely obscured by scaffolding. I find it hard to believe that I am looking at one of the largest domes in the world and am prepared to be unimpressed.

By the time we reach the mausoleum entrance it's stopped snowing but it's incredibly cold; over my mid-thigh-length *manteau* I'm wearing a fleece jacket and Reza's thick padded coat on top. Despite these extra layers I am frozen to the core after just a few minutes out of the van.

'I must be getting soft,' I say, shivering. 'Maybe I'll just look from the van.'

Reza is aghast.

'No! You must trust me – it will be worth it. And this can be one of the coldest places in Iran so it is normal to be cold.'

A lone custodian is crouched inside the ticket booth trying to keep warm over an antique one-bar heater.

We crunch over patches of snow to the base of the mausoleum where the dome soars nearly 50 metres above us with the remains of eight minarets encircling it. Reza ducks under the scaffolding and disappears inside.

I follow him to find that although the leaden skies let very little light into the interior there is enough to illuminate the vast, cavernous space under the 25-metre-diameter dome which Iranians consider it to be the third biggest in the world after the Duomo in Florence and Hagia Sophia in Istanbul. I imagine what those other two places would be like right now; even in midwinter I know there will be hundreds of people passing under the domes, taking photographs, listening to guides, reading their handbooks. Meanwhile Reza and I stand by ourselves in the semi-dark, a lone pigeon rummaging on a ledge high above our heads.

The mausoleum dates from the 14th century and was built by a Mongol sultan, Oljeitu. He had made Soltaniyeh the capital of the Il Khan Mongols who ruled this part of Persia at the time. Originally a pagan, but born to a Christian mother, he'd converted first to Sunni Islam and then become a Shia and in the process had become a devout and enthusiastic convert with big ideas. He wanted to bring the body of the revered Imam Ali from Najaf (now in neighbouring Iraq) and bury him in his purpose-built mausoleum.

Perhaps not surprisingly, the authorities in Najaf were not keen – no doubt for a combination of deeply spiritual reasons but also because the loss of the imam's body would have seriously affected the lucrative pilgrim trade. The sultan did not take the rebuff well – he converted back to Sunni Islam and decided that he'd be buried in the mausoleum instead.

It's a site with personal significance for Reza. Like all young Iranian men he had to complete two years of military service during his early twenties. But as a university graduate he had the option, after six weeks of basic training, of working in a government department. Accordingly he'd chosen the Cultural Heritage and Tourism Organisation and during his term of service was sent to Soltaniyeh to help on an archaeological dig close to the mausoleum.

'Look at the calligraphy around the interior. The artists are playing with geometry and working some very long verses from the Koran, along with the names Allah and Ali, into their designs. I call this a museum of Persian decorative art. It is so complex it is hard even for me to distinguish some of the words. You have to concentrate very hard.'

The mausoleum is appropriately as cold as the proverbial tomb – I'm struggling to concentrate on anything other than not freezing solid.

I thaw out a little as we ascend to the vaulted gallery that runs around the outside of the mausoleum just under the dome and gaze out across the snow-covered grounds.

'I have very happy memories of working here,' Reza says, oblivious to my shaking with cold beside him.

'My best find was a pair of seventeenth-century scissors. They are now in the Zanjan treasury.'

Beyond the village the bleak, snow-strewn plains stretch out to a ring of barren mountains. Reza speculates that the Mongols chose this place partly because it reminded them of their homelands in the steppes of Central Asia.

It would have certainly been cold enough in winter to have summoned up memories of home for them.

Although the dome is the most renowned feature of the mausoleum, it is the ceilings of the gallery that captivate me. Each is decorated with pale pink, terracotta and white moulding so intricate it looks as if Persian carpets have been attached to the roof.

We find a warm *kebabi* restaurant in Soltaniyeh's main street in which to thaw out. The few men sitting at scattered tables and the owner watch, amused, as I position myself in front of the gas-fuelled heater.

'Are you cold?' the restaurateur asks.

I show him my blue hands.

'Today it is quite warm, it is about five degrees. When it reaches minus twenty degrees, then we call it cold,' he tells me.

We drive towards Zanjan, the three of us conjugating Farsi verbs, and in due course arrive at a tourist inn. It's snowing again, the snow sliding off the fir trees in the garden and clinging to the bare rose bushes. Outside the inn, there is little traffic swishing through the slurry and Reza and I have to crunch along the footpath for several minutes before Reza is able to flag down a shared taxi.

I really like the concept of shared taxis – even the smallest most battered Paikan can hold four or five passengers as it traverses a set route. If you are lucky, everyone joins in on the conversation, the topics changing as passengers get out, and newcomers get in.

On this occasion the front-seat passenger is a diminutive elderly man with a bushy black moustache who has a long message for me. Reza translates.

'He says welcome to Iran, welcome to my town. He says he is an old man but he goes to the mountains every week to exercise and eats healthy food every day. He says almonds and walnuts and dates will ensure that you live a long and healthy life. Olive oil is also good for you,' Reza pauses for breath and the man starts talking again. 'Wait a minute, there is more … He says that his children have been very successful. They have been very well educated and one has a master's degree. He is very happy with his life – children should always achieve more than their parents. And please would we go to his humble house to have a cup of tea. He really does mean that but I think we need to keep going – Zanjan has one of the longest bazaars in Iran.'

The taxi driver listens intently and then tells Reza that he would love to be able to talk to foreigners and understand more about their world and could Reza please tell him how to learn to speak a foreign language.

When the car stops near the bazaar the old man gets out and shakes Reza's hand, giving him directions to his house, in case we change our minds. Unusually, the taxi driver also shakes Reza's hand. The conversation has engrossed everyone to such an extent that both Reza and the driver forget about payment and Reza has to slide back through the snow to knock on the passenger side window.

At the entrance to Zanjan's covered bazaar the fruit and vegetable salesmen keep warm by a lot of good-natured shouting and waving about of produce.

It's quieter inside but crowded with shoppers intent on the

brightly lit vaults on each side of the central sinuous corridor which look like a series of Aladdin's caves: a young couple stands in a carpet shop trying to choose between two blue-and-white rugs from Tabriz; women in black chadors cram themselves into tiny gold shops, glittering with displays of bright yellow metal; and the knife shops, stacked with gleaming arrays of knives, including some with extremely nasty-looking serrated edges, are doing a roaring trade.

I spot a shop specialising in surplus military uniforms and equipment and decide it's an ideal place to buy a present for my son but I'm doubtful the two young shopkeepers will sell anything to a tourist like me. But it's no problem at all and soon the other customers, a couple of young soldiers, are debating with the shopkeepers the best present for Jonathan. They choose a selection of badges and tell me that they hope my son will like them very much.

We pass a wooden cart piled with beetroots. A small gas burner sits among the vegetables with a large pot boiling away on top.

'This is a traditional Azeri winter snackfood,' Reza explains. 'I would like you to try it but at the same time I would hate you to get sick if they are not well cooked.'

Steam is rising off the boiled beetroot and the air is filled with an aroma I remember from when my mother used to bottle beetroot.

'I'll live dangerously for once,' I declare. After all, how risky can boiled vegetable be?

One of the young cooks flicks out a large beetroot onto a small paper plate and hands it to us along with two plastic forks. They refuse to take any money, telling Reza that I am a guest and they haven't sold beetroot to a foreigner before.

It is true comfort food, warm and sweet – and I don't get sick.

Back in the labyrinth of the bazaar, Reza turns into a side alley and down a set of steps into the *hammam* that is part of the typical four-part Islamic ensemble of buildings. This one has been converted into an atmospheric teahouse with small octagonal rooms lined with tiles. Fountains splash in the centre of each room.

We pass through the 'men only' frigidarium to the former tepidarium reserved for mixed parties and family groups.

The young couple opposite us stares fixedly at me while they wait for their meal of rice and kebabs to arrive. I stare back but it doesn't deter them.

'It is one thing to look and be interested, another to stare like that,' Reza says. 'I think they are from a village and you are the first foreigner they have seen.'

We drink tea and eat fresh dates until it's time for Reza's graduation dinner. Zanjan had developed along a caravan route that leads into Azerbaijan so a sizeable caravanserai had been built beside the bazaar. It is now one of the most popular restaurants in town.

On our way back through the bazaar we stop to take a photograph of two whiskery broom sellers. Their barrow is piled high with bright orange twig brooms. On impulse we buy one for the van.

In the caravanserai we are led through the internal corridors of two sides of the typical four-sided caravanserai to an unoccupied niche in front of which sails a plaster swan in a small pond.

As this is a graduation feast, Reza orders the regional speciality – *ash reshteh,* a soup of beans, pasta, yoghurt concentrate, vegetables and mint. We follow this with *kashk-e bademjan* – eggplants served with more yoghurt concentrate, onion, mint and walnut paste. A young boy, working at a run along the corridors, keeps us supplied with giant ovals of bread, warm from the oven. We toast Reza's degree with glasses of fizzy yoghurt drink.

Next morning we have to drag our bags through thick snow to the van. The garden is a mass of misshapen white mounds, frozen and still.

'Before we leave Zanjan we are going to visit one of the most unusual laundries you will see anywhere,' Reza tells me.

We pass through a courtyard where the branches of young plane trees are etched in white and snow weighs down the branches of evergreens at their feet.

The Rakht Shuy Khaneh – or house of washing – is one of the world's strangest municipal projects. Built in 1920 it was still in use up to about 40 years ago providing Zanjan's townsfolk with proper laundry facilities. The house of washing was warm in winter, cool in summer and was vastly superior to the previous practice of having to wash in streams. It also provided privacy for the women who did the laundry.

A massive reservoir fed a wide channel that flowed around the four sides of a central platform from which women would do their washing in the fresh, running water.

In an arched alcove overlooking the restored laundry a bearded, grey-haired man with glasses perched at the end of his nose is embroidering a leather shoe of enormous proportions.

Pointing at his shelves of brightly coloured leather slippers, the shoemaker explains that he normally works on more conventional styles but he has decided, just for fun, to make a giant shoe adorned with embroidered depictions of Iran's most famous monuments.

'I think my shoes could sell well to tourists but as we see so few here we have to love our handicrafts very much to keep making them when we have hardly any customers,' he tells us.

'But I am always optimistic about things – I hope tourism will improve. That will of course depend on many factors.'

It's snowing again and above us the clouds, laden with more snow, are pale grey and luminous. Apart from the two black strips of tarmac kept clear by the passing traffic, the world outside the van is utterly white and still.

We stop to feed a flock of tiny birds huddled on the pile of snow at the side of the road with some leftover bread from the night before. They've puffed up their feathers so much they look completely circular.

The road winds over a low pass where, nestled among the hills, are a series of Kurdish villages with their flat-roofed houses. Men and boys armed with brooms stand on the roofs sweeping off slabs of snow.

Further on, along a long stretch of highway devoid of any distinguishing features, we come across an elderly man standing beside the road clad only in wool trousers, a cotton shirt and a thin sports jacket. Reza B stops to allow the old man to climb in. Once he's installed he tells us that his village is snowed in but he needs to get to Tabriz to keep an appointment. Reza ferrets among our food supplies and peels him an orange. Our hitchhiker eats it with shaking hands.

SNOW DRIFTS AT THE BLACK CHURCH

Tabriz and Azerbaijan

As, the sun moving, clouds behind him run
All hearts attend thee, O Tabriz's Sun!

Hafez

Reza B's moustache seems to be bristling with proprietary pride as we drive through a concrete forest of new apartments on the outskirts of Tabriz. Reza B is staunchly Azeri and this city is the capital of Iran's Azerbaijan province; we're also close to his home town. Even I, despite the trouble I usually have differentiating between Iran's ethnic groups, can see the preponderance of Turkish features here.

It's Reza B who checks out the menu at our lunch restaurant and then orders a prodigious quantity of food, even by our standards. As he hands us each an orange as an entrée, he explains that this is his graduation celebration lunch for Reza and because of this we will eat *dolmas*, a local variation on the stuffed vine leaves dish that can be found in several southern Mediterranean countries. We're doing very well using Reza's degree celebrations as an excuse for our prolonged series of culinary blow-outs.

This part of Iran is one of the coldest in the country. When we emerge from the steamy warmth of the restaurant the dry but intense cold has us shivering in seconds. The winter average here is about –2 degrees Celsius, but I doubt if it's that balmy today.

Reza is undeterred, though, as he wants to show me Tabriz's famous Blue Mosque. Built in 1465 it is now partly a ruin due to the frequent severe earthquakes in the region.

What makes this mosque unique is the intricate and beautiful decorative work on its walls, some of which still clings to the ruined shell.

'It's one of the world's great tile-work masterpieces,' Reza says as we circle its rather drab exterior walls. As I'm wondering why it is called the Blue Mosque, he reads my mind.

'Yes, I know what you are thinking but you'll see in a second.'

The mosque's main entrance, a lofty *ivan*, is covered in blue tiles the colour of lapis. Turquoise arabesques and flowing white calligraphy swirl across the sea of blue. It's yet another example of how Iran works on two levels in that while the portal is exuberant and aesthetically beautiful, it is also a visual reminder of the omniscience of Allah. The calligraphy spells out the 1000 different words for God and Reza translates some of them for me.

'Allah the generous, the beneficent, the bounteous, perfect ...'

He tells me such inscriptions are not found on many mosques in Iran.

We pass through the portal into the central domed chamber. The mosque has been restored twice – once about 100 years ago and again in the 1970s at which time master calligraphers were brought in to help repair some of the decorative inlays. Intricate mosaic panels of interlocking black-and-white geometric designs cover some of the walls and I admire the tiles adorned with gold.

The inside of the mosque is colder than an average refrigerator, but it is slightly better than outside. We pause only briefly at the statue of a distinguished-looking robed man who stands between the mosque and the Museum of Azerbaijan.

Khaghani was a 12th-century Persian poet who died in Tabriz after leading a suitably tragic poet's life starting when his father died while Khaghani was young. However, his talent as a writer was officially recognised and this resulted in his being appointed as a court poet. But the constraints of his new life soon became too much (he likened himself to a bird with a broken wing) and he escaped to travel in the Middle East. When he returned his royal employer threw him in jail. It was on his release that he moved to Tabriz with his family, but sadly his son, wife and daughter died in quick succession. He died himself not long after.

Later we track down an excerpt from one of his poems and were not surprised to find it somewhat gloomy.

'Do you know what I benefited from this world? Nothing
And what I gained from the days of life? Nothing
I am a candle of wisdom; but when extinguished, nothing
I am the cup of Jamshid; but when broken, nothing.'

We take refuge from the weather in the museum, which I'm happy to discover is small. There's something about vast museums with innumerable galleries that makes me feel insecure – I always worry that I might miss something significant and, no matter how sensible my shoes, I also suffer from early-onset 'museum feet'.

The Tabriz museum takes a very logical approach to its exhibits, tracing Iran's history in strictly chronological order, which is wonderfully helpful given this country's complex history. There's also a mercifully strictly limited array of pottery and a glittering selection of silver and gold including a hammered gold dish with a delicate cobweb design made by the Achaemenids in at least 300 BC. I also notice a silver rhyton – a curiously curved drinking vessel that sits on a base fashioned as a crouching lion – and a prehistoric squat clay figure with bountiful hips and a enigmatic face that looked astonishingly like a modern-day cartoon figure, which turns out appropriately to be a fertility goddess. My favourite is the collection of stone handbags. Stone snakes with heads entwined form the handles.

'They were probably symbols of wealth for ancient Azeri tribes,' says Reza. 'Apparently the tribal treasurers were in charge of them.'

Reza heads purposefully for the basement. I am less keen – I've had a near-perfect museum experience and am certain the lower floor will probably be crammed with broken pottery.

What we find is a collection of tortured stucco sculptures so graphic I'm surprised there isn't a sign on the door stopping anyone under the age of about 20 from entering. Created by Tabriz sculptor Ahad Hosseini, they are the most terrifying works I've ever seen and include a dragon with five gaping fang-filled mouths chasing petrified humans entitled Anxiety, which seems to me somewhat of an understatement. There is also a massive statue of Primitive Man wielding a club set beside Modern Man carrying a bomb.

Serendipitously there's a tiny refreshment stall just outside the door to the exhibition. Reza orders soothing cups of tea while we contemplate the sculptures from a safe distance.

Daylight is slipping away when we emerge from the museum but it's the perfect time to plunge into Tabriz's bazaar – the largest in Iran if not the whole of West Asia and the Middle East. There are more than 7000 shops and dozens of caravanserai built alongside for the easy transfer of goods from camel to would-be customers.

Although most of the bazaar's buildings are 15th century, its origins probably date back a further 500 years – Silk Road commerce has played a major role here for centuries. We are on a mission to find some of the more unusual wares that are for sale so we pass rapidly through the brick-vaulted arcades glistening with gold jewellery and incongruous neon shop signs. We pause briefly at a conglomeration of kitchenware shops to admire the range of electric samovars and saucepan sets. Five centuries ago camels probably unloaded precious porcelain from the Far East on this spot. Today you can buy cheap Chinese dinner sets. But while dynasties and empires have come and gone and modern-time shopkeepers gossip on mobile phones and order their goods via email, the basic principles of commerce seem little changed.

'We used to produce almost everything ourselves,' Reza comments, turning over a plate to read the label. 'Soon everything will be made in China.'

I tell him that in my part of the world we've been saying the same thing for years.

We're nearly where we want to be but at the end of a T-junction I see a shop-front laden with great glutinous mounds of fat – the raw material for soap. Then we find what we have been looking for – two shops, located on either side of an alleyway thronged with people, both dedicated to the favourite Persian pastime of *qalyan* smoking. One shop specialises in the bases that in Iran almost always carry the bearded likeness of Qajar king Nasser-ed-Din Shah, who ruled Persia for nearly 50 years. The floor-to-ceiling shelves are crammed with them – many in jewel-like glass colours adorned with the bearded face of Shah Abbas, but there are some made of ceramic glazed with multi-coloured flowers, while others are made of brass and silver. Also on display are petite and delicate *qalyan* that look more decorative than functional, but some are sturdier floor-standing models more than half a metre tall. As *qalyan* should always be smoked while drinking tea, there is also a range of teapots and tea glasses for sale.

Across the lane a white-haired man with stubbly cheeks is bent over his workbench wrapping velvet braid around a pink *qalyan* hosepipe. Above our heads, hundreds of finished pipes dangle from the ceiling like brightly coloured plump strands of spaghetti.

These are definitely not made in China. The hoses come from a Tabriz factory and the decorative finishes are added by shopkeepers such as this man whose shop also stocks wooden mouthpieces and the flavoured tobacco especially favoured by younger smokers.

'I have twelve kinds,' he tells us. 'I import them from Syria and Egypt.'

Then he points out the bags of charcoal on the floor. This really is the complete one-stop shop for *qalyan* addicts.

'It's lemonwood charcoal, which enhances the tobacco aroma.'

'I didn't know that,' Reza exclaims. 'You see, even an Iranian can learn about his country on a journey like this.'

A steady stream of customers is coming and going, edging past us politely even though we are clearly cluttering up the tiny space. Smoking *qalyan* might be officially frowned upon, but it's clear many Iranians have taken no notice especially as debate still rages about whether smoking a water-pipe is more or less harmful to one's health than smoking ordinary cigarettes. Based on no scientific evidence at all I have come to the convenient conclusion that it's relatively harmless but I know it's simply to assuage my guilty conscience. At home I'm a committed non-smoker.

Back in the bazaar we wind through the cavernous shadows of the carpet bazaar. Most of the shops have closed for the night, but the sound of rhythmic dull thuds is filtering through a pair of partly closed wooden doors. We peer through the crack at a man in black beanie, pinstriped trousers and an old grey suit jacket thwacking a deep red hand-knotted carpet with a smooth length of tree branch. Even Reza is a little taken aback and he asks the man what he is doing.

Unsurprised by our sudden appearance in his workshop, not to mention our nosiness, he explains he is tightening the pile.

We stop to buy tea from a vendor who seems in imminent danger of being swamped by small black mountains of tea leaves. Behind him and to one side shelves rise up bulging with packets of bulk supplies. He tells us he has varieties from all over the world, including Iranian, but very few tea bags.

'People are going back to loose tea,' he says, shovelling scrunchy black Ceylonese tea into a packet for us.

There are old-fashioned tea chests here, too, which instantly transport me back to my father's grocery shop. I look at the foil lining, remembering how you had to be very careful not to rip your fingers on the splintery wood and how, when no one was watching, I would burrow down to my armpits in the tea. As I take a photo the shopkeeper comments to Reza on the number of tourists that take photos of his tea. I ask Reza to explain that we almost never buy loose tea in the West – and rarely see so many varieties in the one shop.

Reza is now looking thoughtfully up and down the darkened alley.

'I hope I can find the next place I want you to see – it is something very special.'

He ducks in and out of several shops getting a series of conflicting directions, then eventually leads me up a narrow set of stairs between two shops. The smell of tobacco hits me halfway up, and I'm by the time I reach the top I'm engulfed in a pale cloud of smoke.

This is about as serious as an Iranian teahouse gets. There'll be no orange-flavoured tobacco here; the male-only clientele smoke only the hard stuff: pure unadulterated tobacco.

Beside the stairwell is the tiny kitchen where two men are toiling in the heat generated by a charcoal burner. They are constantly in motion – stirring up the charcoal, transferring it to braziers to distribute among the smokers, pouring streams of hot water into vast teapots and sluicing out the used tea glasses. Watching over all this action is a canary in a cage – how it survives in this atmosphere I don't know – maybe it functions the same way as a bird down a mine. When it falls off its perch it's time to air the place out a little.

Along the walls sit the smokers. Almost all are older men in dark jackets or woollen pullovers and though they sit companionably close to their neighbours there is little conversation. Apart from the rattling and clanking from the kitchen, the predominant sound is the gurgle and splutter of several dozen *qalyans*. Some have little metal hoods placed over their lids of glowing embers – apparently these cut down on the smoke emissions.

When the older of the two men who were in the kitchen sweeps past depositing two cups of tea in front of us, he nods in the direction of his fellow worker and identifies him as his son, the owner of the teashop, who in due course arrives to check our charcoal and pauses briefly to chat.

'Most of my clients are regulars. Some come in four or five times a day.' He points to a diminutive old man wearing a fur hat. 'He has been coming here for sixty years. Most are *bazaaris* (bazaar shopkeepers) and coming here gives them a break from work, or for some, from life's hardships. We only allow people of good character in here and cigarette smoking is forbidden. Sometimes poets come and recite their poetry.'

While we watch, one of the smokers stands up stiffly and heads for the door, nodding goodbye to his friends on the way. At the top of the stairs he pauses and stuffs some notes into a charity box affixed to the wall before carefully making his way downstairs, both hands gripped firmly on the banisters.

We follow him soon after. Outside we take gulps of fresh air before making a brief circuit through a semi-open fruit and vegetable market. All the stallholders are shouting out claims and counterclaims about the quality and price of their produce. Trolleys laden with new stock are being pushed through the mêlée. As I take a photo of the scene someone calls out and I turn round to see a shopkeeper smiling at me, clutching the biggest, most knobbly lemons I have ever seen. They would put a good-sized melon to shame.

He's speaking in Azeri and Reza is having a little trouble translating thanks to the noise and the man's accent.

'I think he's wondering why you are taking photos of trolleys when you can take pictures of his wonderful fruit.'

Beyond the bazaar the streets are a little more orderly. Brightly lit shop fronts are festooned with the latest heavily studded handbags, winter boots with impossibly pointy toes and coats trimmed with false fur.

'I need a haircut,' Reza announces. I study his head. There is the slightest suggestion that a few hairs may actually be touching his ears. I wonder about our chances of finding a barber here, at a time of night when most of the shops are starting to close.

But Reza spots the appropriate sign with a small arrow pointing up the stairs above what turns out to be an historic bathhouse about to undergo restoration.

The barber and his assistant are having supper when Reza opens their door but I refuse to step inside until it's clear that they are happy for me to come in. An outbreak of smiles greets me, along with gestures for me to sit down closest to the heater. While Reza is draped in a towel, the assistant brings me tea and offers me the rest of his bread and cheese. I accept the tea, but decline his meal and only then realise we've done the whole thing in mime. The barber's assistant is a deaf mute.

While Reza's hair is washed twice and then dried with towels he is plied with questions about me: where do I come from, what Iranian cities do tourists like visiting, what language is spoken in New Zealand. Reza answers them all, his voice slightly muffled from his head being upside down in a basin before being wrapped in a towel. The assistant vigorously dries off his hair and as the barber begins the trim there is a shout from the hall.

The barber opens the door to reveal a man holding a tray of baked goods balanced on one shoulder. The baker and I regard each other over the top of the barber's head, he with a great deal of astonishment. The barber shrugs nonchalantly, implying that foreign blonde women often call in for tea and a chat. The discussion turns to pastry as the barber selects something from the tray. After salaams all round the barber closes the door and hands me a pistachio-studded macaroon biscuit.

'He bought it especially for you,' Reza says.

The assistant beams at me and gestures at the teapot.

I eat the delicate crumbly macaroon while the barber sharpens a cut-throat razor which he then uses to trim Reza's hairline. He offers him a shave, too, but Reza settles for having a handful of what smells like bay rum massaged into his hair. When it's time to leave I say goodbye with genuine regret.

Neither of us is keen to return to our hotel. Reza has had another outbreak of budget worries and while the place he chooses appears, on first glance, to be acceptable if somewhat basic it is only after we reach our rooms that we discover all is not as it should be. In my bathroom every fitting leaks, the radiator is stuck on high and the sheets have not been changed while Reza's room has an overpowering smell of drains. Before we leave to go sightseeing he asks that my sheets be changed – there is little we can do about the rooms' other shortcomings.

Just a few doors from the hotel we find a brightly lit ice-cream parlour and order ourselves a carrot juice and saffron ice cream each. Three young men in blue camouflage Iranian air force uniforms follow us in and sit nearby drinking banana milkshakes. Before long Reza is in conversation with them and discovers they are from Tehran. They are here doing their military service and it's their first time away from home. They look so young, partly because all three suffer from various degrees of acne.

'They are finding it hard here because they don't understand the language and I sympathise with them,' Reza tells me.

After finishing our snack there's nothing for it – it's time to return to the hotel. We trudge up six flights of stairs to our rooms but when I pull back the bedcover I find that while the bottom sheet has been changed, the new one is dotted with black hairs. I sleep wrapped in a shawl on top of the bed, while the radiator tonks and splutters and water from a selection of leaks drips annoyingly out of sync in the bathroom.

When I wake, I look out the window only to see a concrete wall just an arm's length away. However, when I go downstairs to meet the Rezas at the van, I'm delighted to see that Tabriz is lit by sunshine under blue sky.

We are heading northwest today towards the border with Turkey and deep in the Iranian Azeri heartland. Snow lies thickly on the ground, banked up around the bare trees in the orchards. Poplars line the road and I'm sure I can see the faintest haze of green on their branches but Reza B is doubtful – winter will retain its grip on Azerbaijan for some weeks yet.

The first stop of the day near Sufiyan combines a vital cup of our new tea with a tour of a Saffavid caravanserai. The silk road route that had kept the Tabriz bazaars full passed through Sufiyan on its way to Turkey, the Black Sea and on to Europe. Over the past four years intensive restoration work has been carried out here and in a few months' time it is due to open as a new luxury hotel. The foreman, who is studying English so that one day he can become a teacher, shows us around. It looks impressive: the bricks have been washed and scrubbed clean of soot and grime, the commercial kitchen is stacked with gleaming stainless-steel appliances still partly wrapped in plastic and a carpenter is putting the finishing touches to a teahouse created from the reservoir in the centre of the courtyard.

I think of some of the abandoned and forlorn caravanserais Reza and I have seen on our travels and wish for a windfall so I could rescue at least one of them in the same way.

Beyond the caravanserai the snow deepens. The landscape is

undulating whiteness; everything is moulded and softened by the snow.

The van slips and slides down a track that no one else seems to have travelled on since the last snowfall a few days ago. We are now in the most far-flung western corner of Iran less than 50 km from both the Turkish and Armenian borders. In front of us, rising up behind a high stone wall, is an Armenian church believed to be the last resting place of Thaddeus, disciple of Jesus, who together with fellow disciple Bartholomew is regarded as the founder of Armenian Christianity. Thaddeus is thought to have begun building the first church on the site in about AD 66. Although nothing is left of that first church, there are the remains of a 10th-century chapel that has been added to many times over the centuries. It could well be the site of one of the oldest, if not the oldest, churches in the world.

Kalisa-ye Tadi (the Church of Thaddeus) is also known as Qareh Kalisa, or Black Church, because the oldest surviving part is built of black stone. There are two cylindrical towers (one black-and-white striped) topped with conical towers and fortress-like outer walls of rich cream stone. The entire ensemble contrasts dramatically with the blanket of snow.

As we pass through the arched wooden doorway set in the encircling wall, there's a rumbling sound from the direction of the church followed by a solid thump. Above us, a man is shovelling snow off the roof. The caretaker with us calls up to him, announcing the presence of visitors and presumably asking him not to bury us under an avalanche of snow.

There are some extraordinary carvings on the outer church walls: St George slaying the dragon, gargoyle-like figures with pointy ears and angels with thickly feathered wings.

Armenian and Persian history has been deeply enmeshed throughout the lifetime of this church. In the 17th century, Shah Abbas, the great Persian king, wanted to bring increasing numbers of Armenians from their homeland to work on his new capital of Isfahan as he highly valued their business acumen and craftsmanship, especially with silk textiles.

Reza tells me the story of what happened next as we crunch our way around the church's exterior walls, dodging clumps of snow cascading from the roof.

'The Armenians told the king it would be difficult for them to move because they wanted to be close to their holiest cathedral at Echmiadzin (near Armenia's modern-day capital of Yerevan). Shah Abbas responded by telling them he would move the cathedral stone by stone to Isfahan. The prospect so horrified the Armenians that they agreed to move. Once here, they carved an image of Shah Abbas on the Black Church.'

This church is one of the first places travellers arriving from Turkey stop to visit. Reza tells me it comes as a surprise to many new arrivals that, although only one service is held a year, it is a fully functioning church in the Islamic Republic of Iran.

Every year in July, Armenian Christians who have made their homes in Iran make a pilgrimage here and there can be up to 10,000 people camping in the summer meadows that surround the church. No Moslems are allowed to enter the area during the event and none of the women who participate wear *hijab*.

Priests are kept busy baptising all the new arrivals since the previous year and the pilgrims cleanse themselves of their sins by passing into the church through one of its side doors and out through the other.

Back in the van we snow-plough our way back to the main road and on to the village of Chaldoran, the home of Reza B's sister Farahnaz, her husband Hassan and their two daughters. Yesterday and early today there had been a flurry of phone calls between the family, many of which seem to involve discussions about the lunch menu.

Our driver's two nieces, aged 13 and 11, are home even though it's not yet the Iranian weekend (Thursday and Friday). When there is a shortage of classrooms and teachers, schools often run two teaching sessions a day and as the girls attended a morning session starting at 8.30 am they are now home for the rest of the day. They bring me their English language textbooks and tell me this is the first time they have had a native English speaker with whom they can practise. I wonder what their teacher will think when they arrive back at school with a healthy set of Kiwi vowels.

Our meal, eaten in traditional Iranian style on a tablecloth on the floor, begins with *abgusht* – a classic Persian soup of mutton, lentils and vegetables and given an edge with the addition of dried limes. This is followed by Tabrizi *kufta* – a local speciality of meatballs containing rice, split peas and spices. In the centre of each meatball is either boiled egg or dried plum sprinkled with almonds. The meatballs must be boiled for about two hours, making the dish time-consuming to prepare, especially for a large gathering.

This is Persian home cooking at its best but I am struggling to finish because Farahnaz and both Rezas keep piling more food on my plate, which makes both of the girls giggle.

We leave Chaldoran after lunch on a road that crosses a narrow plain, where, Reza explains, an epic battle between the Persian and Ottoman empires was fought in the 16th century. It was won by the Ottomans who used gunpowder technology, a practice the

Persians refused to follow, regarding it as inhumane. This conflict defined the border between the two empires right up until the present day.

Our afternoon drive takes us ever closer to the border with Turkey. The van labours up a small pass – pristine snow sparkles on the gentle hills all around us. There is little traffic about and it is the perfect place for a snowball fight. Cunningly I ask Reza B to stop so I can take a photo and once we are all out of the van the rest is easy .... As we plunge through the snow, ducking slushy missiles and panting with the effort, both men comment that mixed snow fights among the unrelated are not common.

Clearly they are not the only ones finding this activity such a novelty. A heavily laden car appears over a small rise in the road and not surprisingly slows down almost to stalling speed on seeing us red-faced, puffing, covered with blobs of snow – and me with the ends of my long scarf trailing in the snow. It putters past us, the windows crammed with incredulous faces.

Just how close we are to Turkey becomes evident when we round a corner a few minutes later to see the cone of its highest mountain, Mt Ararat, rising into an ice-blue sky. Although the low mountains between us and the dormant volcano are entirely blanketed in white, the snow on Ararat seems to have cascaded down from the 5137-metre peak and then frozen in place like white lava.

The drive into the border town of Bazargan takes us through canyons of columnar basalt – ample evidence that the now-extinct Mt Ararat once wreaked havoc in the region. We are staying the night with Reza B's brother Ghahreman and his extended family. As is often the case in Iran, a blank nondescript wall reveals an ultra-modern home full of a bewildering array of family and friends.

'They are having a party for us tonight,' Reza explains.

Most astonishing of all is the appearance of Reza B's wife, clearly not Ferengis, the woman with whom we spent three days travelling between Tehran and Mashhad.

In a moment when the tide of visitors abates and Reza and I are briefly on our own I begin a whispered interrogation.

'Ah yes, well, I hadn't quite got round to telling you that Ferengis is Reza's temporary wife. This lady is his other wife. Two of the teenagers you see are his children from this wife.'

At this point wife number one returns to the room and further discussion of Reza B's clearly complex domestic life is put on hold.

Reza had already explained the concept of temporary marriage to me, but this is my first experience of it. A concept found only in the Shia branch of Islam, it is a practice of which Sunnis in particular disapprove and one that many Westerners struggle to understand. Consequently it's a subject about which Iranians are a little sensitive.

There is a very comprehensive set of rules surrounding temporary marriage as well as a great deal of debate among Shias about how, and in some cases even if, it should be instituted. Put at its simplest, it works like this: a man may take a temporary wife for a period of time between one hour and 99 years, but if he is already married he must have the permission of his wife. Normally such a union would need the blessing of a cleric, although some people believe it can be legitimised simply by the couple together reciting certain verses from the Koran. Any children born of a temporary marriage are regarded as legitimate and women in such a relationship are also entitled to financial support and even property. A Moslem man may make a temporary marriage with a Christian or a Jew, but a Moslem woman can only enter into this relationship with another Moslem and she must not be a virgin.

Some Iranians regard temporary marriage as simply prostitution under another name while others believe it is a legitimate solution to the problem faced by young Iranian men in that how else are they supposed to know what to do in the marital bed. Some Iranian feminists point out that as women are still expected to be virgins when they marry, this kind of marriage is of no benefit to young unmarried women. Pre-marital sex is not permitted under Islam but economic realities such as high unemployment and the cost of housing mean that the average age for men to get married has now reached 25 or older. It's a long time to wait for one's first sexual experience.

In Reza B's case a breakdown of his first marriage led to his temporary marriage and as a result he now maintains two households – one in Bazargan and one in Tehran. Without entering into the moral debate over temporary marriages I could certainly understand why he had appeared so happy and relaxed when he was with Ferengis. Meanwhile, the first wife subjects me to a barrage of questioning (via Reza) that is more like an inquisition than the usual well-meaning Iranian enthusiasm to find out about me.

'I think I can see why he has made the choice he has,' Reza mutters to me.

'I've just told her that you are now too tired to answer any more.'

This does not stop her and the two children spending most of the rest of the evening staring at me and from time to time giggling behind their hands.

But this unnerving scrutiny can't spoil the warm tumult of an Iranian extended family's welcome. A tablecloth is spread on the carpet to herald the arrival of the day's second gigantic meal:

soup, salads, yoghurt, saffron rice, bread and chicken cooked in a rich gravy are followed by a sweet rice pudding.

'That was a great party,' I say, as the plates are cleared away. Meeting so many new faces has been exhausting and I'm ready for bed.

'Oh, that wasn't the party,' Reza says. 'That was just dinner – we are going to another relative's house for the party.'

I retire to my room for a minute to regroup. Once again the strain of being surrounded by so many unfamiliar faces, of trying to speak and understand Farsi and being the centre of intense scrutiny is taking its toll.

Most of the family pile into the van with us for the short trip to one of Reza B's sisters' houses. The living room is a vast space with squabs and cushions around the walls and no furniture. I sit on the floor on the side of the room that by some unspoken rule seems to be the domain of the women. Various teenage girls and the smaller children, all of whom beam welcoming smiles at me, join us here, rarely taking their eyes off me. I know it's curiosity rather than rudeness, but I'm grateful when tea and large bowls of oranges and apples are placed on the floor and everyone's attention is temporarily diverted.

One of Reza B's young relatives emerges from a bedroom with an electronic keyboard. Azeri melodies strongly reminiscent of Turkish music fill the room as one of the younger girls gets gracefully to her feet to be joined by three of her uncles. They raise their arms, lightly hold hands and begin to dance in a slow circle around the room, adding dancers, including Reza and me, as they go.

I am surprised to see mixed dancing but Reza B explains this is the Turkish way. 'Remember we are Turkish Azeris first, then Iranians,' he says.

In the morning we eat a cholesterol-laden but delicious breakfast of fresh bread, cream and raspberry jam, fried eggs and tea in the boardroom of Reza B's cousin Seyfollah, whom we had met the night before. We need to keep our strength up – it's only about 10 hours since the last giant meal.

Seyfollah owns one of the country's largest transport firms. From the top floor of his office we can see the Iranian-Turkish border post about two minutes' drive away. He tells us that almost all the European imports to Iran that come by road do so through this border post. No wonder he has his own cook and fully fitted kitchen at the office.

'Well, we spend most of the day and into the night here,' Seyfollah says, 'so the office needs to be like our second home.'

Before we leave the Maku region we stop at the summerhouse of a local ruler known as Baghchichu. In the early 20th century he had been a prominent land-owner and his house was built to befit that status. Set in a garden of bare trees, pools and fountains (now locked in ice), its exterior is a curious mix of Persian, Ottoman and even Russian influences. This fusion of styles flows through the inside, too, with its mirrored halls, stained glass and European furniture.

It is the two large paintings on the dining-room ceiling that Reza especially wants me to see. The first panel features a Persian-style dinner where men, one in a turban and the others in caps, sit on the floor in front of a tablecloth spread with dishes including huge platters of rice which they are eating with their hands. Alongside this is a painting of a European dinner party where men and women sit at a table, carafes of wine clearly visible as are the bare white shoulders of the women.

'It's an interesting portrayal of cultural differences,' says Reza, as we crane our necks to look at them. 'We don't really know if the painter intended it to have any other message.'

Maku town itself is built at the bottom of a spectacularly rugged and steep-sided gorge. Reza points out the remains of houses perched on the cliff face and wedged under overhangs.

'When I first came here not that many years ago many Maku families still lived in those houses – most go back deep into the cliffs – only the very front of the houses are properly man-made. It was a true cave city but now people prefer the comfort of living in modern houses.'

We are now travelling east towards Iran's border with the Republic of Azerbaijan's Nakhichevan enclave. Separated from the rest of Azerbaijan by a wedge of Armenia, its status is still hotly disputed by the two nations and is a prime reason why relations between the two are hostile. Beyond some low hills the road drops down beside a reservoir created by damming a section of the Aras River that forms Iran's northern border with both these Caucasian nations.

We are all startled when my cellphone, which hasn't worked in Iran up until this moment, bursts into life.

'Welcome to Azeri Telecom' it tells me. In the midst of a patch of perfect reception I make a flurry of expensive international phone calls – not a single member of my family nor one friend is at home.

On both sides of the road are shops all but engulfed by bundles of reeds up to three metres long harvested from the Aras River banks.

It's the Azeri side of the border that appears to be more assiduously guarded than the Iranian side, presumably because the Azeris are far more preoccupied with their Armenian neighbours than by the proximity of the Iranians. Watchtowers are dotted at regular intervals along the reservoir and then beside the river as it begins to snake through a spectacular canyon on its journey to the Caspian Sea.

The Aras flows swiftly here and the deep reds and ochres of the rugged shattered rocks of the gorge are a stark contrast to its sky-blue waters. A railway line runs along the far bank and we spot two armed soldiers on patrol.

The gorge deepens until there is only just room for the railway on the Azeri side and the winding narrow road on the Iranian side. We turn up a side road and stop outside the lower walls of the Kalisa Darreh Sham (the church and monastery of St Stephen). Most of the stone buildings built on the mountainside date from the 14th century but it is believed that the first church on the site was founded by St Bartholomew in about AD 62. The monastery remained in use until the 1920s.

Normally a lonely but serene spot, today the car park resounds with the sound of Turkish pop music as half a dozen men cook kebabs over an open fire with their car stereo cranked up to the maximum volume.

Reza and I walk up to the monastery past a series of now abandoned terraced gardens and pools that once provided the monks with vegetables, fruit and fresh fish. The outer walls are heavily fortified with a series of rounded watchtowers which suggests that over the centuries not all visitors came in peace.

The church itself is closed for renovations, but we explore its exterior admiring the Armenian-style carved crosses and their twined borders carved on the walls. On one gable end is a carving of an eagle taking off with a lamb in its talons. Two pigeons had created a nest just under the lamb's dangling hooves. There is also a rather graphic depiction of a stoning. Rising from the centre of the cross-shaped church is a 12-sided tower, also adorned with carvings including distinctive Armenian-style angels with their two sets of wings framing their faces that watch over each angle of the tower.

A caretaker opens a door into the monks' quarters so we can visit one of the tiny cells with its small window, a niche for maybe a cross and wall cupboards in which to store bibles and other religious texts.

Down at the car park the party is in full swing. Movement among the surrounding trees suggests the men may have been dancing – an activity not officially approved of in public in Iran.

But there's a definite feeling in this corner of Iran that traditions, culture and even religious practices that pre-date the Islamic republic and in some cases even Islam itself are deeply embedded in its rocky landscape. At least to the casual observer it seems to be a harmonious co-existence.

The aroma of barbecuing kebabs has both Rezas thinking about lunch so it's time to head for Jolfa, a border crossing point into Nakhichevan. Jolfa was once home to most of Persia's Armenians in the days before the 17th century's Shah Abbas commanded they move to Isfahan. We are spending the night in Tabriz again and once Reza has consumed several of his favourite shish kebabs I explain that I do not want to return to the hotel with the hairy sheets.

'Please do not worry – this time we are going to stay at one of the best hotels in Tabriz. A friend of mine is the manager and he will give us a good rate.'

As the sun sets we stop at Tabriz's Elgoli Park. The centrepiece is a lake encircling a 19th-century palace. In summer the lake would be full of churning paddleboats but at the moment they are chained to the railings, leaving the waters unruffled and the atmosphere peaceful. We circumnavigate the lake past benches on which young couples snuggle as close as they dare. When we glance at them they appear to be engaged in erudite discussions but when they think the coast is clear they often simply sit gazing into each other's eyes. Romance is a tricky operation here when even the eye of the state can be upon you.

Reza's phone rings. It is Mojik, his brother, wanting to make sure we will be back in Tehran in two nights' time. The family is missing us both, Mojik says. I tell him honestly that I'm missing them, too – they have accepted me with generosity and love into their midst and when we reach Tehran it will not just be Reza who feels he's home again.

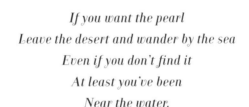

IN HOT WATER

Ardabil, the Caspian and Tehran

If you want the pearl
Leave the desert and wander by the sea
Even if you don't find it
At least you've been
Near the water.

Sanai (13th century Persian poet from Shiraz)

The traffic on the highway that snakes through the mountains between Tabriz and Ardabil has slowed to a crawl. We can see the line of trucks and cars in an unbroken line ahead of us, winding up the hill. Reza B pulls out of the inside lane to pass the truck in front of us. The manoeuvre won't get us very far, but at least we'll escape the truck's exhaust fumes.

There are several vehicles driving directly at us in the downhill lanes, but the truck driver we're passing and the car ahead let us back into line. Unfortunately, however, there is no room for the Peugeot that has also foolishly tried to pass at the same time. Faced with the oncoming traffic the driver simply pulls over directly into the side of our van, just beside my seat. There's a clash of metal and we lurch sideways, Reza B just managing to keep us out of the loose gravel and the drop into the valley below.

Reza B utters a word that has not been covered in my Farsi lessons thus far. Both cars pull over and Reza B jumps out, as does the Peugeot driver. They study the damage together – his car is unscathed but ours now sports a dent. A discussion begins and almost immediately a solidly built bearded man about two metres tall unfolds himself from the back seat of the Peugeot and strolls over to his friend, arms slightly akimbo. Reza now gets out – I'm guessing to try to balance the height and weight discrepancy, which then results in the emergence of the remaining three passengers from the Peugeot. I wonder if I should now emerge, but then remember that as a woman I probably won't count.

No one appears to be getting particular heated so when the Rezas return to the car I ask if the other driver will pay for the damage.

'Nothing more is going to happen,' says Reza. 'The other driver has no insurance.'

Over the brow of the pass we discover why the traffic has been banked up. A police car is parked at the side of the road with a policeman standing beside it utilising a hand-held radar. Once out of sight, normal reckless driving tendencies resume.

We are going to Ardabil to see a carpet. A replica, it's true, but it's a copy of possibly the most famous Persian carpet in the world. There are actually two original Ardabil carpets: the largest and most intact is in London's Victoria and Albert Museum (which Reza has visited several times as it is a magnet for Iranian tourists) and the other is in the Los Angeles County Museum of Art.

The Ardabil carpet in London was created more than 500 years ago and was one of two that graced the mausoleum of Sheikh Safi-od-Din, whose descendants founded Persia's 16th- and 17th-century Safavid dynasty.

In 1892 one of the two carpets surfaced for sale in London where it was seen by designer and writer William Morris who described it as a 'remarkable work of art' with a design of 'singular perfection'. He recommended the Victoria and Albert Museum buy it, which they did for two thousand pounds.

The Ardabil carpet is one of the largest hand-knotted carpets in the world (measuring more than 10 m by 5 m) and contains about 26 million knots. It is believed to have taken the legendary carpet-makers of Tabriz about four years to make.

In 2006 a replica of the Ardabil carpet was finished and now lies in the central hall of the mausoleum.

The gardens around the mausoleum are smothered in snow and inside a walled courtyard Reza and I indulge in a brief snowfight before decorously admiring the stunning decorative brick and tile work on the walls and towers that comprise the mausoleum complex. It is typical of Iran that such exquisite architectural jewels can be found, largely unheralded, in even the most out-of-the way places.

After paying homage at the Sheikh's tomb that is enclosed with intricately carved screens we step, shoeless, onto the carpet. The pile is soft and deep. Flowers and leaves swirl and entwine around us. At each end a vase has been woven into the design, but they are different sizes. This seems strange because usually Persian carpets, even those with such complex floral designs, are symmetrical.

'To understand why this was done, pretend you are sitting on the carpet at this end,' Reza says, pointing to the smaller vase.

'If you are sitting there and looking down the carpet the vases will now seem to be the same size. It is a little like the way the minarets on the Taj Mahal actually lean outwards a little so that from a distance they look perfectly straight – of course it was a Persian who designed that, too.'

In the foyer of the mausoleum Reza stops to talk to a grizzled old man with one arm who sweeps the steps while we put on our shoes. Reza struggles with one of his boots and the elderly cleaner crouches down to help, even though he has only one hand.

Reza B is keen to be on the road again because while Sara'eyn, our next destination, has no historical or cultural significance it is a year-round attraction for Iranians because of its alpine hot water. We are off to the Persian version of a European spa resort.

Sara'eyn sits on the lower flanks of Mt Sabalan. At 4811 metres it is the third-highest mountain in Iran and an inactive volcano. But there is still enough volcanic action underground to produce hot springs – this region is particularly prone to earthquakes; the last one of significant size was in 1997 when 500 people died and about 50,000 people lost their homes.

The Rezas had already discussed the possibility that the 'evil eye' was on us after our accident and their suspicions seem to be confirmed when, on the outskirts of Sara'eyn, a policeman waves us over and fines Reza B for speeding.

A heated discussion follows, which Reza translates.

'Reza is saying that last time he was here a few weeks ago the speed limit along this part of the road was higher and that there should be time for people to get used to the new limit. Of course the policeman is not agreeing with that.'

We pay the fine for him but even so Reza B is still muttering as we drive into town. It is not the money, he says, but the principle.

A building boom is under way. Most of the buildings under construction are hotels and rental apartments; the latter are especially popular with holidaying Iranians as they offer plenty of room for extended family gatherings and a kitchen to ensure a continuous supply of tea and home-cooked meals.

It's a rare quiet day in Sara'eyn making Reza confident he'll be able to strike a good deal at one of the near-empty hotels. However this proves more difficult than he expects at our first choice – even though the lobby is in semi-darkness and the receptionist is asleep, which suggests the place isn't inundated with guests.

'I've pointed out to him that three guests are better than none but I'm wondering if he'd rather sleep and not have us bother him,' Reza explains. He eventually prevails, the man gathering up two sets of room keys with a heavy sigh.

On our way to the public pools we buy a bathing suit for me. I have visions of ladies' bathing suits being sold behind closed doors in women-only enclaves. I could not have been more wrong.

The street between our hotel and the baths is lined with shops selling towels, inflatable toys and bathing suits for both sexes. We fight our way past a bobbing selection of blow-up tigers, Mickey Mouses and donkeys to reach the interior of the shop that Reza judges to have the best selection.

My appearance brings all other retail activity inside (and in the shops on either side) to a complete halt. Under the interested gaze of about a dozen onlookers I search the racks for a suitable bathing suit, my face red with embarrassment. There's no changing room. It's bad enough back home buying a bathing suit even when one can try it on first – to buy without a test drive is terrifying.

I whip along the rows of capacious matronly togs splashed with giant flowers and pull out a pale blue suit complete with short wraparound skirt and a bathing hat.

'What is the largest size you have in this costume?' Reza asks the male shop owner loudly in Farsi.

'Thank you very much,' I hiss.

'Well, don't you think it looks a little small?' he asks.

'I don't care – I just want to get out of here ... everyone's looking.'

The shopkeeper rustles around in a carton of bathing suits still in their cellophane bags. He pulls out one stamped 'L'. All of us (even the inflatable animals seem to have swung round to stare) decide I now have the perfect bathing suit. It costs the equivalent of $US2.50.

I am still traumatised when Reza turns into the bathing complex and stops outside a doorway covered with a long black tarpaulin.

'This is the ladies' entrance because of course the baths are completely segregated. I will see you in maybe one hour?' He starts to walk away.

'Hang on,' I squeak. 'What do I do when I get inside?'

'Um, well I really don't know what happens on your side,' Reza says patiently, 'I've not been into the ladies' section.'

I concede it was a stupid question.

'There will be somewhere to leave your shoes and to pay and then I guess there will be a changing area. I am sure you will be OK.'

I push through the tarpaulin and into a cavernous room to one side of which is a counter surrounded by a gaggle of young girls in bathing suits. Silence falls as I walk towards them. I take out my wallet and ask, in Farsi, 'Where?'

I suspect the conversation that followed between those girls went something like, 'Gosh, I think she's here to swim – she doesn't know what to do. Someone needs to help her. Sara, you help.'

'No, you, Fatima, my English is not good enough.'

After several girls are pushed forward, then retreat giggling, a solidly built teenager edges past them determinedly.

'Shoes here,' she says, pointing at the shoe attendants. 'Now, money.'

I hand over my shoes, pay my money and then my guide, who is 17, and her 11-year-old cousin lead me to the changing room. They choose a locker for me and then stand back and wait.

I am not going to change into a new bathing suit for the first time in front of an audience. Glancing around desperately, I notice three little changing booths and make a dash for one of them.

The bathing suit is skin-tight and the material thin. I have a horrible feeling it is going to prove see-through when wet. Thank God for segregated bathing.

When I emerge my two friends are waiting. They lead me past a steam room full of baths inhabited mostly by older women through to the main pool. Groups of women stand neck deep chatting while youngsters splash around them in water the colour of lager.

I think I've managed an unobtrusive entrance, but once I'm halfway across the pool at a slow breaststroke, I look round to discover at least 10 people swimming alongside me. When I reach the far wall the questions begin.

After 30 minutes of swimming interspersed with faltering conversations in Farsi and English it's time to retreat. To my dismay the changing booths are occupied. I peel off the togs as discreetly as I can and am reaching for my top when I realise the hum of conversation around me has stopped.

Everyone is looking at me. My pool guide explains:

'We are sorry – but we were just saying you have a very beautiful bra.'

Outside, darkness is falling and the slushy snow is starting to refreeze. Reza appears from the men's side.

'That was very relaxing wasn't it?'

We warm up with a local speciality – yoghurt soup made with herbs and beans. It's perfect comfort food after my swim into the unknown.

The next morning we leave Sara'eyn as the light is just starting to slip down the snowy cone of Mt Sabalan. Reza B shields his eyes against the sun as we head due east towards the Caspian Sea.

The road winds through one of the few forests I have seen on our journey. Although most of the trees are deciduous I enjoy even their leafless presence. I can understand why it is one of Reza's favourite roads in spring and autumn. Once this would have been a favoured habitat of the extinct Caspian tiger, the last known sighting of which was in 1947 in the eastern Caspian. This animal was the third-largest sub-species and was the favoured tiger for use in Roman arenas.

Occasionally, hopes are still raised by sightings across its former range from the Caucasus through Iran, Central Asia and into Mongolia, but realistically the chance of meeting this big cat padding through the oak and maple forests of northern Iran are tragically remote. However, Reza tells me wolves, bears and panthers can still be found in the Caspian's forests.

We emerge from the tiger-less hills at Astara right on the border with Azerbaijan and beside the sea.

The air is markedly milder here and as we follow the Caspian towards Rasht, rice fields and tea plantations appear. Iranians are proud of their locally produced rice and tea, although their prodigious consumption of both means they have to import a significant amount of each as well.

Tehranis love the Caspian coast for its mild climate, the sea itself and the holiday atmosphere. But it seems to me that this narrow strip of balmy shore is in danger of being loved to death. Ribbon development stretches almost unbroken along the coastal highway, with hotels, apartments and villas springing apparently unfettered by any kind of planning regulations. And if there is a Caspian waste authority it's clearly not doing its job – nowhere else in Iran is there so much rubbish piled up at the roadside.

Despite these problems the Caspian still holds some fascination for me. I first heard its name while reading C S Lewis's Narnia series – could anything be more exotic for a young reader (albeit one already showing signs of an obsession with geography) than a character called Prince Caspian?

But even today the allure lives on. In Bandar-e Anzali, Reza and I find a boatman to take us out through the Anzali lagoon – one of the largest freshwater lagoons in the world that manages more or less to co-exist with Iran's largest Caspian Sea port nearby.

We zip out through a wide channel past a number of the most unprepossessing waterside shacks into a world of waving reeds and tiny islands. Herons and cormorants perch on logs, peering intently into the water and turtles sunbathe on semi-submerged rocks and hummocks of grass and here and there are a few fishing huts on stilts. Like fishing huts the world over they have evolved over time to become a home-away-from-home; some sport curtains and potted plants.

At water level it's impossible to see anything above the reeds and when the waterway we're on suddenly branches four different ways I have no idea which way I'd have chosen to go back to the dock. But the boatman turns the tiller without hesitation and suddenly we burst out into the Anzali port.

Rusting fishing boats bob gently in our wake – Reza thinks some may once have fished for the Caspian Sea's most valuable inhabitant – the beluga sturgeon, which can grow up to 15 feet long and weigh up to 2000 lb. Of the three sturgeon species in the Caspian it is the black beluga's caviar that is the most sought after – it can command up to $US100 an ounce. But over the last 20 years, sturgeon populations in the Caspian have plunged by 90 per cent and the beluga is perilously close to extinction; it doesn't help that in order to extract its eggs you have to kill a sturgeon. The species is affected by over-fishing because beluga can live up to about 100 years and don't reach breeding age until they are 15. Even then they reproduce only every three or four years.

Pollution, especially from the countries of the former USSR, poaching and over-fishing have all fuelled the decline.

Iran, used to being branded the black sheep of the region in so many other ways, has in the case of the sturgeon been able to bask in the recognition of being the one nation of those bordering the Caspian Sea to do the most to halt the sturgeon's decline through voluntarily reducing its sturgeon quota and appearing be more dedicated and successful in reducing poaching.

But while the relatively new nations of Kazakhstan, Turk-menistan and Azerbaijan along with Russia seem to have more pressing issues to deal with, poaching and over-fishing in their part of the Caspian Sea is still a major threat to the survival of this giant fish.

We leave the fishing fleet in our wake and tear across the main harbour. The ships tied up at the wharves are respectably large ocean-going vessels, graphic evidence of the size of the Caspian Sea which is in fact the world's largest inland body of water containing more than 40 per cent of the world's lake water.

It's windy out here and my headscarf whips off my head and wraps itself around Reza's face. I scramble to retrieve it, worried the boatman will be glaring disapprovingly. But when I turn to look at him he's grinning and indicates that I shouldn't worry.

He guns the engine a bit harder and we shoot out through the arms of the port breakwaters into open sea.

'If we kept going,' I shout at Reza above the engine noise, 'we could travel to four other countries.'

It's an irresistible thought for me.

'We could go north to Russia, visit Astrakhan and boat up the Volga River.'

'Or we could go to Baku in Azerbaijan and see the oil rigs,' adds Reza, getting into the swing of things.

The fact that our little blue boat would struggle to cross the world's largest lake and would probably end up on the sea floor doesn't really enter into our dreaming. That's the trouble when travel addicts start scheming.

Back on dry land we continue driving east towards Ramsar, which despite the best efforts of developers still retains some of its old seaside-resort charm. We eat lunch in the vast empty dining room of the new wing of the Ramsar Grand Hotel perched on red velvet balloon-back chairs, on a red carpet and surrounded by gilded walls and ceiling.

It's hardly cosy but gives us the perfect excuse to walk next door into the old hotel to see the teahouse with which I was very taken when I was here years ago. It is not in the slightest sense traditional; it's actually converted from what used to be the hotel's basement disco. The interior decoration can only be described as Persian boudoir meets Scottish baronial.

Back in pre-revolutionary Iran the hotel used to be a casino. Upstairs grand salons with tall windows look down on Ramsar and along a palm-lined promenade to the sea. The last Shah of Iran, Mohammad Reza Pahlavi and his wife Farah used to come here and Reza shows me the room they used that features two cane chairs with fan-shaped backs. Placed in a bow window, they have attracted the attention of a group of tourists a couple of whom are sitting in them – I'm not sure if is by accident or design that the flimsy cane seems a parody of the magnificent peacock throne that once symbolised Iranian royalty.

Downstairs in the teahouse it's just the two of us and a bored waiter. Set among the dark-stained pillars are banquettes and chairs covered with red and green Scottish tartan. The tartan has also been used to cover floor squabs and tables in a low-ceilinged mezzanine with numerous shadowy niches. Through the gloom I make out a young couple huddled together in the far corner.

A touch of the Middle East has been added to the mix in the form of an alcove with a beaded curtain. We sit in here and order saffron ice cream and tea. Thirty years ago it would have been full of girls in mini-skirts and guys with long hair and tight jeans.

Like the current generation of Iranians, the Shah too enjoyed retreating to the Caspian to escape the dry heat of Tehran's summers and its snowy winters. His summer palace is a short walk away from the hotel, set in gardens filled with palms, flowering sub-tropical plants, citrus trees and ponds.

The palace is now known as the Caspian Museum and with paper bootees on our feet to protect the parquet floors we tour it with the compulsory guide whose delivery is set on fast forward. I'm surprised, given the size of the Shah's other properties in Tehran and his family's predilection for excess, how compact the palace is. It's a delicate light-filled one-storey pavilion that's still full of the family's carpets, furniture, paintings and chandeliers. It seems more like a royal holiday cottage than a sumptuous palace.

We say goodbye to the Caspian at the end of the promenade where teahouses, restaurants and souvenir shops crowd the beachfront. One shop is a little different from the rest in that the window is crammed with taxidermy – if stuffed animals could ever be described as fanciful these certainly fit the bill: ducklings and chickens in nests, rabbits in plus fours, lambs captured in mid-gambol and even what looks like stuffed sturgeon on the walls. Busy among the glassy eyes, furs and feathers is the taxidermist himself who is occupied pushing a polystyrene mould up the inside of a duck carcass. He tells us ducklings and chickens are especially popular as springtime souvenirs for the local tourists.

Outside the weather has changed and waves, whipped up by a strong wind, are crashing onto the gravel. Lines of metal posts stretch out into the sea and Reza tells me they indicate the women's bathing areas. In summer canvas or plastic is strung up along the poles so women can swim behind them unseen.

Iran's highest mountain range, the Alborz, lies between us and Tehran. There are four passes through the mountains and we are going to take the Chalus route. This highway, which zigzags up the northern faces of the mountain in a dizzying series of hairpin bends, took 20 years to build and is regarded by Iranians as an engineering marvel.

The Caspian's mild early spring is soon replaced by the firm grip of winter as snow appears, first on the precipitous mountain slopes on all sides and then in metre-high piles on each side of the road. We stop briefly at a teahouse built above a gorge, its narrow veranda hanging over a gully of jagged rocks, and sadly, a great deal of rubbish. The snows above us are blushing with sunset colours, but there is no time to linger. It's extremely cold and Reza B wants to get over the summit before darkness falls.

Once the southern slopes of the Alborz were home to bandits who used to raid the silk routes that skirted the mountains. Today, however, Tehran is creeping up into what was remote mountain terrain. It feels as if we are in the outer suburbs of the city almost as soon as we are over the top of the pass.

We're all a bit subdued. While we are pleased to be going home, at the same time these are the last few hours of our road trip. When we go to Isfahan and Kashan in a few days' time it will be by bus. The two Rezas calculate how far we have travelled since we left Tehran three weeks earlier and come up with more than 8000 kilometres.

We've stood on the shores of the Persian Gulf and the Caspian Sea, gazed at mountains on the borders of Afghanistan, Iraq, Turkey, Azerbaijan and Armenia, suffered one minor dent, been fined for speeding, but luckily have not had a single flat tyre or breakdown. Most importantly, we've become family. We talk about future trips to explore the few areas of Iran that we haven't visited, but I think we know in our hearts that this is unlikely.

Reza B battles through the Iranian evening traffic towards

central Tehran and Reza's family apartment. On our arrival he rings the bell and Mojik appears. The first thing he does is hug Reza, then, after he shakes my hand he hesitates briefly before hugging me, too.

We unpack the van in silence: bags, piles of coats, our travelling library, the mosque teapot and the numerous bags of fruit and nuts that litter the floor. Reza B and Reza have already *taroffed* at great length over who should take the food and apparently it is staying with us.

Upstairs Reza's mother Sedighe and his sister Nasik are waiting for us. We're enveloped in more hugs as the small family room is swamped with all the gear. I'm perilously close to crying – a result of the warm welcome home and having to say goodbye to Reza B. He's keen to get home, too, so leaves quickly – partly I suspect because none of us wants to prolong the goodbyes. I tell him it might be un-Islamic, but I'm going to hug him anyway. You're like my daughter, he tells me. I can't imagine driving anywhere in Iran without him.

Reza and I add to the chaos by delving among the assorted bags to find the family's presents: nuts soaked in honey from Sara'eyn for Mojik, a pink headscarf from the Persian Gulf for Nasik and saffron and perfume from Mashhad for Sedighe.

The family wants to know everything – we've visited parts of Iran they've never seen. Even though it's late we dig out maps, put the photos on the laptop and relive the journey.

The next day is the first for weeks that we haven't been on the move. I find it an effort even to get from bed to couch, couch to chair. Reza appears to be feeling the same. When I stagger past the kitchen I see him sitting at the table nursing a cup of tea and staring vacantly into space.

It's back to normal the day after, though, as Reza wants to take me on a typical Tehrani day out via metro and shared taxi. The plan is to avoid Tehran's tourist haunts, which are mostly museums, and our starting point is the main bazaar. As we take the efficient Tehran metro into the south of the city I ask Reza why he doesn't bring tourists here.

'You'll see when we get there. In fact I need to tell you now to be very careful once we get inside.'

Immediately I conjure up images of pickpockets, muggers or maybe even rabid fundamentalists on the lookout for escaping blonde hair. But as we pass under the arched entrance into the main bazaar thoroughfare I realise that it's not crime nor religious fanatics that are potentially hazardous. It's the delivery men. Few of the alleyways are open to motorised vehicles (in some cases they are not even wide enough to take them) so most of the goods in this enormous complex are moved from warehouses and trucks to shops on wooden trolleys similar to those found on railway platforms and pushed by men in blue coats. These guys don't stop for anyone, which is understandable because if they were to give way to pedestrians they'd never get anywhere.

A shout from behind is the only warning you get and if you don't jump sideways fast there's a good chance of a crack on the back of the leg at best, or being run over at worst. Reza, who shops here regularly, appears to have a sixth sense about them and keeps shouting 'trolley' as he nudges me (with the minimum of body contact) into doorways. Now I understand why he doesn't bring tourists here; the injury toll could be horrendous.

The Tehran bazaar, perhaps more than any other in Iran, is another example of Iran's 'two wings'. On the surface the bazaar is about buying and selling, but the *bazaaris* themselves are also vital to Iran's wider economy and politics. It's estimated that business done in this bazaar accounts for a third of Iran's entire retail trade, which of course gives the *bazaaris* considerable economic clout. Traditionally they tend to take a politically and religiously conservative stand, which in times of conservative governments gives them particular influence.

Reza turns off one of the main arteries into a side street mercifully free of the shouts of the deliverymen and their rumbling trolleys. We're standing in a caravanserai that still has a pool and fountain in the centre. It's one of many in the bazaar – and evidence that even here in the midst of a modern city of about 14 million people there are still reminders of the importance of the silk route.

'More properly these are serais rather than caravanserais as they functioned more as warehouses for the caravans rather than inns,' Reza explains. 'Downstairs were the warehouses and upstairs the offices. What is fascinating is that these traditional uses still continue today.'

This particular serai is stacked with bolts of fabric – lurid floral velvets, lacy net and plush upholstery fabric. It's quiet, too, except for a gentle clicking sound, which emanates from a tea wholesaler's shopfront where we find an elderly man calculating on an abacus. He tells Reza he finds it as quick and accurate as any electronic calculator.

While we're here Reza wants to visit a friend who has a clothes shop in the depths of the bazaar and we set off to find him, passing dozens of stationery shops on our way. A narrow set of stairs leads us up several storeys, the staircase getting narrower and more rickety until we emerge in a mini-bazaar full of men's and boys' clothing.

Najaf, Reza's friend, is drinking tea in front of his shop, which is piled high with shirts and jackets. He finds a couple of stools for us to sit on and sends a passing minion to bring more tea. We settle in for a chat during which he tells Reza he has just come back from a buying trip to China.

Najaf and Reza met at university where Najaf studied English literature. His favourite writers are W B Yeats and T S Eliot and while he is telling us this suddenly there's a sound of puffing and muttering from the stairs and a man shoots out of the stairwell clutching an enormous carton of clothes slightly wider than the stairs, another bulging cloth bundled tied on to his back. Najaf doesn't bat an eyelid – clearly this is how all the stock is moved around this rabbit warren.

After leaving the bazaar Reza decides that although he's declared this a museum-free day he can't resist taking me into the Golestan Palace as it's not too far away.

'I can't manage a whole day without one cultural visit,' he tells me.

Most of the palace complex dates from the time of the 19th-century Qajar rulers, although it was also the coronation place of the last shah, Mohammand Reza Pahlavi and of his father, Reza Khan. It's a rare outpost of historical architecture in a city that is mostly a chaotic concrete jungle.

Seven buildings from various eras, including one with lofty wind towers, open off a central garden of fountains, pools and tall trees. Normally it would be a tranquil place, but today it's overflowing with school children from tiny new entrants who walk hand-in-hand in crocodile lines to more unruly older groups of giggling teenage girls and carefully segregated boys. Both parties are still managing to size each other up, however.

As the only foreigner I provide something of a diversion, but after being almost buried in successive crushes of enthusiastic students I can't handle any more and tell Reza we need to leave. There's a desperate thirst, especially among young Iranians, for contact with outsiders. It's not just a matter of curiosity but a burning desire to be able to communicate to visitors that they and their country are not as the Western media often portray them.

We use a series of shared taxis to reach another favourite place for Tehranis – Laleh Park. Although this involves changing cars three times, it does mean that in the space of about 15 minutes I get to meet more than a dozen locals at close quarters.

Years earlier Laleh Park had been my first real taste of Tehran and although I didn't really expect to encounter any revolutionary violence or black-clad fist-shaking demonstrators, I was still a little nervous when walking into it that first time. Instead I was rather taken aback to discover people seemed more interested in playing badminton and chess; there were even a few discreetly canoodling under the trees. There was a military presence though – in fact I lost count of the number of soldiers walking around, albeit eating giant cream freezes.

Even today in the depths of winter the park is well used – young men are playing a game of soccer on a miniature pitch, elderly men sit huddled over their games of backgammon and children clutching balloons tear around the maze of paths. We find a seat beside a large pond with a fountain and listen to classical Iranian songs being broadcast through loudspeakers.

Tehranis might be used to having the spectacular Alborz Range towering above them, but they do not take their mountains for granted. Walking, skiing, even climbing Mt Damavand, Iran's highest mountain and an active volcano, are favourite weekend activities. Reza has climbed 5671-metre Damavand three times so when he suggests on our last day in Tehran that we go to the mountains with his sister Nasik I'm a little worried.

Fortunately Reza and Nasik have a much gentler outing in mind – we are going to walk one of the trails at Darband, an alpine village which, thanks to Tehran's sprawl, has now been absorbed into the city.

Nasik drives us, fast and competently through north Tehran with its multi-million-dollar luxury apartments and tree-lined boulevards. These trees are planted in trenches that separate the footpaths from the road and in some places water straight from the mountains swirls fast and deep along them. Once such urban *qanats* (canals) were commonplace, providing residents and trees alike with vital fresh water.

We leave the car beneath a plane tree, a few bedraggled leaves still fluttering on its branches. Nasik disappears into a small bookshop, scans the shelves and exclaims with satisfaction on finding a Persian-English publication of her favourite contemporary poet Sohrab Sepehri. She hands it to me, saying 'This is a present for you'.

Further up the valley the mountains close in and frozen snow covers the tarmacked path which winds up through a haphazard conglomeration of teahouses and restaurants that are built almost on top of one another, architectural styles and paint colours clashing cheerfully. In summer the outside terraces would be full of people. Today, though, only a handful are even open.

We climb to the chairlift ticket office. There's a skifield further up, but today it is mostly walkers who are on the slopes – it's considered a good morning work-out to climb nearby 3957-metre

Mt Tochal (even the lowest parts of Tehran are 1200 metres above sea level so climbers have a head start). They stride past, some carrying ice axes and ropes.

The chairlift glides over a rugged tumble of scree and jagged ridges and as we get to the top, snow starts to fall and the peaks vanish in the flurry. Nasik and I want to walk further up the mountain, but Reza is worried we might get stranded – he lures us down with talk of finding a teahouse.

We choose one that is situated higher than the rest with views between snowfalls of the mountain peaks and comprising a series of small terraces and gazebos linked by icy, slippery steps with a waterfall cascading through the centre. It must be a nightmare being a waiter here.

Its terrace is protected from the elements by plastic sheeting and a roaring gas burner in the doorway is managing to keep the space warm despite all the gaps in the plastic.

We climb onto a *takt* and Nasik orders tea and *qalyan* with her favourite tobacco mix of orange and mint. Outside the snow is falling softly. I remember we have the new poetry book with us and we take turns to read Sepehri's poems, which until this moment I'd never heard before but I'm now captivated as Reza and Nasik recite large chunks by heart.

'We should fold our umbrellas and walk out into the rain, we should take with us all our ideas and memories into the rain,' reads Nastaran.

Brother and sister end the stanza together: 'Life is a series of successive drenchings, Life is taking a dip in the basin of this Moment.'

We prolong our time here by ordering lunch: kebabs, rice and salad. The afternoon passes Tehrani style with conversation, poetry, the gurgle of the *qalyan* and the constant replenishment of our pot of tea. Before we leave Nasik writes in my book: 'Wherever you are remember me'.

That night Reza takes me out to see one of the longest stretches of bookshops in the world. Enqelab Avenue is near Tehran University, Iran's largest and oldest tertiary institution with about 32,000 students. It's dark and near freezing, but the street is brightly lit and the shops full, mostly of students. We find a whole arcade devoted to books in other languages. The best of the English shops is so full there's hardly any space to walk among the towers of books: English classics, self-help books and books devoted to levels of English grammar that I suspect most native speakers would struggle to comprehend.

'Before we go home I want to take you to a café where I think you will find it hard to believe we are in Tehran', says Reza leading me to a death-defying road crossing. Negotiating Tehran's main roads is probably the most risky activity a tourist can attempt in this country. Forget tales of religious police or fundamentalists – if anyone's going to get you in Iran, it's the drivers; not of course that motorists set out to run down pedestrians – it's just that responsibility is very firmly on those on foot to avoid being hit.

Once across the road Reza ushers me into a crowded room heavy with cigarette smoke where a couple sits, heads bent together, hands entwined among the coffee cups. Beside them, three young women are smoking, their sleek black boots emerging below the cuffs of their tight blue jeans. A man with a Father Christmas beard plays the piano accordion.

We are inside Café Godot complete with a photograph of Samuel Beckett on the wall and the only hint that we are in the heart of the Islamic Republic of Iran is that every female present is wearing a headscarf. However, the compulsory decree of Iran's ruling clerics that women should cover their hair is interpreted here in a variety of ways in that headscarves are artfully positioned to allow more than a hint of glossy black hair or billows of streaked, permed hair to peek out. Some head coverings are more the width of a headband than a headscarf, while others are pushed back so far as to defy gravity.

The fascination and curiosity Western women display about the compulsory wearing of *hijab* irritates many Iranian women because while there is a proportion who would choose to wear it – even it wasn't required – there are also thousands of women and girls who do so because they must if they are to get on with their lives.

'Look,' says one woman firmly. '*Hijab* is nothing – it is a minor battle for us. There are much bigger issues in Iran today such as true equality for women. As you say in your culture, "get over it".'

I think of her comments as we leave the café that is now so full it's standing room only. Today more than 60 per cent of Iran's university students are women and 70 per cent of the population are under 30 years old. Clearly, young, educated Iranian women will be a force to be reckoned with in the future.

A NIGHTINGALE SINGS
Kashan and Isfahan

A moment of happiness,
You and I sitting on the verandah
Apparently two, but one in soul, you and I
We feel the flowing water of life here
You and I, with the garden's beauty
And the birds singing.

Jelalludin Rumi

We've only just left the Tehran bus terminal and already there's been a rebellion on our luxury bus (complete with video television, plus a drink and snack service) to Kashan. In the hope that last-minute passengers would arrive, we end up leaving late and because the bus is not quite full, the driver's assistant hangs out the door, touting for business at every city intersection.

The journey is scheduled to take us four hours, which for most of us on board is long enough. If we keep stopping to plead with passers-by to come with us it's going to take a lot longer. Reza sighs and catches the eye of the man across the aisle from our seats. He, too, is annoyed.

As we're only one row from the driver Reza leans forward to tell the driver it's time to get moving. The driver is not impressed, but when everyone else at the front of the bus joins the protest he shrugs, tells the assistant to shut the door, and finally cranks up the speed.

With darkness falling and the bus video inactive (which for me is no bad thing) we have time for an intensive Farsi lesson: compound verbs and comparative adjectives – hardly riveting for the rest of the passengers but Reza and I notice that the man in front of us seems to be listening. Despite the fact he's wearing a Hawaiian shirt and a US baseball cap, Reza is sure he's Iranian.

Suddenly he turns around and speaking in English, albeit with an American accent, tells Reza that along with all the grammar he should teach me some practical stuff, such as 'What the hell is this?'

We both stare at him, surprised.

'You *are* Iranian then,' Reza says, betraying our curiosity. Hossein (not his real name) fills us in on his background including that while he was born in Isfahan, where he is going this evening to visit his parents, he completed most of his high schooling in the States and has worked in Australia.

'Where do you live now, Hawaii?' asks Reza, fishing shamelessly.

'I live part of the year in Ko Samui in Thailand,' Hossein replies. 'I'm in business – it's easy to make money in Iran but hard to spend it.' Now that he's begun talking he's impossible to stop. Reza tries to restart our lesson but Hossein keep interrupting, asking about our travels and why we are going to Isfahan, especially when Reza travels there with tourists many times a year and even I have already been three times. Reza explains we want to spend more time in its beautiful mosques.

'What's that special about the mosques?' Hossein asks.

Reza looks stunned.

'I hate religion – that's why I can only spend a few days here each year because I can't stand the restrictions. Once you've lived outside Iran it's almost impossible to live here again. I've got two daughters living in Spain – they have so much freedom there.'

'But even if you do not like religion surely you appreciate the beauty of our architecture and our poetry,' Reza replies.

'In Ko Samui I have coconut palms on the beach and topless girls in the bars and I love stopping in Dubai,' Hossein answers.

Picking up our Persian language book in an attempt to get back to our lesson Reza asks me to say, 'I like Shiraz but I love Isfahan the best.'

Reza dislikes Dubai intensely because of its lack of history and emphasis on wealth.

'This man has no idea about Iran's culture and history,' he whispers to me, then leaning forward he engages Hossein once more.

'You know, Hossein, not all Moslems have fundamental views,' he says. 'I will draw you a diagram to explain.'

Reza draws what looks like the floor plan of a house with a central room that has many doors. He then explains his theory that some people only reach the outer rooms of their spiritual growth because they are at their limits of understanding; then there are people who go further into the house but who require rules and regulations to feel secure while those who reach the middle are the true seekers of spirituality. The key, explains Reza, is understanding that there are many doors to this room and people arrive there by different routes.

'That's fine,' says Hossein as he points out of the bus window, 'but try telling that to the men over there ...' Is it predestined or simply chance that we are having this discussion while driving past the road leading to Qom? The seat of religious power and learning in Iran, Qom is where Ayatollah Khomeini, the Iranian the West loved to hate, lived and taught before his exile in the years leading up to the Islamic revolution. It is the most conservative place in Iran and unsurprisingly I've never been there and Reza never seems keen to take me.

'There's nothing there, really, apart from the shrine,' he's told me more than once.

I wonder if he is perhaps uncomfortable about letting me see the extent of Qom's religious conservatism.

When our bus pulls in at a roadside café, Reza buys drinks and a box of *sohan*, Qom's other claim to fame. A crunchy biscuit full of pistachios and butter – so much butter it leaves one's fingers shiny – it is utterly irresistible but then our enjoyment is spoiled when Hossein approaches.

'Oh, no,' Reza says. 'I wish he'd leave us alone.'

Hossein, oblivious to his unsettling effect, sits down beside us and Reza, his feelings of hospitality overcoming his reservations, offers him the box of *sohan*.

'Oh, god, I never eat that. Do you know how much cholesterol there is in it? I've already had liposuction once and I don't want to have it done again.'

Reza almost chokes on his biscuit.

Hossein looks at our apple-flavoured non-alcoholic beer drinks.

'Apple beer – in a country where the poetry is full of references to wine. It sums it up, really.' He heads for the counter to buy tea.

'Did you hear what he said? He's had liposuction!' Reza shakes his head.

In Kashan we say goodbye to Hossein. He and Reza thank each other for a stimulating discussion.

Kashan or, more accurately, Fin – a village that has almost been absorbed into the larger town's sprawl – is the site of one of Iran's most famous gardens, Bagh-e Tarikhi-ye Fin.

It's our intention to visit this garden as well as the restored houses of Kashan, which for me epitomise more than perhaps any other place in Iran, other than Isfahan, the duality of Iran and the Persian soul.

We stay in a hotel a short walk from the garden. Reza loathes this particular hotel, but perseveres with it because of its location. Sandwiched between the beauty of Fin and the glories of Kashan's traditional houses, one could realistically expect it to somehow reflect its surroundings. Instead it remains resolutely ordinary. It also has the most unreliable lift in all of Iran and consistently bad breakfasts.

But at least it helps highlight the allure of the Persian garden. For centuries Persians retreated to their gardens inside their high walls to escape the arid barrenness of the desert. Today they are also a haven from concrete mediocrity.

Our walk to the garden follows the channel of one of the spring-fed streams that bring life to Fin. The water gurgles and tumbles beside the road and is diverted through several teahouses, flowing over man-made waterfalls and around, even under, *takts* and tables making it suitable for only the most nimble of waiters. In the garden of one teahouse we spot a gleaming copper still. There's an unmistakable whiff of roses in the air and Reza tells me that this particular teahouse also makes rose water and rose oil.

The Kashan area is famous not only for its houses and garden but for its intensely fragrant roses. The last time I was here the stallholders outside the garden entrance had on display huge plastic bags of bright pink rose petals and the perfume was intoxicating. I watched, intrigued, as men, including Reza and our driver at the time, bought bags of the petals.

'We stir them into our yoghurt,' Reza explained. Just what you would expect deep in the Axis of Evil.

It is too early this year for any roses to be on sale, but the stalls are selling bottles of oils and flagons of rose and mint water.

Fin's garden was created for Shah Abbas the Great, who died in 1629 aged just 42, and was the most successful ruler of the Safavid dynasty as well as one of the greatest of all Persia's kings. Under his command Isfahan became one of the world's most beautiful cities.

All the defining elements of the classic Persian garden lie within Fin's high walls; design features that, partly thanks to the transfer of ideas that took place along the silk roads and in the caravanserais of Persia, were also embraced by the great gardeners of Europe and the Moghul emperors of India.

The walls, in which a stately arched gateway is set, prevent anyone outside from getting even a hint of what lies within other than the gently waving tops of lofty cypress trees. Even from the gateway there is no direct view of the garden; one must pass through a corridor to the left or the right. Not only does this heighten a sense of intrigue, but in days gone by it ensured that if the gate was open, onlookers could not glimpse any unveiled ladies within.

Water is an essential element of a Persian garden and Fin has it in sparkling abundance. Springs fed from the distant hills continue to flow, even in the baking summers of the Iranian plateau.

Water channels, lined with turquoise tiles that accentuate the cooling presence of the water and heighten the contrast with the desert beyond the walls, divide the main garden into four. Aligned down the centre of each channel is a series of bubbling fountains. There are no mechanical pumps; the fountains and water flow are entirely gravity fed.

Over the years nearly 600 cypress trees have been planted in this garden, along with innumerable roses and citrus trees. At its heart is a beautiful arched pavilion, in the centre of which is a deep pool. Swirling spirals of water well up from the springs and shafts of sunlight strike the surface, making the ceiling of the pavilion swim and flicker with reflections.

Those visitors expecting a garden packed with blazing bedding plants and perennial borders tend to be disappointed with Fin. But to the Persian mind, a garden is a piece of paradise created on earth – even the word paradise comes from the ancient Persian word *pairideeza* or *paradis*, meaning a walled garden.

Although paradise is perhaps in the mind of the beholder, the necessities for a Persian paradise on earth comprise a lush haven from the desert where water is abundant and privacy and peace may be found. A garden should also appeal to all the senses. Nothing fills that role more completely than water in a Persian garden: you can taste its sweetness, inhale its freshness, feel its coolness, hear its gurgling, see its sparkle.

Interestingly, given the current regime, no amount of restriction will keep the passionate Iranian temperament completely suppressed. Like the springs of Kashan it bubbles up through poetry, music and art – and in the average or typical Iranian's very nature.

Little sunlight can reach through the dark cypresses this early in spring but we sit on a bench beside the bubbling fountains where above us a bird starts to sing. Intensely melodic, its song seems to waver between happiness and despair leading me to ask Reza what we are listening to.

'That's a nightingale,' he explains. 'Have you never heard one before? But if you are going to hear one for the first time how perfect that it should be here.'

We catch a taxi into Kashan's old quarter where high blank walls protect another of Iran's hidden treasures – its restored 19th-century traditional houses. They are probably the best examples left in the country, but sadly not too many of them remain. Today many rich Iranians prefer to build palatial villas with smoked glass windows, mock Roman pillars and terracotta tiles à la Spanish hacienda.

We enter the first house, Khan-e Abbasin, which used to belong to the Abbasin family, along a windowless corridor at street level that ends in a tiny round foyer from which several more corridors branch. Choosing one, Reza leads me until we step suddenly into the sunshine. I'm astonished to find I'm now on a narrow walkway one storey up above a rectangular courtyard. Below us is a long pool bordered by two gardens planted with citrus trees.

This excavation to create extra depth is a typical feature of these houses. The impact is extraordinary and immediately enforces the feeling of being in a private world.

This particular house is built around two such main courtyards and several smaller ones. It's a mansion, really, designed for an extended family with its communal living spaces and rooms where individual families can find privacy as well as places for meeting visitors.

There are even summer quarters and winter rooms. Steps from the sunken courtyard lead to a spacious underground room where the entire household would sleep in the heat of the day. Wind towers on the roof provide natural air conditioning.

The winter quarters are in the upper storeys in rooms designed to catch warming sunlight, but at the same time preserve the occupants' privacy. This is achieved by the extensive use of stained glass resulting in the whitewashed rooms being dappled with a kaleidoscope of primary colours lit by the sun.

Frescoes and glittering mirror work also adorn many of the rooms. I can't imagine giving up living in one of these elegant and timeless houses, so perfectly in tune with their challenging environment, in favour of a sterile new apartment.

Late that afternoon we board the bus for Isfahan.

Across the aisle from us today is an elderly man sporting a magnificent gauze eye patch on his way home after having had a cataract operation in Tehran. There's also a young woman who needs our help filling out a visa application so she can emigrate to Canada.

'Soon there will be no educated young people left in Iran,' says Reza sadly. 'They feel they will have more success and a better future overseas.'

Near the would-be emigrant is an old woman whose round wrinkled face is framed by a severe black chador. Her heavily made-up daughter sits beside her and spends most of the journey on her mobile phone.

Even the two elderly men in front of us have mobile phones. As we arrive on the outskirts of Isfahan they both take out their phones and call their families to come to collect them.

When we attempt to get our bags out of the baggage compartment under the bus we find a kayak paddle in the way. A young woman, apologising profusely, slides the paddle out along with a lifejacket, explaining to Reza as she does that she's on her way home after a training camp with the Iranian National Women's Kayaking Team.

'You see,' says Reza, as the girl disappears across the car park with her paddle, 'modern-day caravans have as many interesting travellers in them as the old ones.'

We walk along Isfahan's main street, Chahar Bagh. It's still full of trees but during the 17th century when the boulevard was created it featured luxuriant gardens and pools. It was a key element in Shah Abbas's grand design for his new capital city and linked the Royal Square or *maidan* with Isfahan's Zayandeh River.

Shah Abbas relocated the seat of Persian power to Isfahan in 1587. Previously he'd ruled from two capitals, Tabriz and Qazvin, but decided these were too close for comfort to the aggressive Ottoman empire.

As we walk Reza makes me practise the Farsi saying that was coined during Isfahan's brief but glorious time as the centre of the empire: 'Isfahan nesf-e jahan' or 'Isfahan is half the world'.

The shops along both sides of the boulevard are doing plenty of business because *No Ruz* (New Day), Iran's festival to welcome spring, and thus the new year, begins in a few weeks. The traditions of *No Ruz* predate Islam by thousands of years (the Zoroastrians celebrated each of the four seasons). Even after the Persians converted to Islam in the seventh century AD, *No Ruz* stayed as firmly embedded in their psyche as it is today. Periodic attempts since the Islamic revolution to phase out the much-loved festival are met with implacable resistance. It is a measure of the depth of Iranians' feelings about *No Ruz* that the government has so far had to back down, something that does not happen very often.

No Ruz is a time for family and friends to get together, for parties, gifts and travel and is generally preceded by the intensive spring-cleaning of the population's houses and gardens. The giving of presents explains why there are so many people out shopping in Isfahan this evening. It also explains why, on our way to Isfahan, I had seen so many carpets, big and small, hung over balconies, even from the highest of apartment buildings, and spread on footpaths to dry. How the women manage to clean some of these vast carpets and then haul them over the parapets I fail to understand.

What is not so obvious is the reason behind so many goldfish being offered for sale. The most important part of the two-week *No Ruz* celebration is the day on which the sun passes the Aries constellation. This is the spring equinox, which usually occurs between 20 and 22 March. Ready in every house for this moment will be the *haft seen* table, best described as a table set with a white cloth on which will be arranged seven objects symbolising the works of nature and man, each starting with the letter S in Farsi: *sabzi* (germinated seeds of wheat or lentils), *sir* (garlic), *sib* (apples), *senjed* (sweets), *serke* (vinegar), *samanu* (walnut halva) and *sekeh* (a gold coin). Along with these are a mirror, a Koran, some bread, a bowl of water with leaves floating it, hard-boiled eggs the shells of which have been dyed in various colours, salt, lighted candles, flowers (especially violets, hyacinths and narcissi) and a goldfish in a bowl.

Families gather around the *haft seen* table as the moment of the

New Year arrives at which point everyone recites a special prayer for health, happiness and prosperity in the new year. The mother of the house is then supposed to eat one egg for each of her children and the partying and feasting begins.

I've always wanted a *No Ruz* goldfish, especially one of the highly ornate plastic fish bowls in which they come.

'We'll buy you one and take it back on the bus to Tehran and it will go on our *haft seen* table,' Reza says. And this is why we end up walking through Isfahan's most exclusive shopping street carrying a goldfish in a bowl.

Our hotel is serendipitously just across the road from Reza's favourite Isfahan restaurant, Shahrzad. Abandoning our bags and the goldfish we climb the stairs to its dazzling dining room where the maître d' greets Reza like an old friend. Shahrzad's walls are covered with mosaic mirrorwork, mirrored panels and paintings and the windows overlooking the street are framed with diamonds of stained-glass work. It's a perfect setting for eating one of my favourite Iranian dishes, *fesenjan*, made with meat or poultry cooked with spices, chopped walnuts, eggplant and pomegranate juice. It has that delicious sweet-savoury taste so characteristic of Persian cooking.

Meals at Shahrzad always end with a piece of *gaz*, Isfahan's specialty sweet – chewy nougat studded with pistachios. We leave the restaurant, munching our *gaz*, on our way to see the river.

Shah Abbas incorporated the River Zayandeh into his urban planning, commissioning bridges and parks along its banks. Although there are now many more bridges across the river several of the original 17th-century structures remain and it is to Si-o-Se, the bridge of 33 arches, that we are now heading. There are plenty of people around because no matter what the season,

Isfahan's historic bridges and its riverside parks are immensely popular with Iranians, day and night.

The paving stones of Si-o-Se have been worn smooth by centuries of use, and today the bridge is restricted to pedestrians. On each side of the gently curved bridge are its eponymous 33 arches. Narrow ledges, along which it's possible to walk high above the water of the Zayandeh, are on the outside but one needs to duck every metre or so to avoid the supporting side arches. These alcoves are popular trysting places, especially where the floodlights are not working.

After promenading across the bridge we return to the north bank and down the wide steps to the teahouse beneath. Although there are a few seats under cover, most of the teahouse tables are outside on the foot of the bridge abutment where the river foams and gushes just centimetres below our feet.

The metal chairs and tables are rickety and scratched but the setting is incomparable. The bridge, bathed in deep orange light, its arches cast in alternating light and dark shadow, rises up behind us. Downstream a tall plume of water, its spray also illuminated with coloured lights, shoots high into the Persian night competing for attention with a full moon. We sit with glasses of tea and a *qalyan* of apple tobacco and recall how, one year earlier in this very spot, we first discussed the idea of the book.

'I'm not sure exactly how many of Shah Abbas's nine hundred and ninety-nine caravanserais are left, but I think maybe we have visited or at least seen about a hundred of them,' Reza calculates.

'There are still a few left for another time.'

Next morning we discover that our budget hotel does not serve breakfast, but as always Reza has a plan.

'You have yet to try Isfahan's porridge,' he tells me as we walk through the streets on a morning that feels like spring. We turn into a small shop, where disconcertingly for me, the window is piled high with extremely fatty meat.

Reza orders the porridge. Made from wheat and flavoured with rosewater, his portion arrives in a giant bowl, while mine comes in a middle-sized one – I'm expecting the three bears any minute. The porridge is extremely runny and, unfortunately, it becomes the first dish I've been offered in Iran that I cannot eat. While Reza vacuums up his, I'm gagging on mine, albeit as surreptitiously as I can, because I don't want to hurt his feelings. I'm not sure if its the consistency or the fact that I'm facing a refrigerated display case full of what appears to be raw tripe.

Beside us the restaurant staff are setting out their own breakfast of bread, fresh soft cheese and bunches of fresh herbs. Up to this point the most junior of them has been washing the floor, but his boss stops him and apologises to us, saying that as we are guests they will finish cleaning later.

Reza suddenly notices that I'm not eating.

'You don't like it?' he asks, clearly aghast.

I tell him I have always had a bit of a problem with porridge, eventually persuading him it's not a disaster and that as I'm not very hungry he may as well eat my portion. 'It's like a Persian version of Goldilocks and the Three Bears,' I tell him after he's finished and we're once again on the move, this time on our way to Isfahan's grandest hotel, which is also the most spectacularly restored of all Shah Abbas's 999 caravanserai. During the short walk, Reza keeps checking me for signs of imminent collapse. In the end I cave in under his concern and let him buy me a bread roll.

It's been a long time since any camel was near the central

courtyard, the jewel in the crown of the Abassi hotel. Small pools with fountains grace each of the four gardens, jets of water form a shimmering arch over a single long channel of water and rainbows flicker in the droplets. The flowerbeds are planted with roses as well as pink, white and mauve night-flowering stock. In the evenings the perfume is almost overwhelming; even in the daytime the air is heady with scent.

Two storeys of arched doorways surround the courtyard. Once they would have led to lodgings for the caravan travellers. Today, however, Iranian honeymooners and a few foreign tourists lean out the windows.

Although the bedrooms in the Abassi are rather ordinary, no expense has been spared in the public areas such as the lobby with its mirrored mosaic ceiling and the grand dining room where every centimetre of wall space is covered in paintings illuminated by enormous chandeliers. We try to imagine what a dusty, sweaty caravan leader would make of it, but any ghosts have fled long ago.

Reza and I have previously spent many hours in Isfahan's Royal Square or Naghsh-e-Jahan (these days its official name is Emam Khomeini Square), a short walk from the Abassi, but on all those other occasions we had tour groups to look after. Today is a rare treat – no responsibilities, no timetables so we have time to sit back and take in the spectacle of one of the world's truly great public squares – and two of the most magnificent mosques on the planet.

The sky is a cloudless dome over the square when we arrive, and that elusive hint of spring is now most definitely a promise. Actually forming a long rectangle, the square is entirely enclosed by a two-storey arched arcade of shops, most of which sell various examples of Isfahan's vast array of specialist arts and crafts: miniature paintings, enamelwork, block printing, metalwork, carpets, even *gaz*.

We're bypassing the shops for now to visit the Emam Mosque. Architecturally it's regarded as one of the most beautiful mosques in the world, an assessment with which Reza, the expert, and I, the amateur, agree. Despite its 400 years of changing fortunes and millions of visitors, the Emam Mosque retains a deeply spiritual atmosphere. The entrance portal lies exactly in the centre of the southern side of the square. Thirty metres high, it is covered with flowing calligraphy, flowers and geometric designs, all painstakingly created using mosaic faience (a technique whereby tiny pieces of multi-coloured tiles are employed to make the finished design – rather than applying tiles already glazed with a design, which is much less exacting and time-consuming). Reza is 'reading' the façade to me when we hear a distinctive and rather familiar clicking sound behind us and we turn to see the scarf man. For a number of years now this entrepreneurial vendor has been piling up his old black bicycle with ladies' headscarves (he's diversified lately into T-shirts) and wheeling them to the paved courtyard in front of the Emam Mosque. He knows Reza well and, remarkably, remembers me from my previous visits with assorted tour groups.

'You remember me, madam,' he reminds me as he riffles through his latest collection, pulling out a pink scarf shot with silver thread and handing it to me.

'I always have the one-American-dollar scarves for your tourists, but this is a gift for you.' I try to refuse but am out-*taroffed*.

'It's OK,' says Reza. 'He really does want you to have it. He's a kind man and never cheats the visitors.'

We pass through the portal and its magnificent brass doors. Normally in a mosque the central courtyard would lie straight ahead, but the Emam Mosque has a surprise in store for newcomers. The portal was built to harmonise geometrically with the design of the square by balancing a similar portal at the northern end that leads into Isfahan's bazaar. But mosques must face Mecca and if the mosque had been built directly opposite the gateway it would not have done so. Thus, to meet both demands, the 17th-century architect realigned the entire complex beyond the gateway. Winding corridors lead worshippers and visitors around until they emerge in the vast inner courtyard, facing the main *ivan* and its ritual ablution pool and, of course, Mecca.

We perch ourselves on a ledge in a far corner of the courtyard where we can see the main dome covered with its shining gloriously turquoise-blue tiles, across which weave arabesques in white and gold. On each side are minarets completely covered in more of the turquoise tiles. Near the top of these minarets are small circular balconies enclosed with delicately carved wooden screens. Every centimetre of the arches that surround the courtyard is adorned with decorative tiles featuring geometric designs and embellished with calligraphy. The predominant colour is deep blue – we're sitting on the edge of a sea of lapis lazuli.

The call to noon prayers begins and as the courtyard and its *ivans* act as a vast natural amplifier, the sounds reverberate around the space. Gradually, from all corners of the complex, the faithful – including young men in trendy jeans carrying briefcases – approach the doorway to the winter prayer hall.

Even before we see him, we hear a man approaching through the curved corridor singing his own version of the *azan* in a clear tenor voice. Old, bent almost double and using a stick for support, he totters past, achingly slowly, placing his free hand against the wall for support. To produce such a beautiful sound he must be singing from the heart.

'As this is the last time you will be in a mosque for some time,' Reza says, 'shall we say the prayer together?' Over the past weeks, along with my Farsi lessons, Reza has been teaching me the first sura or prayer in Arabic.

A little ploddingly, but without making a mistake, I make it from *Beshmellahe, Rahmane Rahim* (in the name of God) through the tricky *Ehdenasseratal mostaquim* (show me the straight path) through to the wonderful drawn-out vowel sounds of *Alayhem va lazzalin*. In front of us, pigeons flutter down to drink from the placid surface of the ablutions pool. There is peace in this half of the world.

By now I'm sniffling into my headscarf so Reza suggests some retail therapy. We head off to a small studio just off the central corridor of shops that runs around the arcade and which is occupied by two brothers who are widely regarded as the best painters of Persian miniatures in Iran.

Reza is a regular visitor and when we appear in their tiny studio Rasul Fotovvat, one of the brothers, does not jump up to try to sell me anything but instead finds chairs for us, orders tea and hands around a box of *gaz*.

A bout of *No Ruz* spring-cleaning is under way here, too, in that just before we arrived an assistant had been gathering up the shop's collection of flags of the world to dust. For some reason, however, he'd left a flag on the counter and it just happened to be the New Zealand one.

Rasul carries on with his portrait of Shahrazade (better known in the West as Scheherazade), the beautiful Persian royal storyteller from the *Tales of One Thousand and One Nights*. Her delicate face, deep blue dress and the tiny nightingales he is painting on her dress are composed of thousands of dots, almost invisible to the naked eye, made with his paintbrush with just one hair.

'It's a cat hair,' he says in English, 'because cat hair is very fine and flexible. The handle is made from a porcupine spine.'

The brothers use only natural pigments such as saffron and cobalt in their paint and Rasul shows me how he grinds up turquoise stones and mixes the powder with water and gum Arabic to use on Shahrazade's dress.

'Other people do cheap paintings on plastic but we use reconstituted camel bone. On its own the bone splits because it absorbs too much humidity so we grind it up and then compress it. It's still natural, but it means we can also work on large paintings which wouldn't be possible if we were restricted to actual pieces of bone.'

Rasul switches to Farsi in order to speak to Reza and then down puts the portrait he's working on in order to pick up a tiny piece of bone. He then dips a one-hair brush in black paint and in a few deft strokes draws a miniature portrait of Omar Khayyam. Attaching it to a backing sheet he hands it to one of his assistants who slides it into a frame.

'Reza tells me you love our poets so this is a farewell gift for you,' he says.

This display of generosity doesn't help my equilibrium at all and after leaving the studio we pause for a restorative ice cream, inspired by some nearby workmen who have stopped to eat chocolate cream freezes. But today we feel the need for saffron ice cream. Free of time constraints we carry our pale yellow cones onto the lawn in the centre of the square and sprawl on the grass. Behind Reza's head I can see the dome of the Sheikh Lotfallah mosque with its unusual pale gold tiles and swirling white arabesques.

My view is obscured now and then by the *maidan*'s horse-drawn carriages. Today they are full of giggling small girls in pink and blue wimples crammed in three or four to the seat, their multi-coloured backpacks on their laps.

'You know,' says Reza, 'I have never been on one of those touristy carriages and as you haven't either, shall we do now it in the name of research?'

I agree to this plan and slightly embarrassed we climb into a carriage and clop and jingle our way around the square, past the Ali Qapu palace where Shah Abbas used to sit to watch polo matches (two of the goal posts are still in place) and see the portal to the Emam mosque from an entirely new angle. Then we wheel around to our starting point so that the entire square is in front of us, with the shadowy mouth of the bazaar at the far end. It's an immense space – one of the largest public squares in the world.

The day has slid effortlessly into lunchtime and we eat in a restaurant in the arcade next door to the Emam Mosque, which has a reputation for being one of the best places in Iran, to try its famous stews. We choose a *takt* and order plum stew and rice. While we are eating, a large group of Thai tourists walks past, with several pausing to photograph us. Reza is amused.

'Back in Thailand their friends are going to ask if they saw many blonde, blue-eyed Iranians.'

We walk through the eastern arcade after lunch, stopping at a shop selling the giant brass light fittings I've been admiring in various mosques and hotels. The one I really want costs $US7000, which Reza is quick to point out is the same price as a brand-new Kia car.

The second of the square's mosques is Sheikh Lotfallah, which takes visitors on an even longer journey from its portal to its heart. The corridor, lined with mosaics, curves around the mosque's wall like a protective arm – it's a small building but the unusual entrance serves to make it appear bigger. The corridor ends with a sharp turn to the right and a simple doorway leading to the square sanctuary. Above it is the dome's interior, breathtakingly decorated with a lozenge-shaped pattern that diminishes in size as it reaches the most intricate work at the very centre. Shafts of light from the latticed windows high above fall across the mosaics that glisten, the colours changing in the play of light.

We continue our circumnavigation of the square, but are stopped in our tracks when a handsome young man outside a carpet shop says 'Kia ora'. He'd overheard my Kiwi accent and now invites us in to drink tea. We sit on piles of his carpets while he tells of meeting Kiwis and Aussies while on an African safari.

'I'm very happy to hear a New Zealand accent again,' he tells me. He's also impressed how Reza's English vowels sounds (trained by me over past weeks) have developed such an authentic Antipodean twang.

Before we leave I ask him to show me a bright red-and-silver carpet that hangs from the ceiling.

'You have chosen the most expensive carpet in the shop,' he laughs, 'a silk carpet from Qom.'

The price is equivalent to a fleet of Kias.

We now begin the late afternoon teahouse crawl. Our first stop is the Azadegan teahouse tucked away near the entrance to the bazaar and with the most extraordinary interior. Its long narrow room is divided in two by a beaded curtain; at one end sit the hardened male *qalyan* smokers while at the other are couples, families and the very occasional tourist. There almost no headspace, thanks to the most bizarre collection of knick-knacks, antiques and memorabilia dangling from the rafters, including brass lamps, kerosene lamps, Sufi begging bowls, ewers and jugs.

The walls are equally festooned with stuffed animals and black-and-white photographs of old Isfahan, partly obscured by shields, axes and shelves overflowing with old china, battered Aladdin lamps and other treasures that can't be suspended from the ceiling.

We share the family end of the teahouse with two couples who it turns out are studying at Isfahan's school of restoration, the best in the country. At that moment they are supposed to be in a lecture on building materials, but they've skipped it to come to the teahouse.

It's almost sunset, time to climb the narrow sets of stairs (so steep they are really more of a ladder) to the last teahouse on our itinerary. Set immediately beside the portal to the bazaar, its terrace commands a view over the entire square – straight ahead is the Emam Mosque, Lotfallah Mosque is to our left, and the Ali Qapu palace to the right. Below us traffic crawls through the end of the square still open to motorised vehicles. Beyond the traffic chaos the fountains play in the pool and the horses and carriages trot around their circuit.

We sit at the rear of the terrace, our backs against the wall and watch the sunset colours sliding over the gleaming mosque domes and down the minarets, glinting on the brass crescents at their peaks. A *qalyan* arrives along with tea and the teahouse speciality of tiny pastries. The sunset *azan* rises above the noise of the traffic.

'It doesn't get any better than this,' Reza exhales along with a cloud of smoke.

Later in the evening we once again join the Isfahanis down at the river. This time we cross the double-storeyed Khaju Bridge. Built in 1650, it also acts as a dam to regulate the Zayandeh River's flow and, like the other bridges in the city, it's a gathering place. Each bridge pier has steps leading down to the water which, thanks to the first of the spring snow melt, is now roaring through between the abutments. We sit on a step as close to the water as we dare. Only when our shoes are saturated with spray do we move.

Nearby, in the deep shadows of one of the arches, an informal concert is under way. Singing in public is frowned upon in Iran, but almost every evening young men meet under the bridge to sing. If an official of any kind appears they melt away, only to reassemble when the coast is clear.

While we enjoy the view a young man with a beautiful voice sings a traditional Iranian song. It's a haunting melody and his magical voice is attracting a crowd which, like us, stands or sits in the shadows to listen while watching the river tumble under the bridge as the moonlight draws a silvery path across the placid swirling water upstream.

We take a taxi back to the hotel. The driver has met Reza before and when he learns that Reza has just finished his MA, he asks for advice on how to make his son study harder. When we reach the hotel, however, he refuses to take any money.

Today is my last morning in Iran – soon we must take the bus back to Tehran and then at midnight Reza will drive me to the airport for my flight back to New Zealand.

'Try not to cry or my mother will cry and then my sister will cry', Reza tells me.

'We have to remember you will be back soon,' he says.

There is one last thing I want to do before we leave Isfahan. We take a taxi to the square and enter the early-morning silence and emptiness of the Emam Mosque. I lead the way into the main sanctuary and under the central dome with its glittering golden mosaics and concentric circles of roses that seem to tumble from heaven.

Directly under the dome is a spot with perfect acoustics and a remarkable echo (there are supposed to be nearly 50 echoes but the human ear can only hear about a dozen). I ask Reza if he will stand in that spot and sing the *azan*, the call to prayer that has rung out from minarets throughout our travels – a sound that has floated over towns of drab apartments, wafted around gold-clad domes in the holy city of Mashhad, been emitted through spluttering loudspeakers in simple brick towers in timeless villages. It's led us, followed us, and it's become an unbroken thread woven through our journey just as it was part of the lives of the men and women who joined the great caravans that criss-crossed Persia hundreds of years earlier.

Reza stands on the black paving stone under the dome and sings.

'*Allah o akbhar, la elahaellalla* ...' (God is great, there is no god but the almighty, Mohammad is the messenger of Allah, Ali is the vice-regent of Allah, rush to do good deeds. The time for prayer has come. The time for worship has come. The time for good deeds has come.)

His voice fills the dome, encircling it like the mosaic roses, reaching into my soul.

I'd promised that later I would not cry. Now was different.